CW00796304

Digital Fonts and Reading

Series on Language Processing, Pattern Recognition, and Intelligent Systems

Editors

Ching Y. Suen
Concordia University, Canada
parmidir@enes.concordia.ca

Lu Qin
The Hong Kong Polytechnic University, Hong Kong
csluqin@comp.polyu.edu.hk

Published

Forthcoming

Series on Language Processing, Pattern Recognition, and Intelligent Systems — Vol. 1

Digital Fonts and Reading

Edited by

Mary C. Dyson
University of Reading, UK

Ching Y. Suen
Concordia University, Canada

 **World Scientific**

NEW JERSEY · LONDON · SINGAPORE · BEIJING · SHANGHAI · HONG KONG · TAIPEI · CHENNAI · TOKYO

Published by

World Scientific Publishing Co. Pte. Ltd.

5 Toh Tuck Link, Singapore 596224

USA office: 27 Warren Street, Suite 401-402, Hackensack, NJ 07601

UK office: 57 Shelton Street, Covent Garden, London WC2H 9HE

British Library Cataloguing-in-Publication Data

A catalogue record for this book is available from the British Library.

Series on Language Processing, Pattern Recognition, and Intelligent Systems — Vol. 1
DIGITAL FONTS AND READING

First published 2016

ISBN 978-981-4759-53-3

Printed in Singapore by Mainland Press Pte Ltd.

Introduction to the series

Language Processing, Pattern Recognition, and Intelligent Systems

This book is part of a series on *Language Processing, Pattern Recognition, and Intelligent Systems* evolved from the termination of the *International Journal of Computer Processing of Languages* (IJCPOL) in 2013, published by World Scientific Publishing Co. (WSPC) for the Oriental Language Computer Society (OLCS). OLCS was created in 1976 by some prominent professors of Chinese descent in North America, and was initially called the Chinese Language Computer Society (CLCS). The original aim of CLCS was to promote and facilitate the use of Chinese in computer technology. Gradually it received the support from many people in various regions of Asia, notably Hong Kong, Taiwan, Mainland China, Japan, Singapore, Korea, North America, and others. As research and digital technology advanced, a variety of oriental languages became usable for computer input and output, leading to the change in name of the society to OLCS in 2005.

Apart from promoting and organizing numerous international conferences related to the theme of this society, CLCS also started its international quarterly journal called *Computer Processing of Chinese and Oriental Languages* (CPCOL) in 1983, which later changed its name to *International Journal of Computer Processing of Languages* (IJCPOL), published by WSPC. This journal and conferences stimulated substantial research in this area, made many valuable contributions, and played a critical role in international collaborations. As this field and computer science matured, coupled with the rapid growth of digital technology, IJCPOL's role diminished. After successful negotiation with WSPC, a new book series in the field of CPL was founded by Dr. Ching Y. Suen of Concordia University in Canada and Dr. Qin Lu of the Hong Kong Polytechnic University of Hong Kong. To make it more attractive and marketable, we plan to expand the scope of this book series to include subjects like pattern recognition, image processing, neural networks, knowledge engineering and intelligent systems, in which most of the OLCS members have been engaged. Presently two books are already in the pipeline: this one, *Digital Fonts and Reading*, and the next, *Advances in Chinese Document and Text Processing*. As time goes by, it is hoped that others will follow suit covering research and developments in different parts of the world.

The publication of this book series could not have been accomplished without the tremendous help and encouragement from our colleagues, in particular Dr. Shi Kuo Chang of the University of Pittsburgh, Chao Ning Liu formerly with IBM Yorktown Heights, and Ms. Kim Tan of WSPC, as well as the beautiful memory of the founder of CLCS, the late Dr. Yaohan Chu of the University of Maryland.

Ching Y. Suen, Editor of the Book Series,
Montreal, July 2015

Preface

Digital fonts and reading is a collection of invited chapters contributed by different authors, whose writing reveals their perspectives, from science to design, and their experiences as researchers, teachers and practitioners. This diversity introduces a range of approaches to the topic which will resonate with all sorts of readers from academics to students to experienced or novice typographic or interface designers to software engineers, and especially those who have an interest in type.

By focusing on reading, a common thread through all chapters is the reader's perspective. This may seem an unnecessary observation but much is written about fonts without mentioning readers. Chapters which draw on the experience of designing fonts and explain the decisions that are made reveal the importance of judging how the characters or words will be perceived, not focusing only on the marks on paper or pixels on screen.

It should be no surprise to learn that legibility is frequently mentioned as an objective and is defined by several authors in broadly similar ways, with reference to Walter Tracy's *Letters of credit* [1986] which distinguishes between legibility and readability. These issues are addressed through reporting on original studies or reviewing current knowledge, either as the primary focus for the chapter or as a contributory factor in making other judgments (e.g. harmonization of type or appropriateness of typefaces for specific media or purposes).

Traditionally, there has been a separation between researchers and practitioners, with different agendas. Also, knowledge from within each separate discipline has not been accessible to those outside the discipline, either due to the lack of records of craft knowledge, or overly complex scientific articles. The objective of bridging the gap between scientific testing and design experience underpins most of the chapters and is also made explicit by a number of authors. By combining knowledge across disciplines the validity and value of research outcomes are increased through, for example, recognizing the complexity of typographic test material. The seemingly simple task of comparing the legibility of fonts is complicated by the need to consider the interrelationships of many variables within letters (such as x-height, stroke contrast, etc.) and between letters (such as letter-and word-spacing, leading, etc.). The research reported here includes examples demonstrating awareness of the importance of carefully choosing or designing the form of test material alongside how it is tested.

Focusing only on straddling the science-design divide would produce an incomplete account of the interdisciplinary opportunities inherent in the subject of this book. Combining knowledge from related fields is a key objective in putting together this book, which draws on historical and more theoretical analyses, which nonetheless feed into practical applications. The scope is also broadened by including research and analysis of Chinese and Arabic, as well as Latin typography.

From apparently diverse standpoints, consistent themes emerge in addition to the ones already mentioned (considering the reader; managing interrelationships of type variables). These include: optimizing fonts for different types of readers and circumstances; consistency of style; critique of simplistic analyses (of fonts or texts); opposing forces (regularity versus flexibility, economy versus readability); making explicit typographic prac-tice (as an objective or exemplifying the process).

The four sections ('Vision and reading'; 'Scientific approaches to design for reading'; 'Perspectives on type design practice'; 'Using type') perhaps reflect artificial divisions as, for example, scientific approaches are found in 'Using type' as are descriptions of type design practice. There are also overlaps in content but these are reassuring in confirming common threads and convergence of ideas.

Chapters 1 and 2 (Beveratou and Bessemans) both look at visually impaired readers and carry out experiments to explore the optimization of fonts and typesetting parameters for adults or children. The authors use different test methods and test different aspects of fonts, but both start from the premise that increasing the size of print is too simplistic. Beveratou (chapter 1) looks at leading, spacing, type size, thickness of stroke and use of serifs in relation to reading. Bessemans (chapter 2) designed her own test material varying shape characteristics to identify what best supports reading.

Chapters 3 to 6 differ in their objectives but each provides insight into how scientific studies are carried out from perspectives informed by design knowledge. Larson and Carter (chapter 3) demonstrate how collab-oration works in practice by describing the iterative process of testing and refining a new typeface named Sitka. This typeface is also mentioned by

Sorkin (chapter 8) and Shaikh and Chaparro (chapter 13). Slattery (chapter 4) reviews eye movement research as a methodology for studying reading and highlights the disconnect between psycholinguistic research and font design, discussing possible reasons. These resonate with my own explanations of the divergence which have guided my efforts to bridge the gap. Beier (chapter 5) draws on scientific findings and designer's experiences to review what we know about the legibility of fonts that are designed to be read at a distance. This knowledge is converted into practical guidance on how shapes can be improved for optimal distance reading. Wang (chapter 6) reports an investigation of the effects of introducing interword spacing in Chinese text read by children in two age groups. As she found that the younger children (7-8 year olds) benefitted from additional space, the results have implications for the design of learning materials.

Perspectives on type design practice (chapters 7-10) range from an introduction to Chinese typefaces, to coverage of specific issues, to the introduction of a more theoretical approach. Lu, Zhu, Zhang, and Tang (chapter 7) provide a detailed account of the complexities of designing Chinese characters, outline the typical workflow, and discuss particular challenges. Some concepts and methods common to the designs of Chinese and Latin typefaces can be identified. Sorkin (chapter 8) also deals with practicalities by describing the factors to consider when optimizing type for different viewing distances, media, technologies, angle of viewing, and readers. Nemeth (chapter 9) focuses on the harmonization of type design across scripts, touched upon by Lu *et al.* In contrast to the preceding descriptions of practice, this chapter takes a critical look at the practice and questions the case for regularity and uniformity as opposed to flexibility. McKaughan (chapter 10) introduces the design method of pattern languages, illustrating with an example of designing newspaper typefaces. The approach works at a level of abstraction that can handle the multiple variables within and between letters and their interrelationships and can combine knowledge across disciplines.

The final section on using type (chapters 11-14) explores various aspects of fonts in quite diverse ways, from scientific methods to case studies. Dyson, Tam, Leake and Kwok (chapter 11) pick up the theme of consistency of stylistic characteristics of fonts and investigate whether designers have the expertise to enable them to perceive this consistency when they cannot read the (Chinese) characters. Lacava (chapter 12) examines the process of selecting fonts for newspapers through two case studies (one English, one Arabic), providing an interesting complement to the pattern language approach (chapter 10). The personality of the font is also touched upon, which is the subject of chapter 13. Shaikh and Chaparro focus on the perception of onscreen typefaces in terms of personality and the perceived appropriateness of typefaces for various document types. In common with Dyson *et al.*, this research is concerned with the stylistic characteristics of fonts. Almuhajri and Suen (chapter 14) conduct experiments to compare Arabic fonts in terms of legibility and readability with a view to recommending fonts for Personal Digital Assistants.

The publication of this book would not have been possible without the wonderful enthusiasm of authors, the support of colleagues in the Department of Typography & Graphic Communication at the University of Reading, and the patient assistance and skill of Natassia Swulinska in typesetting and laying out pages.

Mary C. Dyson

Contributors

Mrouj Almuhajri
Department of Computer Science, Saudi Electronic
University Dhahran, Saudi Arabia
m.almuhajri@seu.edu.sa

Sofie Beier
School of Design, The Royal Danish Academy of Fine Arts,
Schools of Architecture, Design and Conservation, DK
sbe@kadk.dk

Eleni Beveratou
ebeverat@gmail.com

Ann Bessemans
PXL-MAD (Media, Arts & Design), University Hasselt, Belgium,
READSEARCH
Ann.Bessemans@PXL.be

Matthew Carter
Type designer, Carter & Cone Type Inc., USA
cartermatt@earthlink.net

Barbara Chaparro
Software Usability Research Lab; Department of Psychology;
Wichita State University; Wichita
Barbara.chaparro@wichita.edu

Mary C. Dyson
Department of Typography & Graphic Communication,
University of Reading, UK
M.C.Dyson@reading.ac.uk

Brian Kwok
School of Design, Hong Kong Polytechnic University
brian.k@polyu.edu.hk

Kevin Larson
Advanced Reading Technologies, Microsoft, USA
kevlar@microsoft.com

Lucie Lacava
Lacava Design Inc., Montreal, QC
lucie@lacavadesign.ca

Clare Leake
Department of Typography & Graphic Communication,
University of Reading, UK

Xiaoqing Lu
Institute of Computer Science and Technology, Peking University
lvxiaoqing@pku.edu.cn

Rob McKaughan
Advanced Reading Technologies, Microsoft, USA
robmck@microsoft.com

Titus Nemeth
info@tntypography.eu

A. Dawn Shaikh
Google
dawns@google.com

Timothy J. Slattery
Department of Psychology, Bournemouth University, UK
tslattery@bournemouth.ac.uk

Eben Sorkin
Sorkin Type Co. Easthampton MA, USA
sorkineben@gmail.com

Ching Y. Suen
Centre for Pattern Recognition and Machine Intelligence
Concordia University Montreal, Canada
suen@cenparmi.Concordia.ca

Keith Tam
Department of Typography & Graphic Communication,
University of Reading, UK
k.c.tam@reading.ac.uk

Ting Tang
Founder Fonts Business Division, Beijing Founder
Electronics Co., Ltd
tang.ting@founder.com.cn

Hsiu-Feng Wang
Department of e-Learning Design and Management,
National Chiayi University, Taiwan
robin0612@hotmail.com

Contents

Section 4: Using type

Chapter 1

The effect of type design and typesetting on visually impaired readers

Eleni Beveratou

The term 'visually impaired readers' refers to people who have a sight impairment that cannot be improved with the use of corrective aids. The vast majority of such readers have developed this impairment only in the later years of their lives. Therefore, reading habits and letter recognition patterns have already been established in earlier stages, making the challenge of adaptation to the new situation even harder. Documents referred to as 'large prints' have come to facilitate the reading process. In compliance with a range of guidelines, they manage to bridge the gap between the needs of the readers and their impairment. However, there are factors concerning readability and legibility that are neglected or, often, misinterpreted in their implementation, decreasing the efficiency of large print documents. This chapter analyses the typesetting parameters and the typographic details that optimize typefaces for visually impaired readers. Through a series of conducted experiments, issues concerning the leading, spacing, type size, thickness of the stroke, as well as the use of serifs are examined. The experiments focus mainly on the comparison of various typefaces' reading rates to highlight the typographical details which cause misreading and confusions. As a conclusion, the results will draw attention to the interdependency of all the aforementioned variables; none of them alone can make a typeface ideal for use in documents intended for visually impaired readers.

1.1 Introduction

Visual impairment is a sight deficiency, affecting mainly the elderly, which cannot be improved with the use of correction aids. Having established their reading habits and letter recognition patterns from early years, the disruption becomes harder to adapt to. Documents referred to as 'large prints' have come to facilitate the reading process. In compliance with a range of guidelines, they bridge the gap between the needs of the readers and their impairment. However, factors concerning readability and legibility are neglected or misinterpreted in their implementation, detracting from the efficiency of these documents.

At this stage, it is important to clarify two terms that tend to be mis-used: 'readability' and 'legibility'. Tracy [1986] refers to legibility as the ability to distinguish single typographic characters, and to readability as the comprehension of a text, implying reading ease.

The aim of this chapter is to analyze the typesetting parameters and typographic details that optimize typefaces for visually impaired readers. Through a series of experiments, issues concerning the leading, spacing, type size, thickness of the stroke, as well as the use of serifs will be ex-amined. However, it is important to clarify that this research is qualitative, not quantitative.

1.2   Previous research on the topic

1.2.1   *Type size*

Extensive research underlines type size as the main factor impeding the reading process of sighted [Legge and Bigelow, 2011] and partially sight-ed people [Rubin *et al.*, 2006]. From a simple scientific point of view, a retina is formed by multiple sensors; the smaller the shown element, the fewer sensors are activated, making shapes harder to distinguish [Bailey *et al.*, 1993]. As such, a person with central field vision loss benefits from a larger font size [Chung *et al.*, 1998]. In fact, in order to read with ease people require a much bigger font size than that of their acuity thresh-old [Rubin and Turano, 1994]. Reading speed is optimal for font sizes between 16 to 18 points [Russel *et al.*, 2007]. However, one should take into account that the reading distance will change the perceived size of the typeface [Legge and Bigelow, 2011].

Nonetheless, other research shows that the amelioration of letter iden-tification is non-significant even when letter size is increased [Parish and Sperling, 1991]. Consequently, there are probably some additional factors that affect reading performance. In order to gain insight as to which fea-tures contribute to letter recognition, a comparison will be made between the reading rates of large-sized typefaces and their threshold viewing.

1.2.2   *Leading and spacing*

Leading (the gap between lines) and word and letter spacing are critical for the reading speed of the partially sighted. Larger than default leading is preferred [Paterson and Tinker, 1947], as it helps to identify the start of the next line. For sighted people, generous inter-letter spacing allows better letter recognition [Bouma, 1970]. This way, 'crowding' (the decrease in letter identification when surrounded by other letters [Cline *et al.*, 1997]) is avoided. For the visually impaired, crowding seems worse when peripheral vision is used [Ciuffreda *et al.*, 1991]. Therefore, wider spacing is essential [Levi *et al.*, 2007]. However, so as to avoid reverse results, extensive leading and spacing should not be exaggerated for all kind of readers [Yu *et al.*, 2007; Al Otaibi and Dickinson, 2000]. Optimum figures have been sought and Prince [1967] demonstrated that when typesetting for visually impaired readers 'inter-letter spacing should be 40% and inter-line spacing 140% of the letter 'o''. Researchers seem to agree more on this topic. However, they do not explain how letter spacing may be affected by the use of serifs.

1.2.3   *Serif and sans serif*

There is no apparent preference between serif and sans serif [Minda *et al.*, 2007]. However, when examining the details, there seems to be a differentiation depending on the intended use. Arditi and Cho [2000] discovered that serifs do make a minor positive difference regarding sizes close to the reading acuity limits of readers. Prince [1967] realised that sans serifs were more effective when used for single letters or syllables, but serifs were preferred for normal words. As Unger says: 'Serifs seem to make words and lines hang together better'; their structure is more rigid. Serifs give a personal character to each letter that probably makes it distinguishable [Unger, 2007].

    Nonetheless, these observations do not apply to every situation. As stated by Reece [2008]: 'previous studies differed in methodology, fonts and participant characteristics, which makes comparisons difficult and may account for some variations in results'. Hence, it would be interesting to measure the effect of serifs on readability, when the tested typefaces have similar proportions and features.

1.2.4 *Other typographic details*

A limited set of research has tried to identify whether stroke thickness is another significant variable. Indeed, it was shown that people affected by glaucoma benefit from a bolder typeface [Shaw, 1969]. More specifically, the ideal stroke thickness is thought to be equivalent to 17.5% of the height of an 'o' [Prince, 1967]. This research shows that smaller details could have a great impact; therefore modulation of the stroke and the counters could be a potential area for further exploration.

Figure 1: Example of a testing pack. Original size: 23x12cm.

1.3 Testing each parameter

As a general conclusion, the preceding research seems to not communicate the same message. It was, thus, necessary to conduct an experiment that would clarify, validate and further research some untested—or vaguely—tested parameters (style, size, leading, spacing).

1.3.1 *Testing method and possible risks to consider*

The experiment consisted of a pack of six testing pages, one result sheet and two reading guides (Figure 1). The test was divided into three parts. Each part contained six paragraphs of eighty words varying from 2 to 8 letters. To ensure that the reading speed was not accelerated due to the content of the text [Aitchison, 2003], the paragraphs were formed by placing words in random order [Wilkins, 2003]. The participants had to

Figure 2 (Left): Spectacles simulating loss of peripheral vision (N.1). Width 13cm. (Right): Spectacles simulating loss of central vision (N.7). Width 13cm. Both spectacles are from the Visual Impairment North East simulation package.

read each paragraph aloud for twenty seconds, at their usual reading pace [Tinker, 1963]. The last word read was marked down.

Reading speed can be affected by factors like the reader's experience, the content's familiarity, the vocabulary used and the kind of document read [Smith, 1994]. As one reads and becomes more familiar with the process, the reading speed increases. If the same word order were kept throughout the paragraphs, the results would have been compromised. Therefore, the parts, sequences and paragraphs of the experiment had to be carefully ordered resulting in an experiment with six different packs.

1.3.2 *Selection of participants*

Thirty-three adults took part in this experiment. Twenty-one were partially sighted people aged from 70 to 94 years old. Of these, ten had macular degeneration and eleven had various eye deficiencies. The rest were divided into two categories: six with perfect vision and six with pronounced myopia. They constituted an element of comparison to the results of the partially sighted. Participants with normal visual acuity were tasked to simply read the paragraph. Participants with myopia were asked to remove their glasses and use spectacles simulating two different eye conditions: loss of central vision and loss of peripheral vision (Figure 2). Simulating the sight of the visually impaired would provide examples of how people unaccustomed to these conditions read.

Figure 3: Sample of the typefaces used for this experiment.

1.3.3 *Tested aspects and selection of typefaces*

The testing material consisted of eighteen paragraphs typeset in ten different typefaces. All paragraphs used Latin lowercase letters, due to their common usage [Jones and Mewhort, 2004]. The first part looks at size and readability comparing serif and sans serif. It consists of six paragraphs, each typeset in a different size (Arial in 12, 16 and 20 points and Times New Roman, with its sizes adjusted to match the three x-heights of Arial). See Figure 3.

The sizes were chosen in compliance with the recommendations of the Royal National Institute of the Blind (RNIB). Sizes 12 and 20 pts are the minimum and maximum sizes recommended for clear prints (documents for a wide audience) and 16 points, the ideal size for typesetting large prints [2007]. Therefore, for the second and third part, all fonts were scaled to fit the x-height of Arial, 16 pts (Figure 4).

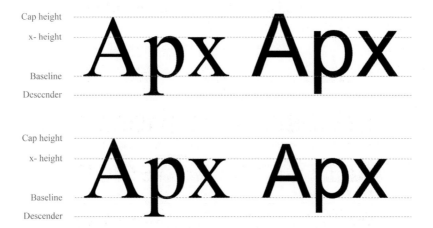

Figure 4 (Top): Two different typefaces displayed at the same font size. (Bottom): Two different typefaces displayed at a different point size but with matching x-heights.

The second part investigates whether spacing affects legibility. Six paragraphs are typeset with varying leading and kerning using Freight Text and Freight Sans. The fonts were selected as they have the same proportions, thus preventing the text's tonality to affect the results.

The third part focuses on whether some typographical design details (thickness, strokes and counters) affect legibility. The selection of the fonts for this last category was less obvious. Minuscule 6, and Freight Micro Book are caption fonts and were chosen based on a hypothesis: if they work in small sizes for normal-sighted people, then they should have the same effect for partially sighted people when enlarged. Palatino, Century Gothic, and Optima, were chosen due to their large counters and their variety in construction (Serif and Sans). The last one was Tiresias, 15.5 points, a font specially designed for large printings, by the RNIB.

1.4 Results and discussion

The results of the three parts of the experiment are summarized in Table 1 and then discussed in the following sections.

Table 1: Results of the experiment.

| | | TOTAL OF WORDS AND LETTERS READ FROM: | | | | | |
| | | 21 Partially Sighted | | 6 Normal Sighted | | 6 Reading with Simulating Specs | |
PART	FONT	Words	Letters	Words	Letters	Words	Letters
1A	Times New Roman 14/14.4/0	380	2039	252	1365	219	1168
	Times New Roman 18/19.2/0	429	2304	248	1342	223	1201
	Times New Roman 23/24/0	506	2719	261	1403	220	1193
1B	Arial Regular 12/14.4/0	376	2056	246	1358	213	1171
	Arial Regular 16/19.2/0	440	2314	249	1377	210	1156
	Arial Regular 20/24/0	438	2267	251	1396	220	1204
PART	FONT	Words	Letters	Words	Letters	Words	Letters
2A	Freight Text Book 18/19.2/0	458	2414	251	1363	233	1262
	Freight Text Book 18/21/20	440	2315	253	1375	231	1245
	Freight Text Book 18/23/50	452	2383	239	1280	233	1248
2B	Freight Sans 18/19.2/0	406	2253	268	1479	237	1315
	Freight Sans 18/21/20	417	2296	256	1418	233	1288
	Freight Sans 18/23/50	434	2412	259	1423	231	1280
PART	FONT	Words	Letters	Words	Letters	Words	Letters
3A	Minuscule 6 16/19.2/0	447	2322	263	1380	221	1147
	Freight Micro Book 18/19.2/0	423	2140	257	1343	219	1131
	Optima 18/19.2/0	443	2259	251	1313	219	1139
3B	Century Gothic 15.5/19.2/0	421	2183	264	1418	226	1205
	Tiresias LP font 15.5/19.2/0	491	2567	259	1382	242	1300
	Palatino 18/19.2/0	438	2314	259	1400	220	1169

1.4.1 *Type size*

Amongst the partially sighted, Times New Roman in its larger size (23 pts), was the typeface with the most read words in the entire experiment, having a difference of 126 words from the same typeface in its smaller size (14 pts). Participants with normal sight and the ones using the simulating spectacles performed better with larger typefaces. However, the difference between the two extreme reading sizes in both Arial (12 and 20 pts) and Times New Roman (14 and 23 pts) was less pronounced than for the partially sighted and differed only by a few words. Consequently, size enhances the reading rate of the visually impaired, as opposed to normal-sighted people.

With Arial, the largest number of words read was at 16 pts with an unnoticeable difference from the results of the same typeface at 20 pts. Interestingly, the difference in reading speed between the most and least read size of Arial (16 and 12 pts) was 64 words, almost half of the equivalent in Times New Roman. Hence, readers benefit from the size increase only in particular typefaces. Thus, additional parameters are contributing towards higher readability.

Lastly, participants commented negatively on the paragraphs typeset in the smallest sizes when introduced at the beginning of the testing process, or after a break. This should be taken into account, as it might determine whether they would engage in reading.

1.4.2　*Visual noise and type size: a complementary study*

When conducting the experiment, one participant suffering from macular degeneration commented twice: 'I've got black spots and they get in the way'. This comment led to an exploratory study based on Liang's [2002] and Pelli's [1994] research, showing that legibility is more affected by 'noise' (any disrupting visual element that renders the recognition of a visual signal more difficult) than size. The aim was to understand which typographical details benefit from a size increase to a deficient eye.

The only noticeable difference after increasing the size of letters was that their thinner parts were more visible and the signal became stronger than the noise (Figure 5).

When using Tiresias LP (bolder typeface with monolinear stems) the word 'limited', was comparably more distinguishable. Therefore, the solution for a legible font seems not to rely only on the size, but also on the thickness of the stroke. Hence, if the exact noise ratio of each deficiency is discovered, a potentially beneficial typeface with higher or lower frequencies than the noise could be designed. Previous research has shown that 'subjects with cloudy media read better when white letters appear on a black background' [Legge *et al.*, 1985]. This statement comes in agreement with the illustration (Figure 6) and therefore the solution in legibility does not rely only on the typeface but also on the background against which it is used.

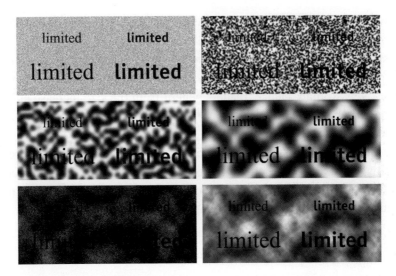

Figure 5: Black letters on white paper, covered by a filter of noise. The typefaces used are Times New Roman and Tiresias.

1.4.3 *Leading and spacing*

The second part investigated how leading and spacing affect legibility for visually impaired people, in both serif and sans serif typefaces. Among the serif version of Freight, the results showed that the default spacing and leading of the font was the most beneficial. Second, yet close to the first, came the widest version of Freight. Wider spacing did not affect legibility contradicting the optimal calculations of Prince [1967]. This may be due to the fact that serifs add a distinguishable gap between letters, thus preventing crowding. However, when reading Freight Text Book one participant commented: 'Big words are tricky, especially with a big magnifier', indicating that results for leading and spacing might differ in larger sizes, as fewer letters will be seen per reading saccade.

In the sans serif sample, the most read words were noted when both spacing and leading were at their widest. Yet, this result fails to reach the lowest legibility rate of the serif one. The results contradict those of sighted people, who read better the samples with the default spacing, with a higher reading rate in the sans serif typeface.

Interestingly, one participant commented for Freight Text Book: 'This is a funny one'. Despite this, his performance for this typeface was the highest among the entire second section. In fact, readers are accustomed

Figure 6: White letters on white paper, covered by a filter of noise. The typefaces used are Times New Roman and Tiresias.

and confident with certain styles of typeface. To change their reading habits would be difficult, even if it could prove to be more beneficial [Unger, 2007].

1.4.4 *Serif and sans serif*

The readability of serif and sans serif typefaces was tested mainly in the first part of the experiment. However, data from the second and third part which used both types of fonts were analyzed. In the two first parts, the typefaces with the overall higher reading rate were serif ones (Times New Roman, 23 pts, and Freight Text Book, 18 pts). It appears that the sans serif typefaces with the most read words fail to reach the lowest legibility rate of the serif ones. In fact, in the top five most read typefaces of this experiment four had serifs. The results contradicted Arditi's comment: when size was reduced almost to the visual acuity limit, the difference in read words was hardly noticeable between serifs and sans. However, this applies only to the results of the visually impaired, as for the other tested groups distribution varies among serif and sans serif. As stated earlier, it is possible that other parameters might be responsible for the efficacy of a typeface. Serifs could be either a positive or redundant feature, depending on the instance.

1.4.5 *Other typographic details*

In the third part, three aspects were tested: the efficiency of a typeface specially designed for the visually impaired; the efficiency of caption designed typefaces enlarged to the equivalent of Arial 16 pts; the efficiency of large counters.

First came Tiresias LP in 15.5 pts, whose results were very close to Times New Roman 23 pts; the typeface with the most words read in the entire test. It also gathered various positive comments. As shown in the study regarding noise and letter recognition, this success may be due to the thickness of the font. Among the readers wearing simulating spectacles, this font had the highest performance but scored only a mediocre reading rate from the normal sighted.

The hypothesis that an enlarged caption typeface would improve legibility was invalid; it did not affect the results. Minuscule 6 was read better than Freight Micro Book probably because of its darker paragraph texture. The big counters of Optima, Palatino and Century Gothic did not handicap nor facilitate the readers. Yet, in this part the least read typeface was Century Gothic, most likely due to the lack of feature diversity that would make a font more recognizable.

One participant commented that the text was getting blurry when reading paragraphs set in bolder typefaces. His performance was not affected by it. However, the thick strokes of the letters reduced the space between details, rendering letter identification more difficult; the letters ultimately became blobs. Therefore, depending on the eye deficiencies, creating typefaces of different thickness and styles to cover different reading needs and limitations should be considered.

1.5 Towards a pattern identification

1.5.1 *Common mistakes found*

Regardless of each typeface's reading rate, participants with low vision and with simulating spectacles made a substantial amount of mistakes compared to the ones without visual deficiencies. Looking for a pattern among these mistakes, they were grouped into three categories.

The first was about words that took a lot of time to read. Consecutive letters with strong vertical stems as in the word 'limited' were the more problematic. Interestingly, most samples with mistaken words involve sans serif letters.

The second one was omitted words. The reader's eye impeded from having an entire view of the line, 'jumped' too far during a saccade and failed to identify small words. The same mistake was seen when short words would appear in the beginning of a line; the readers would pick the wrong starting point. This suggests that tighter word spacing would be beneficial. Also, wider leading should be carefully applied as to not obstruct the readers from finding the beginning of a line.

The third and largest category was misread letters. However, this phenomenon could be because no meaning was deduced from the paragraphs. Hence, the readers could easily proceed to a random false guess, which they would then repeat when the same word would appear again. Nevertheless, even after filtering these results, some ascenders were mistaken for x-height letters. For example: 't', was confused for an 'r' or 'l' for an 'i'. Other x-height letters like 'c' were mistaken for an 'e', or vice versa. Another noticeable mistake was combining two letters, or separating one letter into two (e.g. ti=h, ch=d).

1.5.2   *Eye filtering mechanism and the Fourier Method:*
a complementary study

1.5.2.1   *Testing method and possible risks to consider*

An exploratory study was created in order to locate whether misinterpretation derived from hasty reading or was due to a malfunctioning filtering mechanism in the eye that altered the message. The process used was the Fourier Transform, which is a mathematical description of an image in terms of spatial frequencies. Seven of the participants of the first experiment were selected to partake in this study, based on their previous results. They were presented with six symbols and were asked to reproduce them on a piece of paper. The participants were not informed about the nature of the shown shapes so as to avoid predisposing them. The first symbol was a square. This shape, easy to perceive and draw, would determine the drawing abilities of the participants. The four other symbols were letters, different for each participant based on their individual mistakes. Fifth was the letter 'a', chosen because it was never mistaken during the first experiment. However, the representation of the symbols was often not what the reader had in mind. To control and correct this effect, participants were asked what they were about to draw.

1.5.2.2 *Analyzing the material*

To ensure accuracy of the Fourier Transform, certain adaptations to the drawings in terms of proportions and design were necessary. In order to discover a pattern responsible for the misinterpretation, the given shapes and their drawings were compared. Two symbols from each sample were chosen and input to a program that visualized their respective Fourier frequencies. The next step was to find the filter that simulates the transformation as the deficient eye would. If the used filter was successful, we would be able to analyze which design features for all the letters are beneficial for each eye deficiency. Of the results obtained, only three were worth analyzing. The rest depicted the symbols without difficulty and provided accurate drawings of the shown shapes. Figure 7 illustrates the symbols, participants' drawings, and the effects of the Fourier transform.

1.5.2.3 *The outcomes*

Participants, unaware of the given shape, misinterpreted letters that they were able to read before due to context absence. However, some participants benefited from the letter isolation, probably due to the absence of 'crowding'. The results suggest that accentuating details beyond the normal rules of type design seems like a viable solution. Designing geometrical, angular letters, or accentuating strokes when those form a curve could be some possible paths.

In conclusion, apart from accentuating the responsible features for the distinction of a letter and its counters, the creation of a 'clever' typeface with so-called OpenType alternations should be considered. Thus, when certain letter combinations appear, stylistic alternates of the same characters would replace them, ensuring that they will not be misread. The optimum result will be achieved if inter-word and inter-letter spacing is adjusted according to the number of letters in a word.

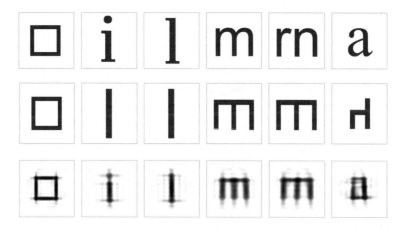

Figure 7 *(Top)*: Initial shapes; Middle: Participant's representation (after drawing adaptations); *(Bottom)*: Initial shapes after applying Fourier Transform filter.

1.6 Conclusion

Visually impaired people are in need of a specially designed font to use in large print documents. In search of the parameters for such a typeface, this research managed to illustrate some of the reasons that make reading a difficult task for the visually impaired. In order to turn these results into reliable statements, a new, quantitative research should be initialized, with a wider selection of participants and more tested aspects.

Generally, the rules that exist so far for readers with normal vision seem to also apply to the visually impaired. Still, these parameters need enhancement in order to achieve equal results to those of sighted people. From a typesetting scope, readability depends on a combination of several typographic features. It seems however that serif fonts in a bigger font size and wider leading are more beneficial.

Regarding typographical details, the majority of visually impaired people read better bolder fonts with large counters; letter and word spacing only needed a few adjustments. Additionally, in order to avoid confusion caused by crowding, adjustments must be made to specific letter combinations. This means that probably two variations of the same letter should be designed, each used when surrounded by different letters. As each individual has different needs, each kind of eye deficiency would need a different solution. In order to provide suitable and customized fonts for each one of them, further research is imperative.

Acknowledgments

This paper could not have been possible without the help of Tom Conlin the chief executive of the Berkshire County Blind Society, Dawn Single-ton, the Manager of the Reading Association for the Blind and each and every participant who embraced this project with so much enthusiasm. I would also like to thank Alexios Beveratos, for sharing his knowledge and time, regarding the Fourier transform methods and Mary Dyson, for guiding me through every step of this research. Lastly, I would like to thank Kleoniki Havaki for her immense support.

References

Aitchison, J. (2003) *Words in the mind: an introduction to the mental lexicon.* (Blackwell, Oxford) pp. 134-136.

Al Otaibi, A. Z. and Dickinson, C. M. (2000) *The effect of some typograph-ical factors on reading performance in visual impairment.* (Swetz and Zeitlinger, NY) p. 309.

Arditi, A. and Cho, J. (2000). Do serifs enhance or diminish text legibility?, *Investigative Ophthalmology and Visual Science*, 41, p. 437.

Bailey, I. L., Clear, R. and Berman, S. M. (1993). Size as a determinant of reading speed, *Journal of the Illuminating Engineering Society*, 22(2), pp. 102-117.

Bouma, H. (1970). Interaction effects in parafoveal letter recognition, *Nature*, 226, pp. 177–178, *Proc.* Yu, D., Cheung, S. H., Legge, G. E. and Chung, S. T. (2007). Effect of letter spacing on visual span and reading speed, *Journal of Vision*, 7(2), p.1.

Chung, S. T., Mansfield, J. S. and Legge, G. E. (1998). Psychophysics of read-ing, XVIII: The effect of print size on reading speed in normal peripheral vision, *Vision Research*, 39, pp. 2949–2962.

Ciuffreda, K. J., Levi, D. M. and Selenow, A. (1991) *Amblyopia: Basic and clinical aspects.* (Butterworth-Heinemann, Boston).

Cline, D., Hofstetter, H. W. and Griffin, J. R. eds. (1997) *Dictionary of visual scienc*e (Butterworth-Heinemann 4th ed., Boston) p. 521.

Jones, M. and Mewhort, D. (2004). Case-sensitive letter and bigram frequency counts from large-scale English corpora, *Behavior Research Methods, Instruments, & Computers*, 36, pp. 388–396.

Liang, Y. X. (2002). Readers beware! Effects of visual noise on the channel for reading. *Intel Science Talent Search*, pp. 1-18.

Legge, G. E, Bigelow, C. A. (2011). Does print size matter for reading? A review of findings from vision science and typography, *Journal of Vision*, 11(5), pp. 1-22.

Legge, G. E., Rubin, G. S., Pelli, D. G. and Schleske, M. M. (1985). Psycho-physics of reading, II: low vision, *Vision Research*, 25(2), pp.253–266.

Levi, D. M., Song, S. and Pelli, D. G. (2007). Amblyopic reading is crowding, *Journal of Vision*, 7(2), pp. 1-17.

Minda, E. R., Jeffrey, W., Jutai, J., Strong, G., Campbell, K. A., Gold, D., Pretty, L., and Wilmot, L. (2007). The legibility of typefaces for readers with low vision: a research review, *Journal of Visual Impairment and Blindness*, p.410.

Paterson, D. G and Tinker, M. A. (1947). Influence of leading upon newspaper type, *Journal of Applied Psychology*, 31, pp. 160-163.

Parish, D. H. and Sperling, G. (1991). Object spatial frequencies, retinal. *Vision Research*, 31, pp. 1399–1416.

Prince, J. H., (1967) Printing for the visually handicapped. *The Australian Journal of Optometry*, 50(6), pp 164-177.

Smith, F. (1994) *Understanding reading: a psycholinguistic analysis of reading and learning to read.* (Erlbaum, Hillsdale) pp. 21, 82.

Reece, G. A., Eubank, T., Rafieetary, M. and Lowther, D. L. (2008). Preferences of reduced vision readers for serif and italic presence on electronic displays, *Association for Education and Rehabilitation Journal*, 1(1), p. 5.

Royal National Institute of the Blind (2007) *See it right: making information accessible for people with sight problems.* (RNIB, London) p.33.

Rubin, G. S., Feely, M., Perera, S., Ekstrom, K. and Williamson, E. (2006). The effect of font and line width on reading speed in people with mild to moderate vision loss, *Ophthalmic and Physiological Optics*, 6, pp. 545–554.

Rubin, G. S. and Turano, K. (1994). Low vision reading with sequential word presentations, *Vision Research*, 32, pp. 895-902.

Russell, E., Jutai, J. W., Strong, J. G., Campbell, K. A., Gold, D., Pretty, L. and Wilmot, L. (2007). The legibility of typefaces for readers with low vision: a research review, *Journal of Visual Impairment & Blindness*, 101(7), pp. 402-415.

Solomon, J., Pelli, D. G. (1994). The visual filter mediating letter identification, *Nature*, 369, pp.395-397.

Shaw, A. (1969). Print for Partial Sight (Library Association, London), *Proc.*
Papadopoulos, K. S. and Goudiras, D .B. (2005). Accessibility assistance
for visually impaired people in digital texts. *The British Journal of Visual Impairment*, 23(2).

Tinker, M. A. (1963) *Legibility of print.* (Iowa State University Press, Iowa)
p. 22.

Tracy, W. (1986) *Letters of credit: a view of type design.* (Gordon Fraser Gallery
Ltd., London) p. 31.

Unger, G. (2007). *While you are Reading.* (Mark Batty Publisher, New York)
pp.77, 166.

Wilkins, A. (2003) *Reading Through Colour: How coloured filters can reduce
reading difficulty, eye strain, and headaches.* (John Wiley, West Sussex)
p. 40.

Yu, D., Cheung, S. H., Legge, G. E. and Chung S T. (2007). Effect of letter
spacing on visual span and reading speed, *Journal of Vision*, 7(2), pp. 1-10.

Chapter 2

Matilda: a typeface for children with low vision

Ann Bessemans

Due to the low quality level of visual input they receive in the form of printed text, visually impaired beginning readers are at a disadvantage in comparison to their peers. In the past, typography has often been regarded as a useful instrument to improve the legibility of the printed reading material that is being offered to children with low vision. However, the legibility research that was at the base of this conception was not always of good quality. In cognitive science for example, many efforts were made that were methodologically correct, yet the test material (typefaces) was unrealistic. On the other hand, typographers themselves introduced many typefaces that were supposed to improve legibility, but the reasoning behind them was hardly ever sufficiently methodologically supported. Moreover, most legibility research focused on people with low vision in general, ignoring the fact that visually impaired children constitute a very particular group with specific issues. This PhD research project approached the issue of legibility for visually impaired beginning readers from a design context. The research is an attempt at bridging the gap between the font designers and the cognitive scientists studying the legibility of letter characters. In the development of the test material, the focus was on parameter design. Parameters are shape characteristics that can be isolated within the same type. Starting from two existing types (one serif, one sans-serif), typefaces were designed based on five parameters that explored the balance between homogeneous and heterogeneous in both form and rhythm. Based on legibility research with test material that conforms to both the scientific and the typographic knowledge in this field, a typeface is proposed that provides support for the target group of visually impaired children in the first stages of the reading process.

1.1 Introduction

Reading is done without consciously recognizing letters [Warde, 1956; Unger, 2007]. Nevertheless letters constitute an important aspect of determining legibility [Rayner and Pollatsek, 1998]. Letters need to be decoded in order to obtain meaning. Reading is a complex, cognitive and fast process. Children having serious problems with reading are at an increased risk to end up in a cycle of failure [Stanovich, 1986; Wolf, 2007]. When reading is a slow and cumbersome process, it will have consequences for cognitive behavior and motivation. A person whose reading process is impeded is less able to develop both intellectually and socially. Because most of the process of learning to read is finished after the age of nine it is important that children who encounter difficulties are supported in the initial stages of this process [Stanovich, 1986; Marquet *et al.*, 2006].

Visually impaired children with no additional disorders do not have problems with reading comprehension, spelling or accuracy. Therefore the reading problems of children with low vision are (initially) visual and not cognitive [Gompel *et al.*, 2003; Gompel, 2005]. A visual impairment has a direct impact on technical reading skills.

Due to the low quality of visual input they receive in the form of printed text, beginning visually impaired readers are at a disadvantage in comparison to their (visually unimpaired) peers. The reading process is disturbed due to a reduction in visual input [Gompel *et al.*, 2003; Gompel, 2005]. Children with a visual impairment have problems with the decoding of words, the deciphering of visual patterns, and the recognition of letters. Because their decoding is hampered, the reading speed is lower, which eventually can lead to cognitive problems necessitating a transfer from regular to special education. To improve visual input, a lot of attention is given to optical reading aids and the use of large print. Large print is often seen as a quick fix to show that efforts have been made for the visually impaired. Research has shown that large print books are not effective for the technical reading process for most children with low vision [Lovie-Kitchin *et al.*, 2001; Corn *et al.*, 2002].

1.2   Typographic research and legibility research

In the past, typography has often been looked upon as a useful instrument to improve the legibility of printed reading material that is being offered to people with low vision. However, legibility research efforts are not always of good quality. In the case of cognitive scientists this is all too often caused by inadequate domain knowledge of typography, pointed out by Spencer [1969], Dyson [1999], Lund [1999] and Bessemans [2012]. This can lead to the use of incorrect terminology, poorly designed letters, poorly motivated and incorrect choice of text material. For the designers, this is due to an intuitive way of approaching legibility research [Dyson, 1999; Lund, 1999; Bessemans, 2012]. Typographers rarely do empirical research. Very few attempts are made by typographers to test their designed material on their target group. They portray their 'findings' as truism, but these lack any scientific validation.

Many legibility studies focusing on the influence of design, both within cognitive science and within the design world, lack internal and/or external validity. Figure 1 shows test material illustrating a common external validity problem. The material is carefully constructed by manipulating isolated parameters (like heaviness of serifs, letter width, letter height). This results in high internal validity. But the external validity is very low. These letters are not considered real typefaces used in everyday life. Figure 2 shows test material illustrating a common internal validity problem. The test material could be present in real life, which means that the external validity is high. However, effects on legibility cannot be attributed to single design parameters. Several design parameters (or even a combination) can influence the legibility effect. For example a difference in legibility between Helvetica and Times New Roman cannot be attributed solely to the serifs as there are other differences between the two types. Therefore the internal validity is rather low. Design parameters are design characteristics within the same font that can be isolated and can be manipulated independently of each other. A design parameter can therefore be related to the internal and external validity.

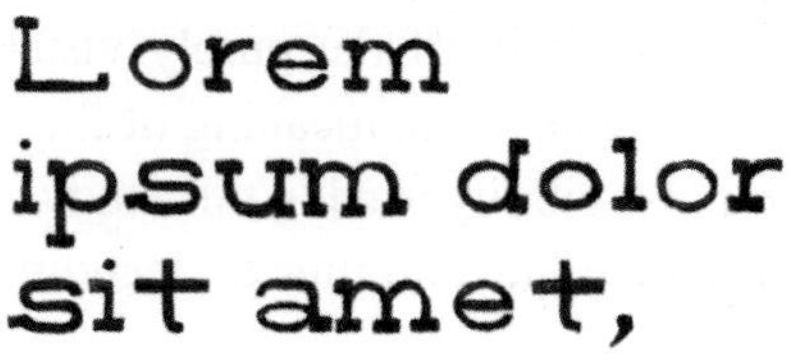

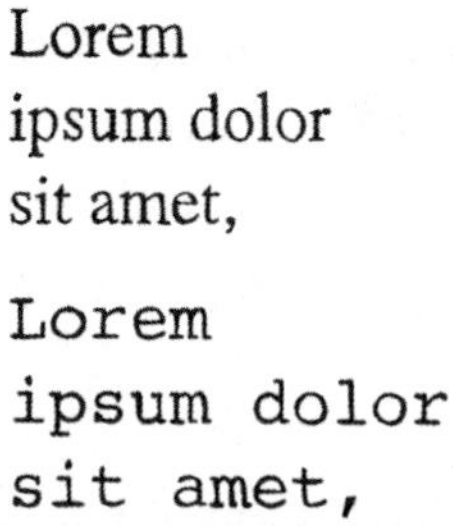

Lorem ipsum dolor sit amet,

Lorem
ipsum dolor
sit amet,

Lorem
ipsum dolor
sit amet,

Figure 1: *(Left)* An example of a common external validity problem. Examples of such material can be found in: [Liu and Arditi, 2000; Arditi, 2004].

Figure 2: *(Right)* An example of a common internal validity problem. Examples of such material where comparisons are made between typefaces can be found in: [Mansfield *et al.*, 1996; Woods *et al.*, 2005].

Moreover, most legibility research has focused on adults with low vision, ignoring the fact that visually impaired children constitute a very particular group with specific issues. Both the fact that their reading process has just started, as well as the fact that their visual impairment is not caused by ageing, makes it difficult or even impossible to simply transfer results. It makes sense to hypothesize that the elderly are more aided by a macro level of typography like the layout of a page or book or even a bigger type size which slows down reading but is more comfortable [Bouwhuis, 1993].

1.3 The term legibility

Another problem within the existing legibility research is confusion regarding the term legibility. Many different groups of people (e.g. typographers, linguists, educationalists, ergonomists, psychologists, etc.) use the term and give it a personal related meaning without explicitly explaining it. This explanation is of importance in order to make legibility studies comparable. Within this research legibility is the ease with which visual symbols are decoded [Bessemans, 2012]. This definition arose from dictionary descriptions of reading. Reading means: transposing visual symbols and converting them into linguistic meanings. To concisely define the term legibility, attention goes to the two global and successive steps that occur when reading: decoding and the acquisition of meaning, or the sensoric and the cognitive aspects of reading (see Figure 3). Decoding or the sensoric aspect in reading is the conversion of the purely visual representation of words (which may not yet relate to the meaning of these words in beginner readers). The definition of legibility used in this study is clearly related to this first sensoric aspect of reading and thus to decoding problems of children with low vision.

1.4 Design methodology applied

Comprehensive legibility research within my own study takes into account a clear definition of legibility and a combination of both scientific methods and typographic practice. A designer-researcher is able to combine these two and thus guarantee the internal and external validity of the test material. The materials of the design research are systematically constructed. The design is the point of focus throughout the research. The methodology starts with the context that is shaped by theoretical research (consisting both of scientific and typographic matter) and practical work

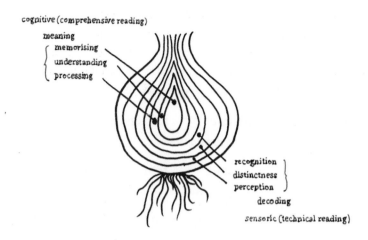

cognitive (comprehensive reading)

meaning
- memorising
- understanding
- processing

recognition
distinctness
perception

decoding

sensoric (technical reading)

Figure 3: An onion model explaining the sensoric and cognitive aspects within reading.

from other designers (mainly typefaces). This context will lead to an initial design that ultimately results in test fonts. These test fonts are used within legibility studies (see 1.5). In turn, the results of the legibility studies provide motivation for a second type design that will eventually lead to the development of a special font for children with low vision. Using this global framework, this study starts with an explicit definition of legibility, and uses methods of measuring that have both internal and external validity. The output is an improved insight into the nature of legibility and some practical guidelines in the realm of type design.

During the process of designing the test typefaces the focus was on parameter designs. Departing from two existing typefaces (serif DTL Documenta and sans-serif Frutiger) a number of derived typefaces were designed with five different parameters: (1) variable x-height; (2) conventional contrast; (3) unconventional contrast; (4) direction; (5) letter width (see Figure 4).

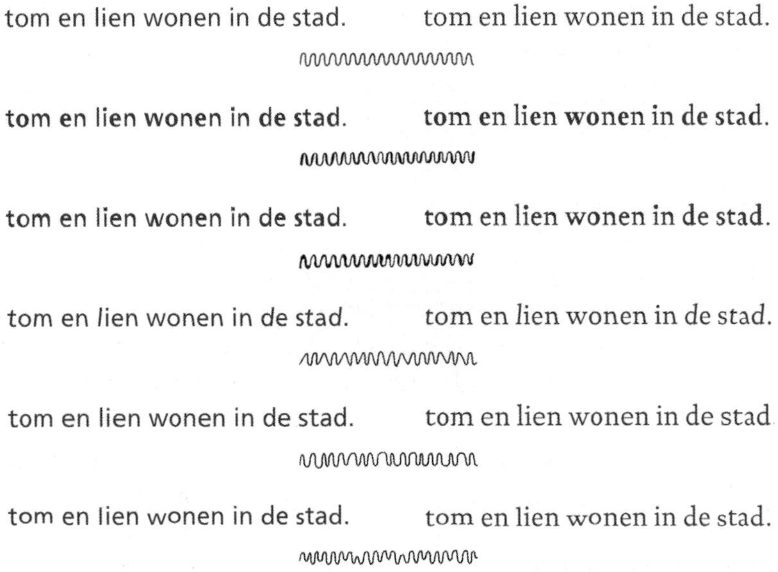

tom en lien wonen in de stad.   tom en lien wonen in de stad.

tom en lien wonen in de stad.   tom en lien wonen in de stad.

tom en lien wonen in de stad.   tom en lien wonen in de stad.

tom en lien wonen in de stad.   tom en lien wonen in de stad.

tom en lien wonen in de stad.   tom en lien wonen in de stad

tom en lien wonen in de stad.   tom en lien wonen in de stad.

Figure 4: The test fonts (sans serif and serif) with their illustrated rhythm. From top to bottom: the basic fonts Frutiger and DTL Documenta; parameter conventional contrast; parameter unconventional contrast; parameter direction; parameter letter width; parameter variable x-heights.

1. Variable x-height: By changing the x-height and the ascender and descender height of the letters, this design parameter induced a lot of heterogeneity, both rhythmically and in terms of letter form.
2. Conventional contrast: This parameter adds contrast to the letter in a conventional way. Certain letter parts were emphasized in a conventional manner. This parameter mainly induced heterogeneity in terms of letter forms.
3. Unconventional contrast: This design parameter emphasized the most distinctive character parts within the letters. This induced in particular the heterogeneity of letter forms (because of less symmetry).
4. Direction: Within this parameter, more heterogeneity was induced within rhythm by playing with the directions of the letter strokes.
5. Letter width: Within this parameter, more heterogeneity was induced within rhythm and letter form by varying the letter widths.

The five parameters were used to examine the balance between homogeneous and heterogeneous in both form and rhythm. The heterogeneity with regard to the letter shape can be illustrated by making related letters less similar (see Figure 5). The heterogeneity with regard to the rhythm of the font can be illustrated by a more irregular stripe pattern which is formed by the vertical letter strokes.

Using the concepts of homogeneity and heterogeneity we can say that in general sans serif typefaces are homogeneous within their letter forms (because of possible mirroring) and heterogeneous within their rhythm (see Figure 6). With serif typefaces it is the other way around (certainly for serif typefaces based on the 20th century model): they are heterogeneous within their letter forms (the serifs and contrasts make mirroring impossible) and homogeneous within their rhythm. Theoretical and practical insights concerning legibility of material for low vision children pointed in the direction of more heterogeneity. Notice that we never tested very extreme forms of heterogeneity.

aeocbd
Welke chique barones verzamelde fijne xyloglyptiek?

aeocbd
Welke chique barones verzamelde fijne xyloglyptiek?

Figure 5: Illustrating the heterogeneity within letter shape. Top: a geometrical sans serif. Bottom: a humanistic sans serif.

1.5 Quantitative and qualitative legibility research

The typefaces were tested by means of experimental (quantitative evaluation) and subjective (qualitative evaluation) legibility research. Both children with good eyesight and low eyesight were selected in order to study the reading skills and reading experiences in visually impaired children. In the study 110 visually impaired children with no additional disorders participated. They were recruited thanks to the cooperation of centers for

Figure 6: Illustrating letter and rhythm heterogeneity. The heterogeneity within the letter shape lies in the serifs and the contrast of the serif typefaces. The heterogeneity within the rhythm lies within the rhythmical pattern formed by sans serifs.

the visually impaired in Belgium and the Netherlands. Also 54 normally sighted children participated in the study and were recruited by regular schools. All readers were five to ten years old.

A psychophysical method was used in the test. Children were presented pseudowords[a,b] in the test typefaces on a computer screen for a short period of time and asked to read aloud the word seen (see Figure 7). The read words were typed and the number of word (letter) reading errors was counted using the software Affect [Spruyt *et al.*, 2010].

In order to allow for differences in error rates between different type faces, the words were followed by a mask and the time in between the word and the mask and/or the word exposure time was adjusted for each child in order to obtain a 50% chance of recognition. This was done in an initial testing phase. Hence, every child had an individual duration at which words were presented. The children who were better at recognizing words were presented with words for a shorter duration. Then, in the main

---

[a] Pseudowords were used because phonological rules and conventions within the letterforms remain, while semantic knowledge and the influence of context are excluded.

[b] 100 pseudowords were created with an equal amount of letters. These pseudowords were used within each parameter and the basic fonts. The software controlling the experiment selected and mixed at random an equal amount of words within the design parameters. Simultaneously the fonts (basic and derived) were chosen at random by the software (Affect).

test, 6 sessions of 60 pseudowords were presented to each child with the child's specific word-duration. Within each session there were 3 breaks to ensure concentration. The statistical analyses were performed on these data.

The effects of the design parameters were measured using statistical analyses based on a General Linear Model (GLM) with repeated measures. The GLM calculates the extent of the connections between a dependent variable (e.g. percentage of words read correctly) and some independent variables (e.g. the different design parameters). Repeated measurements allow you to take multiple observations within a subject (the various sessions of each child can be included within the analysis, taking into account between-subject variability). The GLM identifies those variables that are reliably influencing legibility. Several analyses with percentage correctly read pseudowords as the dependent variable were done: 1) global analyses; 2) analyses within each group of children (low vision and normal); 3) analyses limited to words where at least one letter was correct; 4) analyses in relation to reading level; 5) analyses contrasting Documenta vs Frutiger; 6) analyses for different types of visual problems.

In the subjective part of the study, reading experiences of children who read the test typefaces were examined. The children were (individually) asked to rank the test material, 12 fonts, by the legibility[c] of the fonts (see Figure 8). The children were interviewed about which factors played a role in their subjective judgement by means of dialogue. The feedback and the interaction with the children were of great importance for the design of the final typeface. In contrast with this way of working, a type designer very rarely gets immediate feedback from his readers. Type designers have always been very far behind the frontline when it comes to contact with the readers. In this case there was direct feedback between the readers and the type designer.

The effect of the design parameters on legibility using the subjective method was measured using Kendall's concordance coefficient W. When this coefficient is high, this means that the ranking as observed is a reliable one, i.e. children agreed on the ranking.

---

[c] The children were asked which fonts read the best for them.

Figure 7: Experimental legibility research (quantitative).

Figure 8: Subjective legibility research (qualitative).

1.6   Results

A remarkable finding from the objective legibility research is that children with normal vision read with reliably fewer errors when the serif typeface DTL Documenta was used, rather than the sans serif Frutiger. This result is somewhat surprising because children (especially beginning readers) mainly read with a sans serif in primary school. Zuzano Licko's [1990] well-known quote: '…the readers read best what they read most' is thus jeopardized, certainly for beginning readers in the age group of five to ten years old. The teachers' belief that letters for beginning readers should look as simple as possible and should reflect handwriting is falsified by this study. In visually impaired children the difference in reading accuracy of the two typefaces is less pronounced. During the reading (decoding) process non-visually impaired children appear not to be hampered by a homogeneous rhythm, but rather by a homogeneous form. The children with low vision however, seemed to be hampered more, and in particular, by a homogeneous rhythm. Within the DTL Documenta font set (the basic font with a homogeneous rhythm) the design parameters – rhythm[d] and direction – that made the rhythm the most heterogeneous, had the most positive effect on legibility (in terms of decoding). It appears that for visually impaired children a more irregular rhythm is beneficial for their reading. Also it may be that a certain degree of formal heterogeneity offers support (as we saw with the normally sighted children).

Within the subjective legibility research, the analysis of the rankings showed no significant results. However, the dialogue with the children contained a lot of relevant information. The subjective legibility research results showed a rather early conditioning with daily reading material in beginning readers. Children associated sans serifs with school and considered them to be writable; serifs they associated with literature (e.g. books and newspapers) and they considered them to be difficult to reproduce themselves. The non-visually impaired children generally perceived the most conventional typeface as being the most legible one. Amongst the visually impaired children this was not always the case. Some of the

---

[d] It became clear that the difference with respect to the design parameter rhythm and the basic font is not seen by most of the beginning readers. This parameter can therefore be useful for practical use because it induces legibility while remaining invisible.

children appeared to experience social pressure to choose a normal letter. They were reporting that classmates would laugh at them if they chose a strange looking font to read.

1.7 Matilda

Starting from the results, together with my own understanding, knowledge, intuition and ideas as a design researcher, a typeface called Matilda[e] was designed that is able to provide support for the target group of visually impaired children in the first stages of the reading process. Matilda should be seen as a tool for supporting reading, not as the solution to reading problems.

The new typeface is similar to the basic fonts DTL Documenta and Frutiger in terms of letter width and text color (see Figure 9). Matilda is based on a serif typeface, in order to reduce the gap between the reading material for non-visually impaired children and those with low vision. Furthermore compared to the sans serif font Frutiger, the design parameters within the DTL Documenta font set had the most positive effect on the decoding skills for children with low vision.

The main characteristics of Matilda are wide, open and round letters which are intended to have a friendly feeling (see Figure 10). The letters are dynamic and solid, constructed and organic. The letters are built on a rather stable and vertical axis. The curves are open, the serifs are asymmetric, convex and concave. There are ball terminals to emphasize the letter terminations to augment its individuality and distinctiveness. The low contrast in the letters is necessary to easily enlarge or reduce text. If children with low vision are reading in different contrasts/colors (which they often do on computers) the letters need to remain very clear. Matilda does not have a very large x-height. The ascenders and descenders provide enough room for diacritics.

---

[e] Named after the book 'Matilda' from Roald Dahl (1988).

'Zit je goed, Sofie? Voor de rest van de cursus is het van belang dat
je inziet dat sofisten echte filosofen waren, die hun plaats verdienen
in de geschiedenis van het menselijk denken. De sofisten lieten zich
voor hun werk betalen, omdat ze niet zoals Plato konden rekenen
op een rijkelijk inkomen. Het waren mensen met een ruime belang-
stelling voor intellectuele en ethische problemen, die hun kunde in
dienst stelden van hun studenten. Dergelijke sofisten zijn de hele
geschiedenis door gekomen en gegaan. In zekere zin waren zij de
eerste humanisten en onafhankelijke onderzoekers. Met leraren en
betweters, die ofwel dik tevreden zijn met het weinige dat ze weten
of opscheppen dat ze van een heleboel dingen verstand hebben,
waar ze in werkelijkheid geen snars van begrijpen, hebben ze dus
niks van doen...' !,?.

'Zit je goed, Sofie? Voor de rest van de cursus is het van belang dat
je inziet dat sofisten echte filosofen waren, die hun plaats verdienen
in de geschiedenis van het menselijk denken. De sofisten lieten zich
voor hun werk betalen, omdat ze niet zoals Plato konden rekenen
op een rijkelijk inkomen. Het waren mensen met een ruime belang-
stelling voor intellectuele en ethische problemen, die hun kunde in
dienst stelden van hun studenten. Dergelijke sofisten zijn de hele
geschiedenis door gekomen en gegaan. In zekere zin waren zij de
eerste humanisten en onafhankelijke onderzoekers. Met leraren en
betweters, die ofwel dik tevreden zijn met het weinige dat ze weten
of opscheppen dat ze van een heleboel dingen verstand hebben,
waar ze in werkelijkheid geen snars van begrijpen, hebben ze dus
niks van doen...' !,?.

'Zit je goed, Sofie? Voor de rest van de cursus is het van belang dat
je inziet dat sofisten echte filosofen waren, die hun plaats verdienen
in de geschiedenis van het menselijk denken. De sofisten lieten zich
voor hun werk betalen, omdat ze niet zoals Plato konden rekenen
op een rijkelijk inkomen. Het waren mensen met een ruime belang-
stelling voor intellectuele en ethische problemen, die hun kunde in
dienst stelden van hun studenten. Dergelijke sofisten zijn de hele
geschiedenis door gekomen en gegaan. In zekere zin waren zij de
eerste humanisten en onafhankelijke onderzoekers. Met leraren en
betweters, die ofwel dik tevreden zijn met het weinige dat ze weten
of opscheppen dat ze van een heleboel dingen verstand hebben,
waar ze in werkelijkheid geen snars van begrijpen, hebben ze dus
niks van doen...' !,?.

Figure 9: Comparison of the text color and letter width between Matilda (top), DTL Documenta (middle) and Frutiger (bottom).

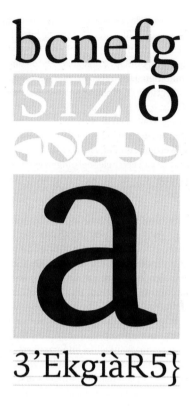

Figure 10: Design features of Matilda.

Matilda is in full development and a growing type family (also ready to test within new legibility research). The typeface includes a serif, an italic, and a bold (see Figure 11). Matilda is also extended by the design parameters that were most helpful to improve the decoding process of children with low vision. These are the parameters rhythm (see Figure 12) and direction (see Figure 13)[f]. More research will be done because it would be interesting to know how the degree of rhythmic heterogeneity affects legibility. Also the outcome of interaction effects such as the combination between the parameter letter width and direction would give more insight into legible fonts for children with low vision (and human perception as more information is revealed about the sensoric aspect when reading).

---

[f] Emphasizing letter parts seems to be helpful for visually impaired children at the lowest reading level.

Matilda
Où est le petit garçon?
ballonnenJA
non'Tok!' AUW 50>36
slim Là bas! Un petit chat.
STOUT peut-être.
Hoe **verrassing**
'Houd daarmee op,' zei de juffrouw.
kijk ZORRO ça va
friet Regarde ici!!
haha WAF C'est gràve?
poney 7-2=5 **hebben**
Snoepje **ai** *bon* KONIJN SPRONG 8 KEER
Een goed boek. Voilà

Figure 11: Matilda Regular, Bold & Italic.

1.8 Conclusion

When legibility is explicitly defined and linked to the reading problems of the target group, methods of measuring legibility become clear while maintaining internal and external validity. It becomes clear that letters influence legibility and that results can be translated into a type design. A design researcher plays an important role in such legibility research.

This research highlights the importance of exploring the balance between homogeneity and heterogeneity. The design research gave clues to design parameters that can successfully improve legibility for low vision children by inducing rhythm heterogeneity. My future aim is to gain more insight into the legibility of printed matter by studying stripe patterns within words during reading, link these to spatial frequencies when reading and translate this information into practical designs. The new envisaged research wants to investigate to what extent the rhythm and spatial frequencies within a typeface can affect legibility for normal and poor readers (e.g. low vision readers). This is in line with the findings of my doctoral dissertation where disturbed stripe patterns within words resulted in better decoding skills (and thus legibility) for those with a less developed perceptual system.

tom en lien wonen in de stad.
ze wonen vier hoog.
ze hebben een hondje, woef.
tom speelt met zijn bal in de kamer.
woef springt wild naar de bal.
pats! de bal vliegt recht op de vaas af.

Figure 12: Matilda Rhythm.

tom en lien wonen in de stad.
ze wonen vier hoog.
ze hebben een hondje, woef.
tom speelt met zijn bal in de kamer.
woef springt wild naar de bal.
pats! de bal vliegt recht op de vaas af.
'tom maakt de vaas stuk', roept zus.

Figure 13: Matilda Direction.

References

Arditi, A. 2004. Adjustable Typography: An Approach to Enhancing Low Vision Test Accessibility. *Ergonomics*, 47 (5) pp. 469-482.

Bessemans, A. (2012). Letterontwerp voor kinderen met een visuele functiebeperking. (Dissertation, Leiden University & Hasselt University).

Bessemans, A. (2012). Research in Typography, *Typo*, 47, pp. 60-63.Bouwhuis, G. D. 1993. Reading rate and letter size, *IPO Annual Progress Report*, 28, pp. 30-36.

Corn, A. L., Wall, R. S., Jose, R. T., Bell, J. K., Wilcox, K. and Perez, A. (2002). An Initial Study of Reading and Comprehension Rates for Students Who Received Optical Devices, *Journal of Visual Impairment & Blindness*, May, pp. 322-334.

Dyson, M. C. (1999). Typography through the eyes of a psychologist. *Hyphen*, 2 (1), pp. 5-13.

Gompel, M. (2005). Literacy Skills of Children with Low Vision. (Dissertation, Radboud University Nijmegen).

Gompel, M. , Janssen, N. M., van Bon, W. H.J. and Schreuder, R. (2003). Visual input and Orhtographic Knowledge in Word Reading of Children with Low Vision, *Journal of Visual impairment and Blindness*, May, pp. 273-284.

Licko, Z. (1990). Do you read me? *Emigre*, 15, pp. 1-36.

Liu, L. and Arditi, A. 2000. Apparent string shortening concomitant with letter crowding. *Vision Research* 40, pp. 1059-1067.

Lovie-Kitchin, J., Bevan, J. D. and Brown, H. (2001). Reading performance in children with low vision, *Clinical and Experimental Optometry*, 84(3), pp. 148-154.

Lund, O. (1999). Knowledge construction in typography: the case of legibility research and the legibility of sans serif typefaces. (Dissertation, The University of Reading).

Mansfield, J. S., Legge, G. E. and Bane, M. C. (1996). Psychofysics of reading XV: font effects in normal and low vision. *Investigative Ophthalmology & Visual Science*, 37 (8), pp 1492-1501.

Marquet, R., Smits, D. and Naegels, G. (2006). Slecht leren begint met slecht zien, Klasse, 163, pp. 10-13.

Rayner, K., and Pollatsek, A. (1989). *The Psychology of Reading*. (New Jersey: Prentice Hall).

Spencer, H. 1969. *The visible word*. (Lund Humphries, London).

Spruyt, A., Clarysse, J., Vansteenwegen, D., Baeyens, F. and Hermans, D. (2010). Affect 4.0: A free software package for implementing psychological and psychophysiological experiments. *Experimental Psychology*, 57, pp. 36-45.

Stanovich, K. (1986). Matthew effects in reading: Some consequences of individual differences in the acquisition of literacy. *Reading Research Quarterly*, XXI/4, pp. 360-407.

Unger, G. (2007). Typografie als voertuig van de wetenschap. (De Buitenkant, Amsterdam).

Warde, B. (1956). *The Crystal Goblet. Sixteen Essays on Typography*. (The world publishing company, Cleveland).

Wolf, M. (2007). *Proust and the Squid*. The Story and Science of the Reading Brain. (HarperCollins: New York).

Woods, R. J., Davis, K., Scharff, L. F. V. and Austin, S. F. (2005). Effects of typeface and font size on legibility for children. *American Journal of Psychological Research*, 1, pp. 86-102.

Chapter 3

Sitka: a collaboration between type design and science

Kevin Larson and Matthew Carter

We recognize words by first recognizing individual letters, then using the letters to build a word [Larson, 2004; Rayner *et al.* 2012]. Words become more readable by making each of the individual letters more recognizable. This chapter is about the development process for a new typeface named Sitka. During the typeface's development, we tested how well peo-ple could read each of the letters in the typeface, and used the test results to inform design decisions. While the test results needed to be applied conscientiously, we discovered that typeface design could be successfully integrated with scientific legibility testing.

1.1 The design brief

A number of requirements for this new typeface were established at the outset. The design was to be a general-purpose typeface primarily for use on screen, a serif design with a family of Roman, Italic and Bold (Bold Italic was added later). Wide Latin language support was essential, with Greek and Cyrillic included. Figure 1 shows a sample of the lowercase Latin letters.

The quick brown fox jumps over the lazy dog

Figure 1: The famous pangram set in the typeface Sitka.

The typeface had to be optically scaled, in other words it would have different versions, each one optimized for setting at a specified output size or narrow range of sizes. Most of the attention would go into the extremes, particularly the smallest size. The number of intermediate masters required to cover the entire range of sizes, from 6 point to 36 point and above, was not decided until late in the development.

One aspect that was fundamental to the design process, and highly un-usual in the practice of type design, was the decision to test the legibility

37

of the design as it progressed. The design was tested at each stage, the results analyzed, and used to improve the next stage. This iterative process was a collaboration between designers and scientists. The aim was to design a typeface as legible as we could make it, and in the course of doing that, to learn more about legibility and the testing of legibility in general. We hoped that what we learned would be helpful beyond this particular exercise.

1.2   The design process

Thirteen tests during the development of Sitka examined many aspects of the typeface: there were tests focused on the lowercase Roman, uppercase Roman, lowercase italic, lowercase Greek, lowercase Cyrillic, and the lowercase large optical size. The studies used a time threshold letter recognition measure to compare the current version of the font to either an earlier version of the font or to a close comparison font.

   A massive amount of data was collected over the course of this design process, too much to discuss here. Instead we will discuss some of the more interesting findings and how we came to our design decisions. The findings include: it's not possible to test everything; a large x-height comes with a cost; a large x-height harms Greek letters; letter width and letter frequency impact letter recognition; it's harder to recognize a letter when next to other letters; large size designs are optimized for elegance not legibility; a typeface is a beautiful collection of letters not a collection of beautiful letters; and sometimes it's necessary to ignore the test results entirely.

1.3   It's not possible to test everything

A goal of this project was to run the studies quickly so design iterations could happen quickly. Each study looked for improvements between subtly different letterforms with a minimal number of study participants (usually 10-12) in order to get results as quickly as possible. We could have tested more people to be more confident of the results, but we decided that it would be better to run more tests with fewer people. As a trade-off we decided it was ok to make decisions with imperfect data. In order to get the most consistent data from each reader we chose to include only people who were 18-38 years old, native readers of English (native Greek and Russian readers for the Greek and Cyrillic studies), and had either normal or corrected-to-normal vision.

Readers were placed 150cm from the high DPI screen (144 DPI), and the letters were 36 points tall. This is three times further than normal reading distance and three times larger than typical text size. This kept the visual angle typical for reading, while allowing us to use large sized letters to test the design without any of the artifacts that can occur when there are too few pixels to represent the design properly.

The reader starts a single trial by looking at a mark on screen, followed by the test material that appeared for only part of a second. The test material was either a single letter displayed at the location of the mark, or was a sequence of three letters with the middle letter centered at the location of the mark. We called the three-letter sequence the context condition as each letter was placed between the letters that it most commonly appears between in written English, though we ensured that the three letters was never a word. In either case, the reader only needed to recognize the letter that appeared at the mark. After the test letters appeared briefly, they were replaced by a letter mask that limited any further processing of the test. When the trial was over, the reader was asked to identify the letter at the mark by pressing that letter on the keyboard. After each trial the reader was told if they identified the letter correctly.

At the beginning of each session a staircase procedure was used to find the fastest presentation time at which a reader could achieve a 50% accuracy rate. It was important for readers to make some errors to detect accuracy differences between letters. If the presentation times are long, even a poor typeface could have an accuracy rate of 100%. The presentation time was decreased by 17ms with each correct response and increased by 17ms with each incorrect response until a stable 50% accuracy was reached over 156 trials.

The testing method was refined over the first couple of studies. As an example, in the first study we compared two designs of the 26 Roman lowercase letters that differed in the openness of some of the letterforms. Under our initial context condition and kind of mask, we found an anomalous number of misrecognitions of the letter n. This didn't make sense; we feared that either flanking every test letter with n, o, or x or the mask was causing this effect. After changing our flanking letters to frequently occurring letter combinations and changing our mask to random letters, we no longer found surprising numbers of misrecognitions for any particular letter.

Another refinement we made during the earliest studies was to change the number of letters we investigated per study. The results from the first study of only 52 letters (26 lowercase letters in two different fonts) were very stable. Letters that were clearly different in design between the two fonts showed differences of only a few percent when tested. For the second study we tried testing many more conditions at once. We investigated the lowercase, uppercase and numbers in three different fonts. The increase from 52 letters to 186 letters led to very unstable results. In some cases there were improbable 20% accuracy differences between letters that were nearly identical.

The method was stable after fixing some of these early problems through trial and error. A tradeoff that we made was to not test every letter; we carefully choose only the most important letters to test. This left many omissions in the testing including extended character sets, uppercase italic letters, and the entire bold weight.

1.4 A large x-height comes with a cost

A commonly held truth among type designers is that legibility is improved by a large x-height [Beier and Dyson, 2014]. The term x-height is commonly used to mean the ratio between the neutral-height letters (e.g. lowercase x) and the overall vertical dimension of the typeface measured from the top of ascending strokes to the bottom of descending strokes. Verdana (Figure 2) is an example of a typeface that has a large x-height and is recognized as being very legible because of it. Sheedy, Tai, Hayes, and Preston [2006] found that Verdana was more legible than an entire suite of highly-touted brand new type designs.

hhhh

Figure 2: A comparison of x-height proportions of Futura, Times New Roman, Verdana, and Sitka. All have been scaled to the same ascender height. Futura on the left has small x-height while Verdana and Sitka on the right have large x-heights.

We found that a large x-height comes with a trade-off. While the large size helps neutral height letters, it hurts the ascending and descending letters. Table 1 shows the accuracies for the lowercase letters in the fourth round (labeled before) of testing. The neutral height letters (acemrorsu-vwxz) are recognized 48% correctly while the ascending (bdfhiklt) and descending (gjpqy) letters are recognized 38% and 33% correctly respectively.

ggjjppqqyy

Figure 3: The descending features are longer in the after (right) version of Sitka.

After discovering the trade-off, we tried slightly increasing the length of the descenders without changing the height of the neutral or ascending letters (Figure 3). This had the effect of slightly increasing the accuracy of the neutral-height letters from 48% to 50%, and the ascending letters from 38% to 39%. The descending letters showed the largest increase from 33% to 37% accuracy (Table 1).

In order to accommodate the longer descenders we planned at first to increase the overall height of the face with the effect of reducing the amount of vertical clearance between successive lines of text. At a later stage we decided instead to retain the overall size of the face which meant a proportional reduction in the height of both neutral and ascending letters. Because lengthening the descenders had proved to benefit not only the descenders but, unexpectedly, the neutral and ascending letters as well we considered extending the ascenders and descenders still further, but we feared this would have come at a cost to the x-height. In the end we abandoned this idea because the neutral height letters contain the most frequently occurring letters in English.

Table 1: Letter recognition accuracies for two versions of the Sitka typeface. The largest change from before to after was a lengthening of the descenders.

	Before	After		Before	After		Before	After
a	56%	54%	j	26%	28%	s	56%	59%
b	35%	33%	k	43%	40%	t	38%	39%
c	30%	34%	l	39%	41%	u	54%	51%
d	26%	33%	m	63%	64%	v	35%	36%
e	71%	75%	n	36%	31%	w	53%	54%
f	43%	46%	o	62%	59%	x	36%	46%
g	35%	41%	p	41%	43%	y	33%	41%
h	40%	41%	q	31%	32%	z	34%	38%
i	40%	38%	r	44%	45%	total	42%	44%

1.5 A large x-height harms Greek letters

The x-height decision for Latin letters determined the x-height for the Greek and Cyrillic scripts. While it is possible to choose different x-heights for different writing systems, having consistent x-heights improves the harmony when scripts are combined in the same document, such as Greek with German, or Russian with English.

When testing the Greek lowercase, we closely followed the procedure that we established for the English tests. While the tests took place in the United States, all of the readers were both native speakers and readers of Greek. We compared letter recognition of the Greek letters in Sitka to the Greek letters in Georgia (Figure 4), the most similar typeface for a comparison in a first study. As with English, the three-letter sequences were chosen for being the most common in Greek, without being a word.

While the neutral height letters in both typefaces were recognized correctly 45% of the time, Table 2 shows that Georgia performed better for both the ascending and descending letters. The ascending letters (δθλ) were recognized 52% correctly in Sitka to 62% in Georgia, and the de-

Figure 4: Georgia Greek (left) and Sitka Greek (right). The x-heights have been scaled to be the same, to show the relatively taller proportions of the ascending letter in Georgia.

scending letters (γημρχ) were recognized 40% correctly in Sitka to 44% in Georgia. Despite the advantages of the Georgia x-height for the Greek letters (Figure 4), we choose to retain the Latin x-height in order to better harmonize across different scripts. If Sitka was designed for Greek only, or for Greek first (with harmonizing Latin and Cyrillic scripts to follow), we would have designed a smaller x-height ratio.

Table 2: Letter recognition accuracies for each Greek letter in the typefaces Georgia and Sitka. The descending letters (γημρχ) perform relatively poorer in Sitka than in Georgia.

	Georgia	Sitka		Georgia	Sitka		Georgia	Sitka
α	51%	48%	ι	41%	41%	ρ	43%	41%
ά	40%	35%	ί	38%	31%	σ	42%	40%
β	67%	61%	κ	52%	49%	τ	45%	41%
γ	41%	37%	λ	57%	50%	υ	32%	32%
δ	66%	60%	μ	42%	37%	ύ	29%	31%
ε	53%	49%	ν	37%	33%	φ	53%	57%
έ	52%	36%	ξ	53%	47%	χ	56%	46%
ζ	58%	49%	ο	46%	44%	ψ	46%	41%
η	40%	37%	ό	41%	34%	ω	49%	55%
ή	29%	28%	π	53%	59%	ώ	40%	35%
θ	62%	47%						

1.6 The entire alphabet should be made of the letter m

There are aspects of letter design which have a big impact, but we cannot control. The first should be obvious, though we haven't found any explicit references to it in the literature. Letters that occur more frequently are more likely to be recognized correctly than letters that are less frequent. This kind of frequency effect in words is perhaps the most robust finding in all of reading psychology. Frequently occurring words are recognized faster than less frequently occurring words. The same appears to be true for letters. There is a very strong correlation ($r = .58$) between the frequency of letters in English and the accuracy that we recorded in our studies (Table 3). The letter best recognized in Sitka was the letter e, and it is by far the most frequent letter in English.

Table 3: English letter frequency correlates with Sitka letter recognition accuracy.

	Frequency	Accuracy		Frequency	Accuracy		Frequency	Accuracy
e	12.7%	74%	d	4.3%	42%	p	1.9%	49%
t	9.1%	46%	l	4.0%	48%	b	1.5%	49%
a	8.2%	59%	c	2.8%	42%	v	1.0%	41%
o	7.5%	66%	u	2.8%	61%	k	0.8%	44%
i	7.0%	46%	m	2.4%	70%	j	0.2%	30%
n	6.7%	44%	w	2.4%	59%	x	0.2%	43%
s	6.3%	62%	f	2.2%	47%	q	0.1%	36%
h	6.1%	52%	g	2.0%	40%	z	0.1%	44%
r	6.0%	50%	y	2.0%	37%			

Another aspect of letter design with a big impact is the width of a letter. Wide letters tend to perform better than narrow letters. Beier and Larson [2010] investigated the well-known issue that certain narrow letters (ijlt) are very difficult to distinguish. They found that designing these letters to be wider helped to improve their recognition performance. This research influenced the Sitka design: the narrow letters were made as wide as feasible. Even with this design influence, there is a very strong correlation ($r = .42$) between the width of a letter and its recognition accuracy (Table 4). We're certainly not the first to recognize that narrow letters are difficult to recognize. The letter m is the second best recognized letter in Sitka, and it is the widest lowercase letter.

To examine the problem of narrow letters we looked not only at accuracy rates, but also at specific misrecognitions. Figure 5 is a complex visualization, but full of interesting data. The first four columns show the mis-recognitions for the letter f. The first column is the letter f when shown in isolation, the second, third, and fourth columns for the letter f when flanked by aft, efo, and ife. There were no misrecognitions for the letter f when it was presented in isolation or when it was flanked with efo. When f was flanked with aft it was frequently misrecognized as the letter k, (visualized as a ¾ full circle). When f was flanked by ife it was very frequently (full circle) misrecognized as the letter k, and sometimes (1/4 circle) as the letter h. The next 16 columns show the same kind of visualizations for the letters i, j, l, and t.

Table 4: The width of each Sitka letter in design units correlates with letter recognition accuracy.

	Width	Accuracy		Width	Accuracy		Width	Accuracy
m	1737	70%	k	1034	44%	c	854	42%
w	1542	59%	o	1030	66%	s	831	62%
n	1149	44%	g	1020	40%	r	830	50%
h	1128	52%	x	998	43%	t	659	46%
u	1120	61%	v	993	41%	f	623	47%
p	1096	49%	y	971	37%	i	537	46%
d	1085	42%	a	964	59%	j	524	30%
b	1065	49%	e	924	74%	l	520	48%
q	1065	36%	z	883	44%			

The letter f is most likely to be misrecognized for the letter k, but only when flanked by other letters. The letter i is likely to be misrecognized for l and j, but only when in isolation. The letter j is more likely to be misrecognized when flanked by other letters, and is misrecognized for f and t as well as for the more surprising g and h. The letter l is more likely to be misrecognized for other ascending letters h and k when flanked by other letters. The letter t is strongly misrecognized for the letter k when flanked by other letters. The fact that narrow letters are often misrecognized as wider letters when flanked is a very interesting finding. It shows that neighboring letters interact with each other and that those interactions need to be considered in more detail.

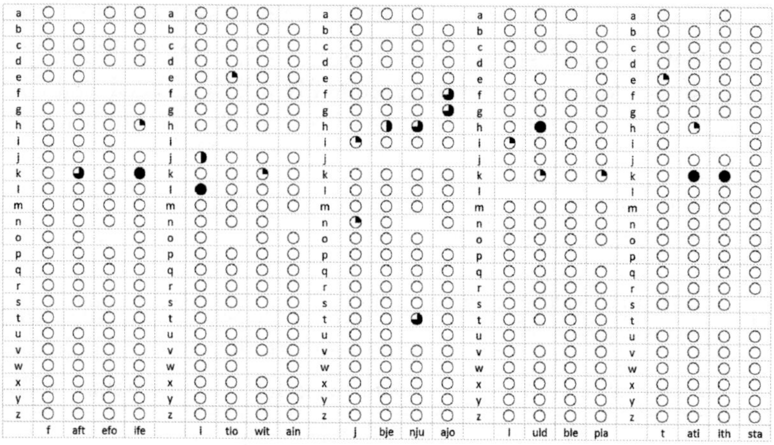

Figure 5: Misrecognitions for the narrow letters in study 4.

1.7 It's harder to recognize a letter when next to other letters

Most words have more than one letter. This greatly complicates the measurement of letter recognition accuracy. It was discovered more than 100 years ago that letters are recognized more accurately when quickly presented as part of a word than when presented in isolation. The Word Superiority Effect comes from our top-down knowledge of language and tells us little about the bottom-up qualities of type design [Larson, 2004]. This effect is contrasted with the more recently discovered Letter Superiority Effect. When letter recognition is size constrained rather than time constrained, letters contained within words needed to be 10-20% larger in order to reach the same level of accuracy as letters in isolation [Sheedy *et. al.*, 2005].

We avoided the Word Superiority Effect by testing each letter in the context of common letter sequences that weren't complete words, in addition to testing each letter in isolation. Without words, our data was more similar to the Letter Superiority Effect. On average letters presented in isolation were recognized 58% correctly compared to 45% correctly for letters in the context of letter sequences.

While letters in isolation were recognized more accurately, most often a letter design that performed better in isolation also performed better when there were flanking letters. In one study where we compared a more open design to a more closed design there were differences between which

aacceess3399

Figure 6: The more open letters (left) performed better when flanked by other letters, while the more closed letters (right) performed better in isolation.

design performed best in isolation and when there were flanking letters. Figure 6 shows the more open design on the left, where the aperture between the inside and outside of each letter is larger, and the more closed design on the right, where the aperture between the inside and outside of each letter is smaller. The more closed design performed better with the letters in isolation while the more open design performed better when the letters were flanked. Because it is far more common to recognize letters within a word, we choose to move towards the more open design than the more closed design.

When a misrecognition occurred for a letter with flanking letters, more than 26% of the misrecognition were for the flanking letter to the left while only 10% were for the flanking letter to the right. We speculate that the left flanking letter was more likely to be reported because of the left-to-right reading direction in the orthographies that we tested, but we would need to confirm that the opposite happens in a right-to-left language to be confident in that conclusion.

Because of the frequent misrecognitions with flanking letters, we considered what we could do to reduce these confusions. Perea and Gomez [2012] showed that word fixation times in continuous reading are faster when there is more space between letters. In more than one iteration of the design we increased the inter-letter spacing to reduce flanking letter confusions with only modest success. We went only so far with this idea because if the space between letters becomes too big the word falls apart.

1.8 The large size-specific designs are optimized for elegance (The Berlow-Hudson Hypothesis)

Historically, typefaces were designed differently for large sizes than for small sizes. This is sometimes called optical scaling or size-specific design. A typeface designed for small size will have a taller x-height, wider letters, less difference between thick and thin strokes, and wider spacing than a typeface designed for larger sizes. In metal type each size had to be made separately. In digital type the same letter can be displayed at any size. The advantage to digital type production is the ease and speed of designing a single version of each letter, but what is lost is the size-specific tuning. Sitka is one of several dozen digital typefaces that have different outlines optimized for different output sizes [Ahrens and Mugikura, 2013].

For the legibility testing aspects of this project we focused our attention on the Sitka Small size because we saw its optimization as having the greatest effect on legibility. In agreement with Harry Carter [1937/1984], we felt that the larger sizes were optimized for elegance and visual interest: 'Shortened descending and ascending strokes are unforgivable on bodies over 18-point. It is quite legitimate to shorten the tails of the small founts to increase legibility and to lengthen them in the display sizes of the same face for the sake of elegance.' An alternative hypothesis that was disputably proposed by David Berlow (personal conversation), and later taken up by John Hudson (personal conversation), claimed that the size-specific adjustments for larger sizes are in fact legibility optimizations for larger text.

To test which hypothesis is correct we used the same letter recognition method, but because typical reading situations were important to the hypothesis we shortened the testing distance in the study to a very typical 50cm distance. We tested a small and large size-specific adjustment, Sitka Small and Sitka Banner respectively (Figure 7), each at two physical sizes, 9 point and 36 point. We did not control for x-height as the x-height difference is one of the key variables that we tested, an element that is fundamental to size-specific adjustments. During piloting of the test we discovered that we could not use the same presentation time for both sizes. 36 point letters are easier to recognize than 9 point letters, so two different calibration times were used. If larger size-specific designs are optimized for legibility than we would expect Sitka Small to perform better at 9 point and expect Sitka Banner to perform better at 36 point. If larger size-specific designs are optimized for elegance than we would expect Sitka Small to perform better both at 9 point and 36 point.

Sitka Small performed better than Sitka Banner at both 9 point and at 36 point. Accuracy at 9 point was 48% for Sitka Small to 39% for Sitka Banner. Accuracy at 36 point was 56% for Sitka Small to 49% for Sitka Banner. The advantage for Sitka Small was statistically reliable, $F=29.3$, p=.0001, and seen for every study participant, and for 25 of 26 letters. The difference between sizes is unfair to compare because we recalibrated the presentation time to present the 36 point size faster. Even with the faster speeds, both Sitka Small and Sitka Banner had higher accuracy rates at 36 point. If we ignore the recalibration and run the statistical test anyway, we find that the size difference is reliable, F=7.0, p=.02, and that there is no interaction between size and font, F=.2, p=.66.

This strongly indicates that the size-specific adjustments made for large sizes do not increase legibility for large sized text. If we want increased legibility at large sizes, we are better served using a small size-specific design. If our goal is instead some level of elegance or personality, then a large size-specific design is appropriate.

The quick brown fox jumps over the lazy dog

The quick brown fox jumps over the lazy dog

The quick brown fox jumps over the lazy dog

The quick brown fox jumps over the lazy dog

The quick brown fox jumps over the lazy dog

The quick brown fox jumps over the lazy dog

Figure 7: Size-specific adjustments in Sitka: Sitka Banner, Sitka Display, Sitka Heading, Sitka Subheading, Sitka Text, and Sitka Small.

1.9 A typeface is a beautiful collection of letters, not a collection of beautiful letters

At the start of the project we analyzed a wide variety of existing research into making legible letters. We were strongly influenced by Sheedy, Tai, Hayes, and Preston's [2006] research on the legibility of individual letters in a dozen top typefaces. Each letter's distance threshold was measured which gave us information about the relative legibility of very different styles of typefaces. One finding of this research was that the best performing typeface for one letter wasn't necessarily the best performing typeface for another letter. Each letter is a unique design. For example the typeface Centaur had the top performing letter s, while Verdana had the top performing letter a, and DIN had the top performing letter m (Figure 8).

An extreme argument could be made that we could create a new typeface by combining the top performing letters into a new Frankenfont. Throughout the project we were cognizant that we wanted to create a typeface and not a collection of letters. We used the earlier studies and our own tests as inspiration for characteristics for each letter that could improve their legibility within a coherently designed typeface.

One example of considered design came from a study of terminals. We measured the performance of the typeface with both teardrop and flared terminals and found that the letters c, f, and j performed 6% better on average with the flared terminal, while the letter a performed slightly better with the teardrop terminal (Figure 9). We could have made the decision to use the flared terminal with c, f, and j, while using the teardrop terminal with a. This inconsistency would have favored the parts over the whole, and resulted in a collection of letters rather than a typeface. We decided to use the flared terminal throughout the design.

Figure 8: Frankenfont of the Centaur s, Verdana a, and DIN m.

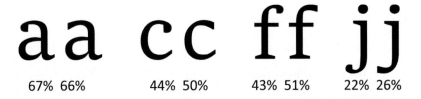

| 67% 66% | 44% 50% | 43% 51% | 22% 26% |

Figure 9: Letter recognition accuracy for four letters with teardrop terminals (left) and with flared terminals (right).

1.10   There can be considerations other than test results

The goal of the legibility research was to provide useful data to influence the design, not to mindlessly determine the design. One example came from the Greek study mentioned earlier in which native Greek readers compared letter recognition between Georgia and Sitka. We tested all of the base letters as well as the seven vowels that can have tonos marks in modern monotonic Greek. Prior to the study we had heard feedback from

Greek type design experts and from Greek readers that the tonos marks in Georgia are a particularly terrible design. For Sitka we designed a tonos mark that experts said was a better and more traditional angled form. We expected the angled design to perform better than the upright tonos mark.

The letter recognition for the unmarked vowels were pretty similar between Georgia and Sitka. 45% of the trials were recognized correctly with Georgia and 44% were recognized correctly with Sitka. The interesting comparison though was how the accuracy changed with the addition of the tonos mark. When the upright tonos mark is added to the Georgia vowels, the recognition accuracy decreased slightly from 45% to 44%. But when the angled tonos mark was added to the Sitka vowels, the recognition accuracy decreased dramatically from 44% correct down to 33% correct (Figure 10).

The results are compelling that Greek readers are more successful at recognizing the upright Georgia tonos marks than the angled tonos mark in Sitka. This left us with the decision between changing the Sitka tonos mark to a more-legible, upright design or staying with the less-legible, angled tonos mark in deference to the advice of experts in contemporary Greek orthography. In this case we decided that it was more important to go with the opinions of experts and readers.

1.11 Conclusions

The novel collaborative process that was used in the development of the Sitka typeface family worked well in the sense that the participants, designers on the one side, scientists on the other, saw very much eye to eye. It never happened that designers produced something that the scientists said was untestable, or the scientists produced results that the designers said were unusable. The process was always a matter of discussion and interpretation between participants who had great confidence in one another's abilities.

Some of the test results were anticipated, such as the problems inherent in narrow letters. In such a case our findings tended to reinforce the conclusions, or suggestions, of earlier researchers. The corollary, that lowercase m is an excellent letter, had perhaps not been so well established, and the superior legibility of the most frequent letters in the language seemed to be a discovery, if not a very surprising one. Despite our best efforts cer-

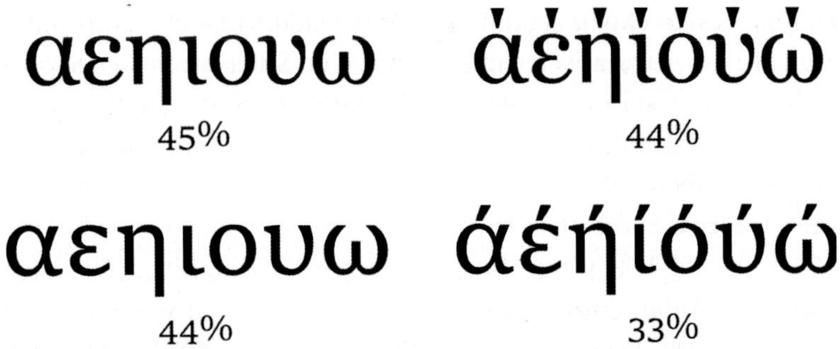

αεηιουω ἀέἠἰὀὐὠ
45%   44%

αεηιουω ἀέἠἰὀὐὠ
44%   33%

Figure 10: Letter recognition accuracy for vowels with (right) and without (left) tonos marks for both Georgia (top) and Sitka (bottom).

tain problems with the Latin alphabet remain intractable; there are practical limits to how wide an f can be stretched, or how long a descender can extend, and it's a hopeless task to try to persuade languages to dispense altogether with diacritics.

Although the type designer will never solve these problems, it is very important to understand the reasons behind them and to mitigate them to the extent that it's possible.

All of us who took part in this project felt that Sitka as it was completed and released was a significant improvement in legibility. We also felt that the design improved dramatically over the course of the development effort. Tantalizingly, we did not demonstrate statistically reliable reading speed benefits as a result of the improvements. We learned a great deal from this project, but it must be said that there is much about the legibility of type and its measurement that is not yet fully understood.

Acknowledgements

The design and development of Sitka was a team effort. It could not have been completed without Geraldine Wade and Michael Duggan, the invaluable project leaders at the beginning and end of the project respectively. We would like to thank the other members of Microsoft's Advanced Reading Technologies, Greg Hitchcock, Paul Linnerud, Tanya Matskewich, and Rob McKaughan for analyzing the study results and so much more, Simon Daniels and Ali Basit our partners on the Microsoft Typography team, Kris Keeker and Libby Hanna for help in conducting the studies, John Hudson and Ross Mills for help on mastering the typeface, Gerry Leonidas for consulting on the Greek design and Greek studies, and Steven Sinofsky for funding the project. The Sitka typeface is dedicated to the memory of Bill Hill. Bill's passion and vision for Reading 2.0 live on in this typeface.

References

Ahrens, T. and Mugikura, S. (2013). *Size specific adjustments to type designs.* (Just Another Foundry).

Beier, S. (2012). *Reading letters: designing for legibility.* (BIS Publishers).

Beier, S. and Dyson, M.C. (2014). The influence of serifs on 'h' and 'i': Useful knowledge from design-led scientific research. *Visible Language*, 47(3), pp. 74-95.

Beier, S. and Larson, K. (2010). Design improvements for frequently misrecognized letters. *Information Design Journal*, 18(2), pp. 118-137.

Carter, H, (1984). Optical scale in type founding. *Printing Historical Society Bulletin*, 13, 144-148. Reprinted from Carter, H. (1937). Optical scale in type founding. *Typog-raphy*, 4.

Legge, G.E. and Bigelow, C.A. (2011). Does print size matter for reading? A review of findings from vision science and typography. *Journal of Vision*, 11(5), pp. 1-22.

Larson, K. (2004). The science of word recognition or how I learned to stop worrying and love the bouma. http://microsoft.com/typography/ctfonts/wordrecognition.aspx

Perea, M. and Gomez, P. (2012). Subtle increases in interletter spacing facilitate the encoding of words during normal reading. *PLoS ONE* 7(10): e47568.

Rayner, K., Pollatsek, A., Ashby, J. and Clifton, C. (2012). *Psychology of Reading*, Second Edition, (Psychology Press).

Roethlein, B.E. (1912). The relative legibility of different faces of printing types. *American Journal of Psychology*, 23(1), pp. 1-36.

Sheedy, J.E., Subbaram, M.V., Zimmerman, A.B., and Hayes, J.R. (2005). Text legibility and the letter superiority effect. *Human Factors*, 47(4), pp. 797-815.

Sheedy, J.E., Tai, Y-C., and Hayes, J.R. (2006). Individual character legibility. http://www.pacificu.edu/sites/default/files/documents/Individualcharacter-legibility.pdf

Chapter 4

Eye movements: from psycholinguistics to font design

Timothy J. Slattery

The study of reading has been greatly advanced in the past 40 years by the examination of eye movements recorded during the reading process. Despite the advances made by reading researchers using eye movement recording as a methodology, this research has resulted in relatively few advances in the way text is displayed to readers. That is not to say that textual displays have not undergone significant improvements over this time, only that the improvements were not driven by eye movement research. This disconnect is of particular interest given the applicability that eye movements offer for understanding all aspects of the reading process. The possible reasons for this disconnect between psycholinguistic research and font design will be discussed. Additionally, current psycholinguistic research trends that overlap with potential font design issues will be explored during a review of the eye movement findings.

1.1 Introduction

Perhaps no experimental methodology has shed more light on the reading process – or offers more promise for continued gains – than eye tracking. This chapter is devoted to the use of eye tracking as a methodology for studying reading, focusing on how this methodology may be useful in guiding decisions on aspects of font design.

Eye movements are a necessary product of the physiology of the retina. The ability to discern fine detail is limited to a small central region of the retina – the fovea. Roughly speaking, the fovea occupies the central two degrees of our vision. At normal reading distances, only 6 or 7 letters will fall inside the fovea. This means that for particularly long words at least some of the letters will fall into a region adjacent to the fovea referred to as the parafovea. Our visual acuity, and therefore our ability to discern letter identities, decreases with increasing eccentricity from the fovea [Bouma, 1970; Klein, Berry, Briand, D'Entremont and Farmer, 1990]. Therefore, we must move our eyes when we read in order to place the image of the word we want to identify onto or near to the fovea for efficient processing.

1.2 Characteristics of reading eye movements

Despite the illusion that our gaze shifts smoothly across the page while we read, reading eye movements consist of a sequence of saccades separated by brief stops (fixations). This jerky appearance of the eyes can be easily seen by anyone with a page of text and a hole punch. Simply punch a hole in the page and find a willing friend to read the text while you peer through the hole to observe their eyes. In fact, recent research confirms that our eyes make saccades between words even in situations in which the text is moving – or scrolling [Valsecchi, Gegenfurtner, and Schütz, 2013].

The size of a typical saccade in English is about 7-9 characters [Rayner, 2009]. However, there is a high degree of variability in the length of reading saccades. Also, the length of reading saccades is determined more by the constraints of the linguistic input (number of letters) than by constraints of the visual system (degree of visual angle) [Morrison and Rayner, 1981]. For instance, readers of Chinese will move their eyes in much smaller saccades (2-3 characters) than readers of English. However, in Chinese, 2 character words are the norm and it's rare to have words composed of 4 characters or more. Therefore, the smaller saccades are required in Chinese reading to prevent the eye from outpacing the mind's language comprehension systems. Saccade lengths are also highly sensitive to the spatial extent of text and the oculomotor system is capable of quickly adapting to the typographical environment [Slattery and Rayner, 2010]. So, a wider font that requires longer saccades, in order to move from word to word, will yield longer average saccade lengths than a narrower font, when measured by visual angle, even though the number of letters traversed may be roughly the same.

Saccades are considered ballistic eye movements that 'fire' from one location to the next. The targeting procedure for saccades a) takes time, and b) is error prone. Estimates on the time to plan and initiate a saccade to a new location are approximately 150-200 ms [Becker and Jürgens, 1979; Rayner, Slowiaczek, Clifton, and Bertera, 1983]. The error involved in saccades is assumed to be composed of two components: saccadic range error, and random error [McConkie, Kerr, Reddix, and Zola, 1988]. Saccadic range error refers to the finding that long saccades tend to undershoot their intended targets while short saccades tend to overshoot their intended targets, with saccadic range error being zero for some idealized saccade length (e.g. 6-7 characters). The random component of saccadic error is assumed to have a mean of zero and a standard deviation that is a function of saccade length being larger for longer than for shorter saccades.

The initial saccade to a word tends to place the eyes in a location just left of word center – the preferred viewing location [Rayner, 1979]. However, there is considerable variability within word fixation locations. In fact, the distributions of within word fixation locations overlap at word boundaries. Therefore, some of the fixations at the beginning of a word (n) were in fact likely intended for the prior word (n-1) and some of the fixations at the end of word n were in fact intended for word n+1. These errant fixations are referred to as mislocated fixations [Nuthmann, Engbert, and Kliegl, 2005; Drieghe, Rayner, and Pollatsek, 2008; Engbert and Nuthmann, 2008].

Another important property of saccades is that new visual information is not typically encoded during them. Therefore, during saccades we are effectively blind – an effect referred to as saccadic suppression [Matin, 1974]. That our minds would suppress the visual information impeding on the retina during a saccade makes intuitive sense, since this information would be little more than a blur. In fact, saccadic suppression extends beyond the end of the saccade as vision remains somewhat suppressed at the very beginning of fixations [Bremmer, Kubischik, Hoffmann, and Krekelberg, 2009; Slattery, Angele and Rayner, 2011].

For English, reading saccades that travel from left to right are classified as 'forward saccades', while those that move from right to left are usually called 'regressive saccades'. It is estimated that ~10-15% of eye movements are regressive during normal reading though this number can be higher in difficult reading situations or with novice readers [Rayner, 1998, 2009]. Saccades that move the eye from one line of text to another are referred to as return sweeps and are not considered regressive saccades. Return sweeps are an important part of normal reading and one where saccadic error can lead to momentary reading difficulties. No doubt you have occasionally made a return sweep to the wrong line of text while reading. Recovering from such oculomotor errors can be time consuming. Based on this, it seems appropriate to follow the basic recommendations of Bouma [1980] that line spacing be adjusted relative to line length so as to keep the angle of the correct return sweep from being too small.

1.3 Eye movement measures of processing

The chief measures of processing time are the fixation durations. While legibility effects, or how easy the letters in a word are to encode, should influence the duration of eye fixations, it is quite clear that these durations are largely influenced by the difficulty associated with the lexical processing of the fixated word [Rayner, 1998, 2009]. For example, readers spend less time fixating high frequency words than low frequency words [Rayner, 1998, 2009]. The word frequency effect is particularly well established having been replicated more times than Earl Grey tea aboard the Starship Enterprise.

One obvious measure of processing time is the average fixation duration on a passage of text. While this can be informative, it can also be misleading if presented alone because passage reading is composed of a highly variable number of fixations. So, when comparing two fonts, a decrease in average fixation duration could be offset by an increased number of fixations. In such offsetting cases, the relative size of each effect would determine the effect on measures of overall processing like total reading time or reading rate.

Recording eye movements has an advantage over just measuring reading time as researchers can examine oculomotor behavior for specific regions of interest (ROI) within a passage. For reading, the ROI are typically individual word units which are standardly defined as the word and the space prior to it [Rayner, 1998]. This standard has made comparison of word processing measures between studies far easier. However, larger ROIs can be useful. For instance, phrases with particular typographical elements (e.g. italics) may be used to examine how changes in these elements influence the natural movement of the eyes. Or, with web page development, the ROIs could be particular advertisements or hyperlinks [Fitzsimmons, Weal and Drieghe, 2014].

Another benefit of eye tracking is that it provides a continuum of processing time measures [Rayner, 1998] For instance, word frequency effects occur very early in word processing with low frequency words eliciting longer first fixation durations than high frequency words. However, alternating case effects first appear in gaze duration [Reingold, Yang, and Rayner, 2010] which adds the duration of the first fixation with the duration of all immediate refixations. First fixation and gaze duration are both considered measures of early word processing, while measures like second pass time (the sum of all rereading fixations) reflect late processes related to comprehension difficulty, such as word mis-readings [Slattery, 2009] and ambiguity resolution [Frazier and Rayner, 1982; Ferreira and Henderson, 1991; Slattery, Sturt, Christianson, Yosida, and Ferreira, 2013].

Blinks are often viewed as a nuisance variable as they represent a major source of data loss. When the eye is shut we do not know how it is behaving. For this reason, participants in eye movement studies are routinely instructed to minimize their blinking during passage reading and to instead blink just prior to and following each reading trial. This strategy is highly effective when the reading passages are only a sentence long. However, with paragraphs, blinks will be an inevitable part of the data record. For typographical research this might not be a big problem. That is, blinks are also a potentially useful measure of eye fatigue [Stern, Boyer, and Schroeder, 1994]. As the total number of blinks will increase with the length of time it takes someone to read a passage, the appropriate measure for examining typographic effects would be blink rate (blinks per minute). Slattery and Rayner [2010] included an analysis of blink rate in their examination of the ClearType anti-aliasing used by Microsoft. They showed that the benefits of anti-aliasing, in terms of reading rate, were not accompanied by any increase in eye fatigue, as measured by blink rate. As reading from screen increases, the need to assess changes in screen technology may make blink rate an even more important measure.

1.4 Gaze-contingent eye movement methods

We have learned a considerable amount about the processes involved in reading by monitoring eye movements while people read static passages of text. In such studies, the texts are carefully constructed ahead of time in order to examine how a variable (e.g. word frequency, syntactic structure, contextual constraint) influences eye movements. However, with eye tracking researchers can do so much more. For instance, it is possible to change what is presented on the screen based on where the reader is looking. While the range of manipulations available with gaze contingent display changes is seemingly endless, I will be discussing three techniques that may be valuable in the study of typography.

1.4.1 *Moving window*

The moving window paradigm [McConkie and Rayner, 1975; Rayner and Bertera, 1979] presents text to readers in a manner in which the letters outside of a readable 'window' are replaced with masking letters. This readable window is tethered to the fixation and therefore moves through the text with the eyes (see Figure 1). In studies using the moving window paradigm, researchers manipulate the size of the window as well as the types of information maintained outside the window. For instance, in the example shown in Figure 1, information about word boundaries (inter-word spaces) are still present outside the readable window but letter identities have been masked with the letter 'x'.[a] Using the moving window technique researchers have explored the perceptual span (i.e. the area around fixation from which useful information for reading can be obtained). These studies have found that the perceptual span for reading English is asymmetric, extending 3-4 letter spaces to the left of fixation and 14-15 letter spaces to the right [McConkie and Rayner, 1975; McConkie and Rayner, 1976; Rayner and Bertera, 1979; Rayner, Well, and Pollatsek, 1980; Rayner, Well, Pollatsek, and Bertera, 1982; Underwood and McConkie, 1985; Underwood and Zola, 1986]. The size and asymmetry of the perceptual span depends on language characteristics. It is smaller in Chinese [Chen and Tang, 1998; Inhoff and Lui, 1998] and the asymmetry is reversed for Hebrew [Pollatsek, Bolozky, Well, and Rayner, 1981]. Additionally, the perceptual span does not extend to upcoming lines of text [Inhoff and Briihl, 1991; Inhoff and Topolski, 1992; Pollatsek, Raney, LaGasse, and Rayner, 1993]. Finally, the perceptual span is not a fixed property; it is smaller for beginning readers compared to skilled readers [Rayner, 1986], for older readers compared to younger readers [Rayner, Castelhano, and Yang, 2009], and for slower readers compared to faster readers [Rayner, Slattery, and Bélanger, 2010]. With the moving window technique, researchers could explore the extent to which a typographical element was useful by varying the size of the window around which this element was available. For instance, would the presence of serifs within the moving window increase or decrease the perceptual span?

---

[a] Note that the letter 'x' in the word 'fox' is not actually masked in this particular manipulation.

1.4.2 *Boundary change*

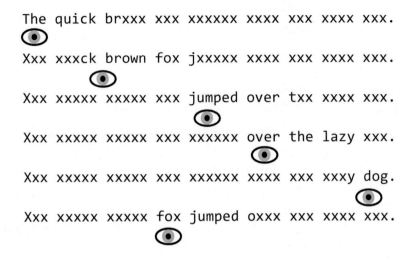

The quick brxxx xxx xxxxxx xxxx xxx xxxx xxx.

Xxx xxxck brown fox jxxxxx xxxx xxx xxxx xxx.

Xxx xxxxx xxxxx xxx jumped over txx xxxx xxx.

Xxx xxxxx xxxxx xxx xxxxxx over the lazy xxx.

Xxx xxxxx xxxxx xxx xxxxxx xxxx xxx xxxy dog.

Xxx xxxxx xxxxx fox jumped oxxx xxx xxxx xxx.

Figure 1: Moving window illustration.

The boundary change paradigm initiates a change to the text only after the eyes cross an invisible boundary (see Figure 2). This boundary is routinely placed just prior to the inter-word space preceding some word of interest. The text in the region prior to the change is referred to as the preview and the text after the change is referred to as the target. Researchers then compare reading time measures on the word of interest for different preview conditions. In Figure 2, the preview and target have different letters but maintain the same vowel consonant structure and basic word shape. The benefit of having an identical preview compared to various non-identical preview conditions is usually in the order of 30-50 ms [Rayner, 1998, 2009].

Most research utilizing boundary changes seeks to uncover the representational structure of words that can be processed in the parafovea [for a review see Schotter, Angele, and Rayner, 2012] and it may be difficult to see how it relates to typography. However, there is one boundary change effect with special significance for font design as it relates to word shape. A recent eye movement study has shown that the upper half of words is more important for reading than the bottom half [Perea, 2012] which may

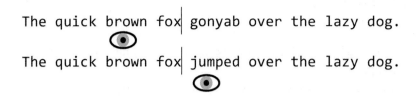

Figure 2: Boundary change illustration. The vertical lines in the figure are shown only for description and aren't viewable by readers in such studies.

be the result of word shape information. However, transposed letter effects provide strong evidence against the notion that words are recognized by their outline shape alone rather than by their constituent letters [see also Perea and Rosa, 2002]. Single word priming studies have also shown that transposed letter non-words are better primes for words than substitution non-words. So, 'jugde' is a better prime for the word 'judge' than 'judpe' [Perea and Lupker, 2003]. Recent boundary change experiments confirm that transposed letter non-words provide greater preview benefit effects during normal reading than substitution letter non-words [Johnson, Perea, and Rayner, 2007] and the effect is the same whether the transpositions maintain word shape (crown, corwn) or not (clerk, celrk). This would not be the case if word shape was more important than letter identities. Other research has shown that reading requires the individual letters in words be individually discriminable [Pelli, Farell, and Moore, 2003; Pelli, Tillman, Freeman, Su, Berger, and Majad, 2007].

Another important effect revealed by boundary change experiments, that is relevant for the more general use of the technique, relates to 'foveal load'. The amount of parafoveal preprocessing a reader can accomplish is inversely related to the difficulty associated with foveal processing [Henderson and Ferreira, 1990]. That is, difficulty processing the currently fixated word results in the focusing of attentional resources on the fovea and away from the parafovea – shrinking the perceptual span. So, when the text is especially difficult due to low frequency words or difficult semantic integration, readers will not get as much useful information from upcoming words. An open question is whether difficult fonts would result in increased foveal load.

1.4.3 *Disappearing text*

Both the moving window and boundary change techniques attempt to implement display changes during saccades so as to take advantage of saccadic suppression. When executed well, subjects are hardly, if ever, aware that something has happened [but see Slattery, Angele, and Rayner 2011]. However, other display change techniques make no attempt to hide their existence and initiate changes during a fixation. The disappearing text method [Rayner, Liversedge, White, and Vergilino-Perez, 2003] falls into this category of display changes. It involves removing words from view at varying times after they are fixated. The words reappear only after the eyes move on to another word. What is surprising is that, compared to normal reading, text can be read without much disruption when the words disappear just 60 milliseconds after fixation. Additionally, reader's fixation durations on words are still influenced by word frequency. That is, readers continue fixating the blank region left by the disappearance of a low frequency word for a longer amount of time than they spend fixating the blank region left by the disappearance of a high frequency word [Blythe, Liversedge, Joseph, White, and Rayner, 2009; Rayner *et al.*, 2003; Rayner, Liversedge, and White, 2006]. While Rayner *et al.* [2003] only used a 60 millisecond timing for the disappearance, more recent research examining the influence of disappearing text on children [Blythe *et al.*, 2009], and on older readers [Rayner, Yang, Castelhano, and Liversedge, 2011] used a range of timings. Blythe *et al.* [2009] revealed that children were only somewhat disrupted by text that disappeared after even the shortest timing tested – 40 milliseconds. In stark contrast, Rayner *et al.* [2011] reported that older readers (65+ years of age) were disrupted significantly more by the disappearing text manipulation than college age readers. However, timings tested included only 60, 50, and 40 milliseconds. It is possible that at longer delays the disruption experienced by older readers may have been significantly minimized.

There are a few aspects of the disappearing text technique that might make it suitable for investigating typographical factors related to font design. The first is that the timing of the disappearance is assumed to influence the initial visual encoding of words. As long as the text is presented for a duration sufficient for visual encoding, reading can progress normally. If fonts differ in the ease with which they can be encoded then researchers should be able to adjust the duration in order to determine the timing profile of different fonts. Additionally, the disappearing text manipulation has been shown to be sensitive to reader's individual differences (i.e. age) and thus may be useful in determining what font related factors are most important to maximize readability at different ages.

These three gaze contingent display change methods are only the tip of the iceberg. There are many other examples of the general method that have yielded great insight [e.g. fast priming: Sereno and Rayner, 1992] and new uses occur on a regular basis. These techniques offer creative typographical researchers a wealth of options that remain largely untapped for investigations into font characteristics and page layouts.

1.5 Eye movement studies of typography

Given the great success that eye tracking has had for illuminating the cognitive processes related to reading [Rayner, 1998, 2009], it may come as some surprise that there are very few studies of eye movements designed to examine aspects of typography. A Google scholar search, at the time of this writing, using the terms 'eye movements' and 'reading', yielded approximately 124,000 hits. Adding the search term 'typography' reduced that number to 964 hits – less than 1% of the total.[b]

With so much research into the way readers move their eyes, why are so few studies concerned about the influence of typography? Surely there are many factors responsible for the dearth of eye movement studies of typography, such as the cost of eye trackers and the expertise required to collect and analyze eye movement data. Additionally, the relevant variables in the design of a font are likely to be strongly interdependent. For instance, when typesetting text, Bouma [1980] argued that longer line lengths require additional interlinear spacing to avoid problems with shallow angled return sweeps. This does not preclude the scientific study of these variables [Tinker, 1963] and their potential interactions but it does make it more complicated and laborious. Given this added level of difficulty, it is unsurprising that many early typographical researchers did not tackle the additional challenge of acquiring the expertise needed to collect expensive eye movement data.

---

[b] If instead of adding the search term 'typography' we add the term 'font legibility' or 'font readability' the situation is far worse with only 9 and 23 hits respectively.

So why weren't the psycholinguists who studied eye movements during reading more interested in the influence of typography? When I was a graduate student in the early 2000s, there seemed to be a common belief that as long as the text was presented in a reasonable manner, a reader's eye movements would be determined more by the characteristics of the language than by differences in the typographic presentation. Along with this belief was the tacit assumption that any difference related to typography would represent a main effect only and would not interact with language variables. So, Times New Roman might be read faster than 𝔒𝔩𝔡 𝔈𝔫𝔤𝔩𝔦𝔰𝔥 but this difference would be the same for all words and sentences. Since psycholinguists were concerned with the processing of the words and sentences, it seemed a safe and simplifying assumption to ignore typography so long as it was held constant within a study. This assumption also had empirical support from an early study utilizing display changes. McConkie and Zola [1979] presented passages of text in aLtErNaTiNg CaSe then on specific saccades the case alternation was switched (AlTeRnAtInG cAsE). The astonishing finding was that fixations following a case switch were no longer than fixations that did not follow a switch. The authors conclude that readers integrate abstract letter identities (where 'A' and 'a' are the same) from one fixation to the next. If a change in a letter's case did not increase fixation durations, it is difficult to imagine that a relatively small change in font would influence such durations. However, as you might guess, reading alternating case is more effortful than reading all lower case or all uppercase text [Rayner, McConkie, and Zola, 1980; Juhasz, Liversedge, White, and Rayner, 2006; Reingold, Yang, and Rayner, 2010]. It may be that alternating case disrupts normal word identification processes [Coltheart and Freeman, 1974] and that under more normal circumstances changes in fonts would influence fixation durations. Additionally, the foveal load hypothesis predicts that the additional foveal difficulty associated with processing a word written in aLtErNaTiNg CaSe would result in reduced parafoveal processing of upcoming words. This could explain why McConkie and Zola [1979] were unable to find a significant difference between their case switch and no-switch conditions. Still, few psycholinguists have seemed interested in examining the role of typography.

1.6 Fonts

It may be surprising to learn that the most prevalent font family used in eye movement studies of reading is `Courier`. This has far less to do with `Courier`'s legibility, and far more to do with its fixed width characteristic. In a fixed width font, every letter occupies the same amount of horizontal space. This property has a number of benefits in the eyes of psycholinguists. First, with a fixed width font controlling the number of letters in target words also controls their physical size. Additionally, fixed width fonts make it easy to implement display changes in moving window and boundary change studies. These experiments would be far more complicated if the letters in the mask or preview were a different size than those in the target. Initiating such changes is possible but would result in perceived changes in the length of the line of text unless the size of the mask or preview letters were made to fit those of the target letters. Rayner, Slattery, and Belanger [2010] conducted such a moving window experiment using both the fixed width font `Consolas` and the proportional width font Georgia for texts. In order to create the masks needed for the moving window with Georgia, the space between the letters of the mask were adjusted so that the size of the mask would exactly equal the size of the target word that would replace it. They found no significant differences in the size of the perceptual span for the different fonts. Despite similar reading rates for the two fonts across the different window size conditions, there were significant differences in fixation durations and the number of fixations required for reading. The average fixation duration was longer for Georgia, while `Consolas` required more forward and regressive fixations for reading. The forward saccade differences were due to shorter saccades (measured in characters) for `Consolas` than for Georgia. In interpreting these differences it is important to note that Georgia has a higher character density than `Consolas`. So in this study, the higher density font led to longer fixation durations but fewer fixations overall compared to the lower density font. The same pattern of effects with respect to density was reported by Kolers, Duchnicky, and Ferguson [1981] – higher density text led to fewer but longer fixations.

While fixed width fonts like `Courier` and `Consolas` are preferred by psycholinguists, there are plenty of eye movement studies that use proportional width fonts like Arial and Times New Roman. However, few eye

movement experiments have designs that allow for direct font comparisons. One recent study examined how younger and older (65+) readers
handle the task of reading a difficult font compared to an easy one [Ray-
ner, Reichle, Stroud, Williams, and Pollatsek, 2006]. They chose Times
New Roman as their easy font and 𝔒𝔩𝔡 𝔈𝔫𝔤𝔩𝔦𝔰𝔥 as their difficult font.
One benefit of using these fonts was that they had nearly identical character densities. As predicted, 𝔒𝔩𝔡 𝔈𝔫𝔤𝔩𝔦𝔰𝔥 texts took longer to read than
Times New Roman ones. This effect was due to an increase in both the
average fixation duration and number of fixations for 𝔒𝔩𝔡 𝔈𝔫𝔤𝔩𝔦𝔰𝔥 compared to Times New Roman. Moreover, the increased reading time associated with the difficult font was considerably larger for the older readers
than for the younger ones. Rayner *et al.* [2006] also examined the effects
of target word frequency and predictability. An analysis of the specific
predictability of manipulated target words found that when these words
were of high (86% cloze completion) predictability, based on prior sentence context, they were fixated for less time than when they were of low
(4% cloze completion) predictability. More interesting was the fact that
words presented in a difficult font benefitted more from high predictable
contexts than words presented in an easy font – font difficulty and word
predictability interacted. An analysis of the gaze durations on specific frequency manipulated target words replicated the standard frequency effect.
Additionally, the word frequency did ***not*** interact with the difficulty of
the font. That is, low frequency words were fixated for longer amounts of
time than high frequency words but the difference between low and high
frequency words was similar for both fonts. However, other research utilizing distorted fonts to produce perceptual difficulty found interactions in
gaze durations between font distortions and word frequency [Sheridan and
Reingold, 2012]. The interactions between lexical and typographical variables are important because they illustrate that typography can influence
certain words more than others.

    While the font comparisons in Rayner *et al.* [2006] and Sheridan and
Reingold [2012] examined what happens when fonts are made more difficult, other studies have examined the influence of variables designed
to make fonts more legible. Slattery and Rayner [2010] conducted a pair
of eye movement studies examining Microsoft's ClearType anti-aliasing
technique which involves sub-pixel rendering to smooth the outline of letters [see Larson, 2007]. Examining ClearType scientifically was aided by

clear theoretical predictions. For instance, ClearType should have a larger impact for fonts with more curved or slanted features since these suffer most from aliasing. Consistent with this prediction, they found benefits for ClearType in total time and average fixation duration that interacted with font; effects were larger for Harrington, and *Script MJ* than for Times New Roman. So ClearType anti-aliasing improved legibility more for fonts that suffer more aliasing. Based on the shorter fixation duration measures for Times New Roman compared to the other two fonts we could also conclude that it was the more legible font. Additionally, in total time there was an interaction between word frequency and font as Times New Roman had smaller frequency effects than the Harrington, or *Script MJ*. Moreover, in gaze duration there was a significant interaction between ClearType and word frequency. A second experiment, compared regular, italic, and bold text for two fixed width fonts – Consolas and Andale Mono. Andale Mono was more legible than Consolas as evidenced by shorter gaze durations and total time on target words. Additionally, the italic style was more legible in Andale Mono than Consolas as indicated by interactions in gaze duration and total time. The word frequency effect interacted with style being larger for the italic than for regular or bold text. ClearType also improved the legibility of italic text more than regular or bold text. And there were again indications that word frequency effects were smaller with ClearType anti-aliasing than without it. This complex pattern of effects and interactions is in direct opposition with the tacit psycholinguistic assumption that font differences will have the same influence on all words.

1.6.1 *Serif vs. sans serif*

There has also been a renewed interest in using eye movements to explore font characteristics such as the presence or absence of serifs. However, all of these studies have at least one serious flaw that leaves unresolved the question of whether serif or sans serif fonts are more legible in general. For instance, Josephson [2008] reported a study that examined two serif fonts (Times New Roman and Georgia) and two sans serif fonts (Arial and Verdana). Choosing multiple fonts to estimate the influence of serifs is a plus for this study. Additionally, the study used a within subjects design which is crucial for detecting effects when subject variability is high.

However, passages were not counterbalanced across font conditions. So the language variables known to influence fixation durations were different for each font. Additionally, only six participants were included in the study and no inferential statistics were reported – only condition means. A somewhat improved study was reported by Beymer, Russell, and Orton [2008]. They collected eye movements from 82 adult readers using **Georgia** and **Helvetica**. However, they failed to find any significant differences in the eye movement records for the two fonts. They did however report many significant differences between groups of readers. For instance, readers in their 30s spent more time rereading words than readers in their 50s. Additionally, they found large significant differences between native English readers and readers for whom English was a second language. The flaw in the design of the study was that they manipulated font as a between subject variable. So, 41 subjects read in **Georgia** and a different 41 read in **Helvetica**. With large differences between readers, such a design will be severely underpowered to find font differences. More recently, Perea [2013] conducted a much improved study using **Lucida** and **Lucida Sans** to address the serif question. The only significant difference between the two fonts was that the serif font received slightly more fixations during reading. However, all other measures were equivalent between the two fonts – including total reading time. The only drawback to the Perea [2013] study was that only one serif and one sans serif font were used. Perhaps with a different selection of fonts, serif effects would have been found.

1.6.2 *Inter-letter and inter-word spacing*

Recently there has been an increased interest in exploring the effects of horizontal text spacing. Moreover, this interest spans a number of different subfields within reading research: vision scientists [Chung, 2002, 2004; Arditi, 2004; Arditi and Cho 2005; Blackmore-Wright, Georgeson, and Anderson, 2013;], psycholinguists [Perea, Moret-Tatay, and Gomez, 2011; Risko, Lanthier, and Besner, 2011; Slattery and Rayner, 2013] and typographical researchers [Reynolds and Walker, 2004].

The spacing between letters influences our ability to discern them [Bouma, 1970; Erikson and Erikson, 1974; Chung, Levi, and Legge, 2001; Marzouki, and Grainger, 2014]. As letters are pushed closer together their identification becomes less accurate. However, identifying a word is different from identifying a letter. With word identification tasks like lexical decision, increases to inter-letter spacing can result in faster reaction times [Perea, and Gomez 2012], but beyond a critical point additional space slows performance [Chung, 2002; Pelli, Tillman, Freeman, Su, Berger, and Majad, 2007; Paterson and Jordan 2010; Risko, Lanthier, and Besner, 2011; Vinckier, Qiao, Pallier, Dehaene, and Cohen, 2011]. This suggests an optimal inter-letter spacing value at which any change would cause inhibition. This optimal value may differ across readers. When Arditi [2004] allowed low vision readers to make real time adjustments to various font variables, the largest adjustments were made to inter-letter spacing. Additionally, fonts differ widely in their amount of inter-letter space. Perea, Moret-Tatay, and Gomez [2011] noted that the results of studies of spacing are somewhat inconsistent due in part to the use of different fonts. For instance, Perea *et al.* [2011] manipulated the spacing of Times New Roman and found facilitation for increased inter-letter space while Cohen, Dehaene, Vinckier, Jobert, and Montavont, [2008] found inhibition for increased inter-letter space using `Courier`.

In English and other alphabetic languages, word boundaries are signified by an inter-word space. These spaces benefit reading and reading rate drops when they are removed [Pollatsek and Rayner, 1982; Rayner, Fischer, and Pollatsek, 1998; Perea and Acha, 2009; Rayner, Yang, Schuett, and Slattery, 2013; Sheridan, Rayner, and Reingold, 2013]. The size of inter-word spaces varies across font, just as inter-letter space does. Therefore, the benefits of inter-word spaces should differ between fonts based on the size of their inter-word space.

There are now a number of studies which have explored horizontal text spacing on eye movements [Drieghe, Brysbaert, and Desmet, 2005; Paterson and Jordan, 2010; Perea, and Gomez 2012; Perea, Panadero, Moret-Tatay, and Gomez, 2012; Zorzi, *et al.* 2012; Slattery and Rayner, 2013; Blackmore-Wright, Georgeson, and Anderson, 2014]. Most of these studies report benefits to reading from increased spacing. For instance, Perea *et al.* [2012] found faster reading rates with small increases in inter-letter spacing with Times New Roman. Additionally, these benefits were greater for readers with developmental dyslexia [see also Zorzi *et al.*, 2012]. However, in these studies inter-letter spacing was confounded with inter-word spacing. That is, these studies added or removed space between all characters including the inter-word space character. Therefore, they can't separate the influence of one type of spacing from the other.

Another study found detrimental effects of increased spacing on eye movements [Paterson and Jordan, 2010] when using the fixed width font `Courier`. However, the smallest addition to inter-letter spacing in their experiment added an extra space b e t w e e n   e a c h   l e t t e r (as in the prior three words) which likely disrupted the overall integrity of the words in the sentences. Paterson and Jordan also reported larger word frequency effects for all increased spacing conditions relative to standard spacing. Their study also manipulated both inter-letter and inter-word spacing but not in a fully factorial manner. Therefore, the individual contributions of each type of space could not be assessed.

Slattery and Rayner [2013] also manipulated inter-letter and inter-word spacing in two eye movement studies. Their first experiment manipulated spacing between all characters for Cambria and Times New Roman fonts. They found that changing the space between the characters of these fonts increased total reading times. In a follow up study they used a novel manipulation which reduced inter-letter spacing within words then added the saved space to the end of the word thereby increasing inter-word spacing. This condition was then compared to a normal spaced condition for Georgia and `Consolas`. The adjusted spacing condition yielded shorter gaze durations than standard spacing and this benefit was largely limited to the Georgia font. Blackmore-Wright, Georgeson, and Anderson [2014] also report benefits to reading rate with increased inter-word spaces for readers with macular disease.

More research is needed to explore inter-letter and inter-word spacing. This research should focus on potential interactions between these spacing variables as well as differences in optimal use of space for proportional versus fixed width fonts.

1.7 Concluding remarks

In recent years, eye movement recording, in conjunction with appropriate experimental design, has helped dispel the assumption that typographical variables can only have a main effect on reading performance. These studies have not only found reliable typographic effects, they have also shown that these effects differ for different words and different readers. The field now seems primed to explore reading from the viewpoint that it represents a complex interplay between language, typographic display, and reader ability. The outcome of such future explorations has the potential to uncover the ways in which font and language variables combine to influence legibility.

References

Arditi, A. (2004). Adjustable typography: an approach to enhancing low vision text accessibility. *Ergonomics*, 47(5), pp. 469-482.

Arditi, A., and Cho, J. (2005). Serifs and font legibility. *Vision research*, 45(23), pp. 2926-2933.

Becker, W. W., and Jürgens, R. R. (1979). An analysis of the saccadic system by means of double step stimuli. *Vision Research*, 19(9), pp. 967-983. doi:10.1016/0042-6989(79)90222-0

Beymer, D., Russell, D., and Orton, P. (2008, September). An eye tracking study of how font size and type influence online reading. In *Proceedings of the 22nd British HCI Group Annual Conference on People and Computers: Culture, Creativity, Interaction-Volume 2* (pp. 15-18). British Computer Society.

Blackmore-Wright, S., Georgeson, M.A., and Anderson, S.J. (2013). Enhanced text spacing improves reading performance in individuals with macular disease. *PLoS ONE* 8(11): e80325. doi:10.1371/journal.pone.0080325

Blythe, H. I., Liversedge, S. P., Joseph, H. L., White, S. J., and Rayner, K. (2009). Visual information capture during fixations in reading for children and adults. *Vision Research*, 49(12), pp. 1583-1591. doi:10.1016/j.visres.2009.03.015

Bouma, H. (1970). Interaction effects in parafoveal letter recognition. *Nature*, 226, pp. 177-178.

Bouma, H. (1980). Visual reading processes and the quality of text displays. *IPO Annual Progress Report*, 15, pp. 83-90.

Bremmer, F., Kubischik, M., Hoffmann, K., and Krekelberg, B. (2009). Neural dynamics of saccadic suppression. *The Journal Of Neuroscience*, 29(40), pp. 12374-12383. doi:10.1523/JNEUROSCI.2908-09.2009

Chen, H., and Tang, C. (1998). The effective visual field in reading Chinese. *Reading and Writing*, 10(3-5), pp. 245-254. doi:10.1023/A:1008043900392

Chung, S. T. L. (2002). The effect of letter spacing on reading speed in central and peripheral vision. *Investigative Ophthalmology and Visual Science*, 43, pp. 1270-1276.

Chung, S. T. L. (2004). Reading speed benefits from increased vertical word spacing in normal peripheral vision. *Optometry and Vision Science*, 81, pp. 525-535.

Chung, S. L., Levi, D. M., and Legge, G. E. (2001). Spatial-frequency and contrast properties of crowding. *Vision Research*, 41(14), pp. 1833-1850. doi:10.1016/S0042-6989(01)00071-2

Cohen, L., Dehaene, S., Vinckier, F., Jobert, A., andMontavont, A. (2008). Reading normal and degraded words: Contributions of the dorsal and ventral visual pathways. *NeuroImage*, 40, pp. 353-366.

Coltheart, M., and Freeman, R. (1974). Case alternation impairs word identification. *Bulletin of the Psychonomic Society*, 3(2), pp. 102-104.

Drieghe, D., Brysbaert, M., and Desmet, T. (2005). Parafoveal-on-foveal effects on eye movements in text reading: Does an extra space make a difference? *Vision Research*, 45, pp. 1693–1706.

Drieghe, D., Rayner, K., and Pollatsek, A. (2008). Mislocated fixations can account for parafoveal-on-foveal effects in eye movements during reading. *The Quarterly Journal of Experimental Psychology*, 61(8), pp. 1239-1249.

Engbert, R., and Nuthmann, A. (2008). Self consistent estimation of mislocated fixations during reading. *PLoS One*, 3(2), e1534. doi:10.1371/journal.pone.0001534

Eriksen, B. A., and Eriksen, C.W., (1974). Effects of noise letters upon the identification of a target letter in a nonsearch task. *Perception and Psychophysics*, 16, pp. 143–149.

Fitzsimmons, G., Weal, M. J. and Drieghe, D. (2014) Skim Reading: An Adaptive Strategy for Reading on the Web. In proceedings, of the 6th Annual ACM Web Science Conference held in Bloomington, IN, 23-26 June, (pp. 211-219).

Ferreira, F., and Henderson, J. M. (1991). Recovery from misanalyses of garden-path sentences. *Journal of Memory and Language*, 30(6), pp. 725-745. doi:10.1016/0749-596X(91)90034-H

Frazier, L., and Rayner, K. (1982). Making and correcting errors during sentence comprehension: Eye movements in the analysis of structurally ambiguous sentences. *Cognitive Psychology*, 14(2), pp. 178-210. doi:10.1016/0010-0285(82)90008-1

Henderson, J. M., and Ferreira, F. (1990). Effects of foveal processing difficulty on the perceptual span in reading: Implications for attention and eye movement control. *Journal of Experimental Psychology: Learning, Memory, and Cognition*, 16(3), pp. 417-429. doi:10.1037/0278-7393.16.3.417

Inhoff, A. W. and Liu, W. (1998). The perceptual span and oculomotor activity during the reading of Chinese sentences. *Journal of Experimental Psychology: Human Perception and Performance*, 24, pp. 20-34.

Inhoff, A. W., and Briihl, D. (1991). Semantic processing of unattended text during selective reading: How the eyes see it. *Perception and Psychophysics*, 49(3), pp. 289-294. doi:10.3758/BF03214312

Inhoff, A. W., and Topolski, R. (1992). Lack of semantic activation from unattended text during passage reading. *Bulletin of the Psychonomic Society*, 30(5), pp. 365-366.

Johnson, R. L., Perea, M., and Rayner, K. (2007). Transposed-letter effects in reading: Evidence from eye movements and parafoveal preview. *Journal of Experimental Psychology: Human Perception and Performance*, 33(1), pp. 209-229. doi:10.1037/0096-1523.33.1.209

Josephson, S. (2008). Keeping your readers' eyes on the screen: An eye-tracking study comparing sans serif and serif typefaces. *Visual Communication Quarterly*, 15(1-2), pp. 67-79.

Juhasz, B. J., Liversedge, S. P., White, S. J., and Rayner, K. (2006). Binocular coordination of the eyes during reading: Word frequency and case alternation affect fixation duration but not fixation disparity. *The Quarterly Journal of Experimental Psychology*, 59(9), pp. 1614-1625.

Klein, R., Berry, G., Briand, K., D'Entremont, B., and Farmer, M. (1990). Letter identification declines with increasing retinal eccentricity at the same rate for normal and dyslexic readers. *Perception and Psychophysics*, 47(6), pp. 601-606. doi:10.3758/BF03203112

Kolers, P. A., Duchnicky, R. L., and Ferguson, D. C. (1981). Eye movement measurement of readability of CRT displays. *Human Factors*, 23(5), pp. 517-527.

Larson, K. (2007). The technology of text. *IEEE Spectrum*, 44, pp. 26–31.

Marzouki, Y., Grainger, J. (2014). Effects of stimulus duration and inter-letter spacing on letter-in-string identification. *Acta Psychologica*, 148, pp. 49-55.

Matin, E. (1974). Saccadic suppression: A review and an analysis. *Psychological Bulletin*, Vol 81(12), pp. 899-917.

McConkie, G. W., Kerr, P. W., Reddix, M. D., and Zola, D. (1988). Eye movement control during reading: I. The location of initial fixations on words. *Vision Research*, 28, pp. 1107–1118.

McConkie, G. W., and Rayner, K. (1975). The span of the effective stimulus during a fixation in reading. *Perception and Psychophysics*, 17(6), pp. 578-586. doi:10.3758/BF03203972

McConkie, G. W., and Rayner, K. (1976). Asymmetry of the perceptual span in reading. *Bulletin of The Psychonomic Society*, 8(5), pp. 365-368.

McConkie, G. W., and Zola, D. (1979). Is visual information integrated across successive fixations in reading? *Perception and Psychophysics*, 25(3), pp. 221-224.

Morrison, R. E., and Rayner, K. (1981). Saccade size in reading depends upon character spaces and not visual angle. *Perception and Psychophysics*, 30, pp. 395-396.

Nuthmann, A., Engbert, R., and Kliegl, R. (2005). Mislocated fixations during reading and the inverted optimal viewing position effect. *Vision Research*, 45(17), pp. 2201-2217. doi:10.1016/j.visres.2005.02.014

Paterson, K. B., and Jordan, T. R. (2010). Effects of increased letter spacing on word identification and eye guidance during reading. *Memory and Cognition*, 38, pp. 502-512.

Pelli, D. G., Farell, B., Moore, D. C. (2003). The remarkable inefficiency of word recognition. *Nature*, 423, pp. 752–756.

Pelli, D. G., Tillman, K. A., Freeman, J., Su, M., Berger, T. D. and Majad, N. J. (2007). Crowding and eccentricity determine reading rate. *Journal of Vision,* 7(2):20, pp. 1–36

Perea, M. (2012). Revisiting Huey: On the importance of the upper part of words during reading. *Psychonomic Bulletin and Review*, 19(6), pp. 1148-1153. doi:10.3758/s13423-012-0304-0

Perea, M. (2013). Why does the APA recommend the use of serif fonts? *Psicothema*, 25(1), pp. 13-17.

Perea, M., and Acha, J. (2009). Space information is important for reading. *Vision Research*, 49, pp. 1994-2000.

Perea, M., and Gomez, P., (2012). Increasing interletter spacing facilitates encoding of words. *Psychonomic Bulletin and Review*, online DOI 10.3758/s13423-011-0214-6

Perea, M., and Lupker, S. J. (2003a). Does jugde activate COURT? Transposed-letter similarity effects in masked associative priming. *Memory and Cognition*, 31, pp. 829-841.

Perea, M., Moret-Tatay, C., and Gomez, P. (2011). The effects of interletter spacing in visual-word recognition. *Acta Psychologica*, 13, pp. 345-351.

Perea, M., Panadero, V., Moret-Tatay, C., and Gómez, P. (2012). The effects of inter-letter spacing in visual-word recognition: Evidence with young normal readers and developmental dyslexics. *Learning and Instruction*, 22(6), pp. 420-430. doi:10.1016/j.learninstruc.2012.04.001

Perea, M., and Rosa, E. (2002). Does 'whole-word shape' play a role in visual word recognition? *Perception and Psychophysics*, 64(5), pp. 785-794. doi:10.3758/BF03194745

Pollatsek, A., Bolozky, S., Well, A. D., and Rayner, K. (1981). Asymmetries in the perceptual span for Israeli readers. *Brain and Language*, 14(1), pp. 174-180. doi:10.1016/0093-934X(81)90073-0

Pollatsek, A., Raney, G. E., Lagasse, L., and Rayner, K. (1993). The use of information below fixation in reading and in visual search. *Canadian Journal of Experimental Psychology/Revue Canadienne De Psychologie Expérimentale*, 47(2), pp. 179-200. doi:10.1037/h0078824

Pollatsek, A., and Rayner, K. (1982). Eye movement control in reading: The role of word boundaries. *Journal of Experimental Psychology: Human Perception and Performance*, 8(6), pp. 817-833. doi:10.1037/0096-1523.8.6.817

Rayner, K. (1979). Eye guidance in reading: Fixation locations within words. *Perception*, 8(1), pp. 21-30.

Rayner, K. (1986). Eye movements and the perceptual span in beginning and skilled readers. *Journal of Experimental Child Psychology*, 41(2), pp. 211-236. doi:10.1016/0022-0965(86)90037-8

Rayner, K. (1998). Eye movements in reading and information processing: 20 years of research. *Psychological Bulletin*, 124, pp. 372-422.

Rayner, K. (2009). The Thirty-fifth Sir Frederick Bartlett lecture: Eye movements and attention in reading, scene perception, and visual search. *The Quarterly Journal of Experimental Psychology*, 68, pp. 1457-1506.

Rayner, K., and Bertera, J. H. (1979). Reading without a fovea. *Science*, 206(4417), pp. 468-469. doi:10.1126/science.504987

Rayner, K., Castelhano, M. S., and Yang, J. (2009). Eye movements and the perceptual span in older and younger readers. *Psychology and Aging*, 24(3), pp. 755-760. doi:10.1037/a0014300

Rayner, K., Fischer, M.H.., and Pollatsek, A. (1998). Unspaced text interferes with both word identification and eye movement control. *Vision Research*, 38, pp. 1129-1144.

Rayner, K., Liversedge, S. P., and White, S. J. (2006). Eye movements when reading disappearing text: The importance of the word to the right of fixation. *Vision Research*, 46(3), pp. 310-323. doi:10.1016/j.visres.2005.06.018

Rayner, K., Liversedge, S. P., White, S. J., and Vergilino-Perez, D. (2003). Reading disappearing text: Cognitive control of eye movements. *Psychological Science*, 14(4), pp. 385-388. doi:10.1111/1467-9280.24483

Rayner, K., McConkie, G. W., and Zola, D. (1980). Integrating information across eye movements. *Cognitive Psychology*, 12(2), pp. 206-226. doi:10.1016/0010-0285(80)90009-2

Rayner, K., Pollatsek, A., Ashby, J., and Clifton, C. (2012). *The Psychology of Reading*. New York: Psychology Press.

Rayner, K., Reichle, E. D., Stroud, M. J., Williams, C. C., and Pollatsek, A. (2006). The effect of word frequency, word predictability, and font difficulty on the eye movements of young and older readers. *Psychology and Aging*, 21(3), pp. 448-465. doi:10.1037/0882-7974.21.3.448

Rayner, K., Slattery, T. J., and Bélanger, N. N. (2010). Eye movements, the perceptual span, and reading speed. *Psychonomic Bulletin and Review*, 17(6), pp. 834-839.

Rayner, K., Slowiaczek, M.L., Clifton, C., and Bertera, J.H. (1983). Latency of sequential eye movements: Implications for reading. *Journal of Experimental Psychology: Human Perception and Performance*, 9, pp. 912-922.

Rayner, K., Well, A. D., and Pollatsek, A. (1980). Asymmetry of the effective visual field in reading. *Perception and Psychophysics*, 27(6), pp. 537-544. doi:10.3758/BF03198682

Rayner, K., Well, A. D., Pollatsek, A., and Bertera, J. H. (1982). The availability of useful information to the right of fixation in reading. Perception *and Psychophysics*,31(6), pp. 537-550. doi:10.3758/BF03204186

Rayner, K., Yang, J., Castelhano, M. S., and Liversedge, S. P. (2011). Eye movements of older and younger readers when reading disappearing text. *Psychology and Aging*, 26(1), pp. 214-223. doi:10.1037/a0021279

Rayner, K., Yang, J., Schuett, S., and Slattery, T. J. (2014). The effect of foveal and parafoveal masks on the eye movements of older and younger readers. *Psychology and Aging*, 29(2), pp. 205-212. doi:10.1037/a0036015

Reingold, E.M., Yang, J., Rayner, K. (2010). The time course of word frequency and case alternation effects on fixation times in reading: Evidence for lexical control of eye movements. *Journal of Experimental Psychology: Human Perception and Performance*, 36(6), pp. 1677-1683.

Reynolds, L., and Walker, S. (2004). 'You can't see what the words say': Word spacing and letter spacing in children's reading books. *Journal of Research in Reading*, 27(1), pp. 87-98. doi:10.1111/j.1467-9817.2004.00216.x

Risko, E. F., Lanthier, S. N., and Besner, D. (2011). Basic processes in reading: The effect of interletter spacing. *Journal of Experimental Psychology: Learning, Memory, and Cognition*, 37(6), pp. 1449-1457. doi:10.1037/a0024332

Schotter, E. R., Angele, B., and Rayner, K. (2012). Parafoveal processing in reading. *Attention, Perception, and Psychophysics*, *74*(1), pp. 5-35.

Sereno, S. C., and Rayner, K. (1992). Fast priming during eye fixations in reading. *Journal of Experimental Psychology: Human Perception and Performance*, 18(1), pp. 173-184. doi:10.1037/0096-1523.18.1.173

Sheridan, H., Rayner, K., and Reingold, E. M. (2013). Unsegmented text delays word identification: evidence from a survival analysis of fixation durations. *Visual Cognition*, 21(1), pp. 38-60.

Sheridan, H., and Reingold, E. M. (2012). Perceptually specific and perceptually non-specific influences on rereading benefits for spatially transformed text: Evidence from eye movements. *Consciousness And Cognition: An International Journal,* 21(4), pp. 1739-1747. doi:10.1016/j.concog.2012.10.002

Slattery, T.J., (2009). Word misperception, the neighbor frequency effect, and the role of sentence context: Evidence from eye movements. *Journal of Experimental Psychology: Human Perception and Performance*, 35(6), pp. 1969-1975.

Slattery, T.J., Angele, B., Rayner, K., (2011). Eye movements and display change detection during reading. *Journal of Experimental Psychology: Human Perception and Performance*, 37, pp. 1924-1938.

Slattery, T. J., and Rayner, K. (2010). The influence of text legibility on eye movements during reading. *Applied Cognitive Psychology*, 24(8), pp. 1129-1148.

Slattery, T. J., and Rayner, K. (2013). Effects of intraword and interword spacing on eye movements during reading: Exploring the optimal use of space in a line of text. *Attention, Perception, and Psychophysics*, *75*(6), pp. 1275-1292.

Slattery, T.J., Sturt, P., Christianson, K., Yoshida, M., Ferreira, F. (2013). Lingering misinterpretations of garden path sentences arise from competing syntactic representations processing. *Journal of Memory and Language*, 69(2), pp. 104-120.

Stern, J. A., Boyer, D., and Schroeder, D. (1994). Blink rate: a possible measure of fatigue. *Human Factors: The Journal of the Human Factors and Ergonomics Society,* 36(2), pp. 285-297.

Tinker, M. A. (1963). Legibility of print. Ames, Iowa: University of Iowa Press.

Underwood, N. R., and McConkie, G. W. (1985). Perceptual span for letter distinctions during reading. *Reading Research Quarterly,* 20(2), pp. 153-162. doi:10.2307/747752

Underwood, N. R., and Zola, D. (1986). The span of letter recognition of good and poor readers. *Reading Research Quarterly,* 21(1), pp. 6-19. doi:10.2307/747956

Valsecchi, M., Gegenfurtner, K. R., and Schütz, A. C. (2013). Saccadic and smooth-pursuit eye movements during reading of drifting texts. *Journal of Vision,* 13(10), doi:10.1167/13.10.8

Vinckier, F., Qiao, E., Pallier, C., Dehaene, S., and Cohen, L. (2011). The impact of letter spacing on reading: A test of the bigram coding hypothesis. *Journal of Vision,* 11(6), doi:10.1167/11.6.8

Zorzi, M., Barbiero, C., Facoetti, A., Lonciari, I., Carrozzi, M., Montico, M., and ... Ziegler, J. C. (2012). Extra-large letter spacing improves reading in dyslexia. *PNAS Proceedings Of The National Academy Of Sciences Of The United States Of America,* 109(28), pp. 11455-11459. doi:10.1073/pnas.1205566109

Chapter 5

Designing legible fonts for distance reading

Sofie Beier

This chapter reviews existing knowledge on distance legibility of fonts, and finds that for optimal distance reading, letters and numbers benefit from relative wide shapes, open inner counters and a large x-height; fonts should further be widely spaced, and the weight should not be too heavy or too light (Figure 1). Research also indicates that serifs on the vertical extremes improve legibility under such reading conditions.

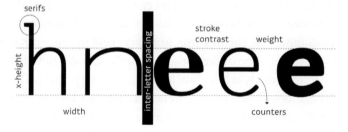

Figure 1: Matters to consider when choosing and designing type for distance reading: the placement of serifs; the size of the x-height; the horizontal width of letters; the spacing between letters; the stroke contrast; the letter counters and the weight of the typeface.

1.1 Introduction

The further away we can read the text on a sign, the longer we have to make the right navigational decision or the sooner we know if we are moving in the right direction. This question of performance is particularly important in road signage, where the added time in extreme cases, may help to prevent accidents. In airports or in dense urban areas, legible signs contribute to smoother traffic patterns and less frustrated users. Optimizing the distance legibility of signage fonts can therefore have a significant impact on people's everyday lives.

Drawing on both scientific findings, and on designer's experiences, this chapter will present the different factors that influence the legibility of fonts when read from a distance.

1.2 Disappearing details

A significant effect of distance is the loss of information in the smaller features and details. This can have a range of effects on reading performance. It appears that the information loss can partly be worked around if we understand how to compensate for this loss. When Jock Kinneir and Margaret Calvert created the British traffic sign system from 1957 to 1963, their font development resulted in a public debate on letterform legibility. Their chief critic was rival type designer, stone carver and lettering artist David Kindersley [for a detailed description see Lund, 2003]. Like others, Kindersley had observed that: 'In very small type, or in larger letters to be read at a great distance – in fact, wherever there is a question of distance in relation to size – there is always a loss of definition' [Kindersley 1960, p. 465]. To compensate for this loss in the corners of letters, Kindersley argued for the importance of the serif as it 'reinforces the individual character of the letter exactly where this loss is greatest' [p. 465]. This notion has partly been confirmed by researchers Beier and Dyson [2014] who found no difference in the overall distance legibility between sans serif and serif fonts, yet when looking at the group of letters with serifs at the vertical extremes (Figure 2), the data showed higher distance legibility. Kindersley's proposal emphasized these corners.

Figure 2: Beier and Dyson [2014] found that serifs on the vertical extremes improve distance legibility.

The lazy dog

Figure 3: The intention with the round corners of the typeface FF Info was to create an even appearance of the letter stroke on backlit signs (by Erik Spiekermann and Ole Schäfer).

In contrast other designers have chosen to create stroke endings that accept and integrate the loss of detail that can be expected. This has led to round sans serif corners. When type designer Gerard Unger [2014] was working on the font for the Amsterdam Metro early in his career (1974) , many of the signs were illuminated from within. Unger observed that when light shines through a hole of any shape or form, the light tends to soften the form and this softening appears circular. He decided to integrate this observation in the final design of the font, and consequently created round corners on the letters. A similar solution was applied in the more recent typeface family FF Info by Erik Spiekermann and Ole Schäfer (Figure 3).

1.3   Open inner counters

It may seem logical to assume that the larger the letter size, the greater the distance at which a text can be read. We might therefore think that because signs often have to fit within a limited horizontal surface area that narrow letters will be more legible because they will be able to fit in the surface area, while having a larger point size (Figure 4).

This objective, that a font for signage should be economic in the use of horizontal space, was part of the brief given to Gerard Unger, when he de-signed the font for the Dutch small signposts (ANWB-U) in 1996. During the development process the font was exposed to empirical distance test-ing [Walraven *et al.*, 1996]. The study compared the new font with two versions of the font it was replacing; one of these was both narrower and lighter in weight (ANWB-C) than the Unger font, and one was slightly wider than the Unger font with similar weight (ANWB-E).

Both fonts were altered variations of fonts found in the American road signage typeface family FHWA Series (often referred to as Highway Goth-ic) (Figure 5). The experiment found the performance of the new font ex-

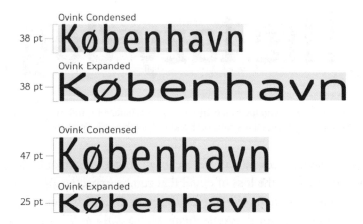

Figure 4: The two fonts at the top are set in the same point size, yet take up very different horizontal space. The two fonts at the bottom, take up the same amount of horizontal space, yet the condensed version is in 47 point size while the expanded version is in 25 point size.

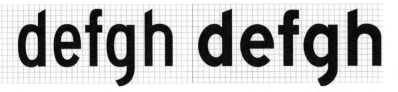

Figure 5: The Highway Gothic Series was originally developed for the American road system. This example shows ANWB-C or Series C with narrow letter shapes (left) and ANWB-E or Series E, which has wider letter shapes (right) (MUTCD 2000).

ceeded that of the narrow version by 13%. It was, however, slightly inferior to the wider version by 3%. Unger[a] has said that the results confirmed to him that large inner letter counters improve distance legibility, a feature he emphasized as much as possible within the limited horizontal width that he had to work with (Figure 6).

Quite a few other designers of traffic typefaces have spoken in favor of large counters. On several occasions, Jock Kinneir [1978, p. 344; 1980, p. 66] noted the significance of having clear and open counters, to avoid clogged counters and therefore more ambiguous letter shapes when the letters and numbers are viewed through the glare of headlights. He also

---

[a] Personal communication (December 2012)

The quick brown fox jumps over a lazy dog

Figure 6: In the font ANWB-U, Gerard Unger aimed at creating large inner counters, while working on saving horizontal space as well.

emphasized that even while narrow glyphs can be set larger and taller, this will not improve on the legibility if the two opposite sides of the counters are too close and begin to seem to merge [Kinneir 1980, p. 66]. More recently, type designer James Montalbano collaborated with Meeker & Associates on the design of the typeface ClearviewHwy that is intended to eventually replace Highway Gothic on American roads. In an interview with the New York Times, Montalbano voiced his opinion of the letter counters of Highway Gothic, finding them too small. He too refers to the problem of headlights' illumination causing problems with recognizing letters and numbers. In the case of the letters 'o' and 'e' Montalbano describes them as appearing like 'bullets that you couldn't put a pin through' [Yaffa 2007, p. 4] meaning that the counters seem to disappear. A similar observation has been made by type designer Adrian Frutiger in relation to his traffic sign typeface Frutiger Astra, where he enlarged the counters as a way of ensuring that letters like 'e' and 'a' can be easily distinguished and do not appear like dots from a distance [Linotype, 2009].

These designers all realized the significance of opening up the counters for distance legibility and found that it is essential to produce fonts where the inner white area is as big as possible.

Large counters can be created in several ways. One way is related to the x-height, and another way is related to the width of the glyph.

1.3.1 *The x-height*

In many of the lowercase letters, the majority of the details are found within the x-height. Hence it is the x-height and not the point size that defines the perceptual size of the font, a fact that has been overlooked in the history of legibility research too often (Figure 7). Therefore the larger the x-height the larger the font is perceived to be.

An early legibility study by Elisabeth Roethlein [1912] confirms this. Roethlein tested the distance legibility of the individual letter in a series of different fonts, and as shown in Figure 8, the fonts of the larger x-height were also the fonts that were legible from the greatest distance.

There is, however, a limit to how big the x-height can be. In his publication 'Letters of Credit' from 1986, typography writer Walter Tracy ar-

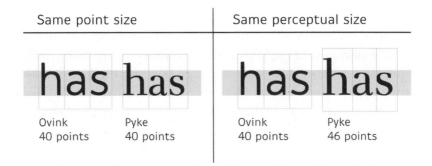

Same point size		Same perceptual size	
has	has	has	has
Ovink	Pyke	Ovink	Pyke
40 points	40 points	40 points	46 points

Figure 7: The font Ovink has a larger x-height than the font Pyke; when set in the same point size Ovink will appear larger than Pyke while working on saving horizontal space as well.

New Gothic	236.4
Bulfinch	233.6
Clearface	229.5
Century O.S.	228.0
Century Exp.	226.7
Cheltenham W	224.3
Jenson	214.7
Della Robbia	214.7
Cushing O.S.	206.4
Cheltenham O.S.	206.4
De Vinne	204.8

Figure 8: A selection of the fonts tested by Elisabeth Roethlein [1912] with their distance thresholds (right column). This table demonstrates that large x-heights tend to be read at greater distances than small x-heights.

gued that, although short descenders on letters such as g, j, p, q and y may be 'displeasing to the eye' [p. 50], this is not as problematic as too short ascenders on letters such as b, d, h, k and l, which can result in the letters losing their individuality. A classic example of this problem is the confusability between h and n (Figure 9).

There is consequently a limit to how big the x-height can be before it starts to interfere with the parts that differentiate one letter from the other.

Figure 9: If the x-height is too big, it can result in misreading of certain letters.

1.3.2 *Letter width*

In order to inform the choice of typeface for signs at London's Heathrow Airport, Robert Waller [2007] compared the fonts BA Signs, Frutiger Bold, Frutiger Roman, Vialog, and Garamond Italic. He gradually enlarged the test material until the participant was able to identify the word. The data showed that the narrow Vialog was less legible than the two Frutiger weights and the BA Sign fonts, all of which were wider in horizontal proportions than Vialog (Figure 10).

In another investigation, researchers [Beier and Larson, 2010] measured the number of errors made by participants while identifying letters at a short exposure and at a distance, and found that at distance reading, narrow designed characters tended to produce more errors than wider designed characters (Figure 11); this was most evident in fonts of low stroke contrast.

Over the years, several studies have looked into the legibility of the Highway Gothic family. In 1939, Forbes and Holmes compared the legibility distances of the narrow series B with the wider series D (Figure 12), and found that both at day and night time conditions, the wider versions delivered the best performance. Another researcher, Thomas Schnell

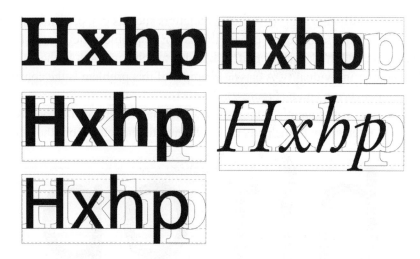

Figure 10: The fonts BA Signs, Frutiger Bold, Frutiger Roman (left), Vialog, and Garamond Italic (right), tested by Robert Waller [2007].

[1998] also looked into different aspects of the distance legibility of the Highway Gothic family. As part of his PhD studies, Schnell investigated the contrast threshold on a computer screen, starting out with the same luminance between stimulus and background, and then gradually adding visual contrast until participants could identify the test material built out of uppercase letters and numerals. Under these conditions, Schnell found that the wider fonts resulted in better performances than the narrow.

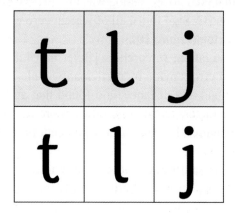

Figure 11: At distance reading and at short exposure, wider letters (top) produced a higher identification rate than did narrow letters [Beier and Larson, 2010].

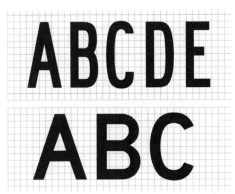

Figure 12: Highway Gothic series B (top) and series D (bottom).

Applying two methods, one based on luminance, and one based on distance threshold, Curt Berger [1948] studied different variations of the digits 5 and 0, all of same height, stroke weight, and contrast, but varying in horizontal size. The findings demonstrated that the wider the digits the more legible they became. Elisabeth Roethlein [1912] further reported a distance legibility investigation of a number of fonts within the family Cheltenham Oldstyle, which found the Wide and the Bold versions to be legible at a greater distance than the Bold Condensed, the Ordinary, and the Italic versions (Figure 13).

A font of wider proportions would need to be scaled down in size to fit a limited surface area; which then will result in a smaller point size (Figure 4). The challenge is to identify the optimal height-width ratio that enables open inner counters without having to scale down the letter size too much.

1.4 Letter weight

Defining the optimal letter weight is a difficult matter. If the stroke is too light, the characters might become invisible when viewed from a distance. The opposite is also a problem. If the stroke is too heavy, the counters will become too small and result in illegible letter shapes.

When white text is placed on a dark background; when light is projected through the glyphs; or when a sign is made out of reflective material, the phenomenon known as halation or irradiation can cause problems for readers (Figure 14). The blurring of light around the bright area of the

Bold	**Bold Condensed**
Wide	Ordinary
	Italic

Figure 13: The different styles of the Cheltenham Old Style font family tested by Roethlein [1912]. The fonts in the left column of fonts were read at a greater distance than those in the right column.

Figure 14: A simulation of halation.

sign results in a 'halo', which makes it visually bleed into the surrounding areas. The effect of halation appears to vary depending on the nature of the 'halo'. In an extended review of relevant legibility research Helmut T. Zwahlen and his colleagues [1995] found that white text on dark background, generally requires a lighter stroke weight than dark text on white background. In some situations this will be solely an aesthetic adjustment, while in others the 'halo' surrounding the glyphs will cause significant reductions of legibility. This phenomenon is further evident in the data of the test studies carried out in connection with the ClearviewHwy typeface family [Garvey *et. al*, 1997; Holick *et. al*, 2006]. These studies found that in nighttime conditions the Clearview font could be read from farther away than the slightly heavier Highway Gothic series E. The same difference was not seen in daytime conditions, where the two were read equally well.

1.5 Inter-letter spacing

'Inter-letter spacing' (also called fitting or metrics) is the amount of space between all characters in a font, this being in contrast to 'kerning', which is the adjusted amount of space between two specific characters. In a design guide for the implementation of the Highway Gothic Series, the Federal Highway Administration stated that: '...tests have shown that, for any given legend, better legibility can be obtained by using a relatively wide spacing between letters than by using wider and taller letters with a cramped space' [MUTCD, 2000, p. 8-1]. The statement suggests that inter letter spacing is one of the most central parameters when creating type for distance reading, however, the Highway Administration does not provide any references to their sources. In an investigation into distance legibility of night-time guide signs, Holick and Carlson [2003] set out to study the effect of four different spacing settings: one in Highway Gothic Series E, and three in the sans serif typeface family ClearviewHwy 5W. One of the ClearviewHwy fonts had a 3% reduction of the default spacing value, and another had a 6% reduction of the default spacing value. All fonts were tested with white text on green background. The experiment found no statistically significant difference between the three spacing values of the ClearviewHwy font, suggesting that for a significant difference to be found, the difference between spacing values may need to be greater than 6%.

Several renowned type designers have emphasized the importance of large inter-letter spacing in fonts designed for distance reading. One of these, designer Erik Spiekermann, has pointed out that too narrow letter spacing is a common flaw in signage systems [Spiekermann, 2006]. He further puts the argument forward that when reading a sign we do not read it in the same way as we do in continuous text, but instead decipher each letter of the text. As signs often contain single words with no additional context, Spiekermann finds that all characters under these circumstances need to be more clearly separated from each other.

Jock Kinneir [1978] made a similar observation. He referred to the phenomenon shown by pointillist painters that forms tend to merge when viewed from afar. These designers have observed a phenomenon identified by researchers as the 'crowding effect' or 'contour interaction', where neighboring letters within a word interfere with each other. This interference makes it harder to identify the individual letters. The phenomenon is most evident under perceptual conditions of low resolution, which occur when reading at a distance [Hess *et al.*, 2000; Liu *et al.*, 2001].

A couple of field experiments in the 1950s looked into the inter-letter spacing of the Highway Gothic Series. One of these, carried out by Harry

W. Case and his colleagues [1952] was concerned with the distance legibility of individual uppercase letters of the Highway Gothic Series E font
(Figure 5). The study showed a difference in legibility depending on the
type being set in positive or negative contrast, and found that black type
on a white background was slightly more legible under a narrower spacing
setting, and that white type on a black background was most legible under
a wider spacing setting (Figure 15).

In another experiment from the same period, David Soloman [1956]
looked into the influence different spacing values have on words set in the
three Highway Gothic Series fonts E, C, and ED (the latter being similar in
width but slightly thinner than series E) (Figure 5). The study was carried
out in a dark parking lot using dipped headlights, with test material made
out of white reflectorized material mounted on a black non-reflectorized
panel. The findings confirmed the earlier results of Case and his colleagues
by showing that distance legibility of white type on a black background
increases as the spacing value increases. It appears that to reach a high level of legibility, the irradiation that affects the type under these conditions
calls for a larger amount of space between the glyphs, and this effect is not
as strong when dark text is set on light background.

Figure 15: Due to the bleeding of white into the dark background, Harry W. Case and his
colleagues [1952] found that light text on black is more legible with a larger amount
of inter-letter spacing (here illustrated with the typeface Interstate designed by Tobias
Frere-Jones).

1.6 Summary and conclusion

To meet the problem of lost details at great distances, serifs on the vertical
stems improve distance legibility, yet when the type is influenced by halation, or in situations where light is projected from the back of the sign, the

letters might benefit from being designed as low contrast sans serif fonts instead.

Open inner counters generally tend to improve distance legibility; this can be achieved by making the x-height relatively large and the letter shapes relatively wide. That being said, there is a limit to the size of the x-height if certain glyphs are not to be misread for others, and there is a limit to the letter width, if the text is to fit horizontally on a specified surface area without having a point size that is too small.

Due to the effect of crowding, it further appears that large inter letter spacing – in general – benefits distance reading, and that this is most evident when light text is placed on a dark background. Furthermore, since the color white tends to bleed into a darker surface, text set white on a dark background should be lighter in weight than the corresponding dark text on a light background.

A practicing designer's knowledge and understanding of the craft is often attained through trial and error, or through experimentation with the material, while scientific findings often stem from controlled investigations that aim to either confirm or disconfirm a predefined hypothesis. By combining these distinct approaches, and by considering them as equally valid in the search for answers, it is possible to gather information that can help us better understand the field of type design.

References

Beier. S., and Dyson, M. (2014) The influence of serifs on 'h' and 'i': useful knowledge from design-led scientific research, *Visible Language*, 47(3), pp. 74-95.

Beier, S. and Larson, K. (2010) Design improvements for frequently misrecognized letters, *Information Design Journal*, 18(2), pp. 118-137.

Berger, C. (1948) Some experiments on the width of symbols as determinant of legibility, *Acta Ophthalmologica*, 26(4), pp. 517-55.

Case, H.W., Michael, J.L., Mount, G.E., and Brenner, R., (1952) Analysis of certain variables related to sign legibility, *Hway. Res. Bd. Bull*, 60, pp. 44-54. Abstract and short summary reported in: *A study of Traffic Sign Requirements*, T.W. Forbes, Snyder, T.E., and R.F. Pain (eds.), Department of Psychology Division of Engineering Research, Michigan State University, pp. 53-54.

Forbes, T.W. and Holmes, R.S., (1939) Legibility distances of highway destination signs in relation to letter height, letter width and reflectorization', *Proceedings of the Highway Research Board*, 19, pp. 321-355.

Garvey, P.M., Pietrucha, M.T., and Meeker, D.T. (1997) Effects of font and capitalization on legibility of guide signs', *Research on Traffic Control Devices*, 1605.

Hess, R.F., Dakin, S.C. and Kapoor, N. (2000) The foveal 'crowding' effect: physics or physiology?, *Vision Research*, 40, pp. 365-370.

Holick, A.J. and Carlson J. (2003) *Nighttime Guide Sign Legibility for Microprismatic Clearview legend on High Intensity Background*, [online], available from: http://d2dtl5nnlpfr0r.cloudfront.net/tti.tamu.edu/documents/0-1796-4.pdf [accessed 5. August 2014].

Holick, A.J., Chrysler, S.T., Park, E.S., and Carlson, P.J. (2006) *Evaluation of the Clearview font for negative contrast traffic signs*, Texas Transportation Institute.

Kindersley, D. (1960) Motorway sign lettering, *Traffic Engineering and Control*, 2(8), pp. 463-465.

Kinneir, J. (1978) The practical and graphic problems of road sign design, in: R. Easterby and H. Zwaga, (eds), *Information design: the design and evaluation of signs and technical information*, Chichester: John Wiley and Sons Ltd., pp. 341-58.

Kinneir, J. (1980) Words and buildings: the art and practice of public letterings, London: The Architectural Press.

Linotype (2009) Typography as the highest form of visual communication: A talk with Adrian Frutiger, [online] available from: http://www.linotype.com/de/2316-17757/servingapurpose.html?lang=de [accessed 5. August 2014].

Liu, L. & Arditi, A. (2001) How crowding affects letter confusion', *Optometry and Vision Science*, 78(1), pp. 50-55.

Lund, O. (2003) The public debate on Jock Kinneir's road sign alphabet, *Typography Papers*, 5, pp. 103-126.

MUTCD (2000) Design Guidelines *Manual on Uniform Traffic Control*, available online: http://mutcd.fhwa.dot.gov/SHSe/Design.pdf [accessed 5. August 2014]

Roethlein, B.E. (1912) 'The relative legibility of different faces of printed types, *American Journal of Psychology*, 23(1), pp. 1-36.

Schnell, T. (1998) *Legibility optimization of uppercase alphanumeric text for display messages in traffic applications*, PhD Thesis (unpublished), College of Engineering and Technology, Ohio University.

Soloman, D., (1956) The Effect of letter width and spacing on night legibility of highway signs, *Proc.Hway, Res. Bd.* 35, 600-617, Abstract and short summary in: *A Study of Traffic sign requirements*, T.W. Forbes, T.E. Snyder, R.F. Pain (eds.), Department of Psychology Division of Engineering Research, Michigan State university, pp. 67-68.

Spiekermann, E. (2006) Infography: On FF Info, in: J. Middendorp & E. Spiekermann, (eds), *Made with FontFont: Type for independent minds*, Amsterdam: BIS Publishers, pp. 54-57.

Tracy, W. (1986) *Letters of Credit: a view of type Design*, London: Gordon Fraser.

Unger, G. (2014) M.O.L. (1974), available online: http://www.gerardunger.com/allmytypedesigns/allmytypedesigns03.html [accessed 5. August 2014].

Waller, R. (2007) Comparing typefaces for airport signs, *Information Design Journal*, 15(1), pp. 1-15.

Walraven, J., Varkevisser, J. & But, P. (1996) *Evaluatie van de leesbaarheid van een nieuw ANWB-alfabet voor*, TNO Technische Menskunde bewegwijzering.

Yaffa, J. (2007) The Road to Clarity, *The New York Times*, Aug. 12, available online: http://www.nytimes.com/2007/08/12/magazine/12fonts-t.html?pagewanted=4&_r=3 [accessed 5. August 2014].

Zwahlen, H.T., Sunkara, M. and Schnell, T. (1995) A review of legibility relationships within the context of textual information presentation', *Transportation Research Board*, 1485, pp. 61-70.

Chapter 6

Effects of interword spacing on Chinese children's reading abilities

Hsiu-Feng Wang

This experiment investigated whether different interword spacing arrangements in Chinese text affected the reading speed and comprehension of Taiwanese children. The text was shown on a tablet computer. The experiment used standard interword spacing (i.e. that typically used in Chinese text) and three arrangements with larger sized gaps. It also used two groups of children. One group comprised 7 to 8 year-olds and the other comprised 10 to 11 year-olds. In the experiment the children read text that had different sized spacing arrangements; their reading speeds were recorded and they completed a series of tests in which they had to identify substituted words that were incongruous to the rest of the text. The results showed that those different interword spacing arrangements and age groups affected children's reading times and their reading performance. It also found that the younger children benefited significantly from interword spacing that was larger than that typically used in Chinese. These findings are likely to be of interest to people designing reading materials, learning resources and text messaging systems for children who read Chinese.

1.1 Introduction

Interword spacing is the act of leaving gap between words to enable readers to easily and quickly identify where one word ends and another begins. Many languages use interword spacing. Chinese, however, does not. In Chinese, gaps exist after each character, regardless of whether a character forms an entire word or part of a word. Instead of relying on visual cues, Chinese readers determine where one word ends and another begins exclusively through reading experience.

Over 70% of Chinese words are made up of two or more characters [Yu *et al.*, 1985]. This method of forming words, while immensely flexible, can lead to confusion as it is possible for a reader to erroneously combine characters that belong to one word with characters that belong to another. An example of this is given in Figure 1. Either the first two characters in the sentence can be combined to form the word 'pencil' and the sentence reads: 'It is important to use a pencil to take notes' or the first three characters in the sentence can be combined to form the word 'sketch' and the sentence reads: 'It is important to make notes on how to sketch'. In other words, the meaning of the sentence depends entirely on how the reader mentally groups the characters. Other examples of sentences that have more than one meaning when the characters are grouped differently are given by Hsu and Huang [2000a, 2000b].

鉛筆/畫重點很重要

'It is important to use a pencil to take notes'

鉛筆畫/重點很重要

'It is important to make notes on how to sketch'

Figure 1: Different interpretations of the same sentence.

Students of Chinese often find it difficult to determine which characters in a sentence should be grouped together to form the words the author intended [Bassetti, 2009; Yao, 2011; Bai *et al.*, 2013]. Unfortunately, this problem often persists throughout many students' entire schooling as the more vocabulary they learn, the more word permutations exist.

In order to help children identify and learn correct character groupings, teachers in Taiwanese primary schools typically circle characters that form common words. This technique differs from that used in books directed at foreigners learning Chinese. In these books interword spacing is typically used. This raises the question of whether interword spacing would assist Taiwanese children learning Chinese. Interword spacing has the advantage over character circling in that it can be incorporated into an electronic text speedily without the use of special graphic tools. Furthermore, it does not add aesthetic clutter to the page. This is particularly helpful if the text has annotation or uses highlighting techniques, such as italic or underline.

This study explores the relationship between interword spacing and age with respect to Taiwanese children reading Chinese text. It is envisaged that the findings of the study may promote the development of better reading materials for Taiwanese children. The study addresses the following research questions: Do different levels of interword spacing have an impact on Taiwanese children's reading speeds and their ability to recognize text correctly? Does age have an impact upon Taiwanese children's reading speeds and their ability to recognize text correctly? Is there any interaction between different levels of interword spacing and age in relation to Chinese text with respect to Taiwanese children?

1.2 Background to the study

1.2.1 *Interword spacing and the reading of Chinese text*

A number of researchers have investigated the effects of interword spacing on Chinese text. Some of these studies have involved native speakers while others have involved foreign language learners.

One study that involved native speakers was conducted by Hsu and Huang [2000b]. In this study Taiwanese adults were shown several articles on a computer screen. These articles were presented in three different interword spacing formats: conventional no spacing, half-character spacing and whole-character spacing. The articles that had conventional no spacing used the same spacing as that used traditionally in Chinese (i.e. all the characters were equally spaced); the articles that had half-character spacing used an additional half-character space between words; and the articles that had whole-character spacing used an additional whole-character space between words. The researchers found that the articles that had half-character spacing were understood better and read more quickly than the articles that had either conventional no spacing or whole-character spacing. However, other researchers have obtained different results. For example, Liu *et al.* [1974] found that interword spacing did not improve the reading speed of Chinese readers reading Chinese; Inhoff *et al.* [1997] also found this to be the case.

More recently, Bai *et al.* [2013] investigated whether interword spacing could help foreigners learning Chinese to acquire new vocabulary. The study, which involved language learners from the University of Wisconsin-Madison, had two parts: a learning session, in which participants read sentences that contained new words, and a testing session. In the learning session, half of the participants read conventionally unspaced text and half read interword spaced text. In the testing session, all the participants read conventionally unspaced text. The researchers found that the participants who initially read the new words in the interword spaced sentences read them most speedily in the testing session.

However, research by Yao [2011] suggested that interword spacing may not assist all non-native Chinese readers. In an experiment that involved participants from different orthographic backgrounds, Yao found that participants whose first language did not use interword spacing slowed down when they read interword spaced text, while participants whose first language did use interword spacing were unaffected by the gaps between words.

Although a number of researchers have conducted experiments that investigate interword spacing with respect to Chinese text, most of these experiments have been conducted with adults. Still little is known about how interword spacing affects the reading speeds of different aged children and how it affects their ability to find typographic errors.

1.2.2   Theory related to reading

Gestaltists argue that the mind has a tendency to organise individual elements into groups; they assert that the whole is other than the sum of its parts [Wertheimer, 1923; Koffka, 1935]. Arguably, the Gestalt principle that is most pertinent to this study is that of proximity. According to this principle, people perceive entities that are close to each other as a group.

One study that investigated the principle of proximity was conducted by Hsu and Huang [2000b]. The researchers investigated whether splitting two-character Chinese words across lines, so that one character was at the end of one line and one was at the beginning of the next, reduced reading speed. The researchers found that it did. They argued that this was because readers did not see the two characters as related: the characters were not next to each other and thus were not perceived to be a single entity.

Li *et al.* [2009] offered a model that explained how people segment Chinese text into words as they are reading. The model displayed a process of both top-down and bottom-up information processing. It had three interactive levels: visual perception, character recognition and word recognition. The researchers explained that the first layer, visual perception, was where the features that make up characters were recognized. They stated that information from this level was then combined in the second level, character recognition, with feedback from the third level, word recognition. The researchers added that the third level received information from the lexicon and from the character recognizers in the second level.

However, whilst Li *et al.*'s [2009] model is helpful in explaining how Chinese words are recognized, it assumes that a reader is familiar with Chinese characters and words. Early learners are not. While some may recognize specific characters, they often do not know how these characters are combined to form words. As such, they can look at the last character of a word and incorrectly assume it belongs to the next word.

1.2.3 *Age difference*

A number of studies have looked at differences between adults and children with respect to reading text on screen [e.g. Bernard *et al.*, 2002]. However, in the majority of these studies children are not divided into age groups. It is thus possible that certain age related issues in the design of text on screen have been overlooked.

One study that divided children into age groups was conducted by Hughes and Wilkins [2000]. In this study, children aged 5 to 7 years (younger) and children aged 8 to 11 years (older) were shown four passages of text that employed different font sizes and spacing arrangements. The researchers found that the reading speeds of the younger children decreased as font size decreased. This was unlike the reading speeds of the older children which remained the same. Wilkins later conducted a set of similar studies with other colleagues [see Wilkins *et al.*, 2009]. In these studies, which involved children aged 7 to 9, comprehension and reading age were investigated with respect to font size. The studies revealed that children comprehended sentences more quickly and had a higher reading age when the text was printed in a large font rather than a small font.

Another study that divided children by age was conducted by Wang *et al.* [2013]. In this study the researchers investigated whether there was an interaction between age and e-book adaptive design with respect to learning achievements and motivation. The children involved in the study were 10 year-olds and 11 year-olds. The researchers found that the 10 year-olds had better recall, transfer and attention scores when their e-books were set to the adaptive setting rather than any other setting. The performance of 11 year-olds was the same for all the settings.

With respect to studies involving websites, Nielsen [2010] found that children of different ages preferred different sized text. He also discovered that if a website's content was presented for a school grade other than that of the viewer it was often disliked.

Considering that variation has been found in the way different aged children react to font size and typeface design and respond to age-related reading with adaptive design e-books, it seems reasonable to assume that they might have preferences and perform differently when it comes to reading on screen.

1.3 Methods

1.3.1 *Participants*

Thirty-two 1st grade students (15 male and 17 female) and thirty-two 4th grade students (14 male and 18 female) were randomly selected from an urban primary school in the south of Taiwan. The 1st grade students were aged between 7 and 8 years old (M=7.61, SD=.590) and the 4th grade students were aged between 10 and 11 years old (M=10.23, SD=.423). The students in each grade had a similar reading standard to each other; this was confirmed by looking at their examination results. All the students were regular tablet computer users, went online at least three times a week. On completing the experiment each received a small toy as a gift.

1.3.2 *Experimental design*

To test the effects of interword spacing and age on reading time and reading performance a 2 x 3 mixed design was used. The two independent variables were: interword spacing and age. Interword spacing used a within-subjects factorial design and had three levels: unspaced, semi-spaced and fully-spaced. Age used a between-subjects factorial design and had two levels: younger (this level consisted of participants who were 7-8 years old) and older (this level consisted of participants who were 10-11 years old).

The two dependent variables were reading time (the time it took a participant to read an article) and reading performance (the accuracy with which a participant found incongruous Chinese characters placed in an article).

1.3.3 *Materials*

Three primary school teachers were asked to jointly select the reading materials used in the study. First they selected three articles for the 1st year students. They were chosen from a collection of twelve articles accredited by the Ministry of Culture in Taiwan as being suitable for 1st grade primary school students. Each article contained between 450 and 480 characters. The teachers then selected three articles for the 4th grade students. These were chosen from a collection of twelve articles accredited by the Ministry of Culture in Taiwan as being suitable for 4th grade primary school students. Each article contained between 520 and 550 characters. All the articles used in the study were about aboriginal tribes that lived in Taiwan.

Once the articles had been selected, fifteen Chinese characters in each were substituted. These characters were chosen randomly and replaced with characters that looked similar. For example, in one article the character '日 (sun) was replaced with the character '目'(eye): A character that would be viewed as being out of place if it were read carefully. The altered articles were shown to students from another class prior to the test. All the students agreed that the substituted characters used in the articles did not make sense in the context in which they were found.

Each article contained three pages. Each page contained between 11 and 13 lines of text (between 165 and 186 characters per page). The text filled the entire screen of the tablet computer. The text was displayed at 14 point font size, with 28 point line spacing and in the Ming typeface, a typeface found to be highly legible on a computer screen [Chi *et al.*, 2003]. The text was written horizontally. This alignment is used in science textbooks in Taiwanese school.

The text was shown to the participants in three formats (see Figure 2). The first format was unspaced. This format reflected the spacing traditionally used in written Chinese: it used spaces of approximately one fifth of the width of a character between each and every character. The second format was semi-spaced; it employed spaces of approximately one third of the width of a character between words and one fifth the width of a character between characters that formed words. The third format was fully-spaced; it employed spaces of approximately the width of a character between words and one fifth the width of a character between characters that formed words. The three formats conformed to guidelines developed by Liu *et al.* [1987].

The study used an Asus Eee Pad tablet computer with a 10.1 inch IPS multi-touch screen. The screen had a resolution of 1280 × 800 pixels; it was used in a landscape orientation.

Unspaced	從前，部落裡有兩個非常優秀的青年勇士，他們能力好，狩獵技巧高超，對於傳統舞蹈及歌曲，也都很厲害。
Semi-spaced	從前，部落裡 有 兩個 非常優秀 的 青年勇士，他們能力好，狩獵技巧 高超，對於 傳統舞蹈 及 歌曲，也都 很厲害。
Fully-spaced	從前，部落裡 有 兩個 非常優秀 的 青年勇士，他們能力好，狩獵技巧 高超，對於 傳統舞蹈 及 歌曲，也都 很厲害。
Translation	Once upon a time, there were two intelligent men who lived in an aboriginal tribe; both were highly skilled hunters, singers and dancers

Figure 2: Examples of the test pages with interword spacing used in the experiment.

1.3.4 *Procedure*

The experiment was conducted in a number of computer laboratories at the participants' school. The participants were split into two groups according to their grade level. These groups were then subdivided to form six groups: three 1st grade groups and three 4th grade groups. The participants were placed into these groups randomly. In total there were 10 to 13 participants in each group. Each group was assigned two assistants. These assistants answered any procedural questions and helped the participants complete their paperwork. Each participant was given his/her own tablet computer.

Before the experiment commenced, the participants undertook a set of familiarisation exercises using onscreen materials similar to those used in the experiment. In these exercises they touched an onscreen button to make an article appear/disappear. This button also controlled the timing clock, and selected Chinese characters that they thought were out of place in the text by touching them (touching them made the characters change colour).

Once all the participants understood what to do, the experiment began. The participants were informed that they would see three articles in succession. They were told that they should read the articles as quickly and as accurately as possible and select any characters that they thought were incongruous with respect to the text. They were told that they should work alone. Each participant saw one unspaced article, one semi-spaced article and one fully-spaced article. The articles were shown in a random order for each participant. Reading times and characters selected were logged automatically by each participant's tablet computer.

The participants took around 20 minutes to perform the reading tasks. On leaving, they completed a short form that collected their demographic details.

1.4 Results

As the articles used for 1st and 4th grade students differed in length, each participant's reading times were transformed into seconds per 100 characters. The performance scores were taken as the percentage of substituted characters found.

Analysis of variance was carried out on participants' reading times and the percentage of substituted words found. All data undergoing analysis of variance (ANOVA) were tested for the assumption of sphericity. The mean reading times and the percentage of substituted words found for each experimental condition are shown in Table 1.

1.4.1 *Reading time*

A significant difference was observed between the effects of interword spacings on reading time, $F(2, 124) = 4.87, p = .009$. The reading times of the effects of interword spacing were fully-spaced interword text, followed by semi-spaced interword text, and last, the unspaced interword text. Further multiple comparisons using the Scheffé statistical test showed that the text reading time for fully-spaced text was significantly shorter than that for unspaced text ($p=.004$); and times for semi-spaced text were significantly shorter than those for unspaced text ($p=.038$). However, when examining the difference between fully-spaced and semi-spaced text, no significant difference was found. It seems that interword spacing was helpful for a child's speed of reading at age 7 years and age 10 years.

Analyses identified a main effect for children's age. Older children read text faster than younger children, $F(1, 62) = 13.40, p = .001$.

1.4.2 *Reading performance*

Examining reading performance for different age groups in relation to the percentage of detected substituted words revealed a main effect for children's age. Older children's achievement was better than that of younger children in relation to their reading performance, $F(1, 62) = 7.39, p = .009$. However, analyzing the percentage of detected substituted words for the effect of interword spacing showed no significant difference with regard to reading performance.

Table 1: Means and standard deviations of reading times (sec.) and reading performance (%) under different experimental conditions.

	Reading time		Reading performance	
	M	SD	M	SD
Word arrangement				
Unspaced	237.19	56.61	63.87	21.38
Semi-spaced	219.61	50.54	69.53	28.68
Fully-spaced	216.48	41.58	72.26	23.61
Age				
Younger	240.19	49.69	62.89	24.56
Older	208.67	44.33	74.21	22.16

The results revealed an interaction between the three different interword spacing arrangements and the two different age groups in relation to children's reading performance, $F(2, 124) = 4.78, p = .010$; this is illustrated in Figure 3. Children's reading performances for fully-spaced text were better than those for unspaced text, regardless of the children's age.

Children's reading performances for the three different interword spacing arrangements showed a significant difference for younger children, $F(2, 62) = 6.692, p = .002$, but there was no significant difference for older children, $F(2, 62) = .844, p = .435$. Looking at age groups separately, multiple comparisons with the Scheffé test showed that younger children read fully-spaced text significantly better than unspaced text. They also read semi-spaced text better than unspaced text. However, the difference between semi-spaced and fully-spaced text was not significant. For older children, there was no significant difference between interword spacing. In other words, interword spacing significantly affected younger children's reading performance, but had no effect on older children.

The results also revealed that older children's reading performance with unspaced text was significantly better than younger children's reading performance, F (5, 64) = 5.909 p = .035. However, no significant difference was found between semi-spaced and fully-spaced text layouts in relation to age groups. This suggests that unspaced text layout (traditional text) has an age related effect on reading performance, but spaced text does not.

1.5 Discussion and conclusion

The experiment examined the influence of interword spacing and children's age on Taiwanese children's reading materials. It measured chil-

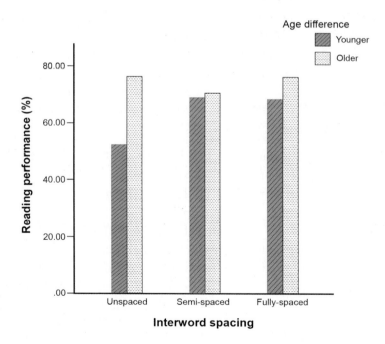

Figure 3: Reading performance (%) for different interword spacing arrangements and age difference.

dren's reading times, and assessed their reading performance with respect to these materials. The data revealed those different interword spacing arrangements and age groups affected children's reading times and their reading performance.

Data analysis revealed that the Taiwanese children read interword spaced text significantly more quickly than the unspaced text layout (traditional text). This finding reflects that of Hsu and Huang [2000b] who, in an experiment that investigated interword spacing and Taiwanese adults with respect to reading times and comprehension, found that interword spacing with a similar sized gap between words to those in this experiment, produced the fastest reading times compared to other interword spacing arrangements. It should be noted, however, that Hsu and Huang's experiment measured participants' reading performance through a post-reading comprehension test. This experiment investigated reading performance by identifying substituted words that were inappropriately placed in the text. This type of task reduced participants' skimming behavior and provided an extra visual cue which guided them to find the substituted words [Bernard et al., 2002, 2003]. In addition, Hsu and Huang's experiment only involved Taiwanese adults. This experiment therefore extends their findings by confirming that interword spacing also helps Taiwanese children to read faster, although it uses different measures of reading performance.

There were differences between younger and older children with respect to the percentage of detected substituted words. These results mirrored the finding of Hughes and Wilkins [2000] who, in a reading task, found that older children have no differences with regard to font size and typeface design in reading materials. However, the reading time of younger children decreased as the text size decreased.

Further analyses of reading performance demonstrated that, with respect to the percentage of detected substituted words, older children performed better than younger children. According to Li et al.'s [2009] Chinese word recognition model, the recognition of Chinese characters involves both topdown and bottomup cognitive processing. This experiment additionally found that interword spacing, which is not used in written Chinese, assisted younger children to recognise words in text. It is possible that this finding can be attributed to the law of proximity [Wertheimer, 1923; Koffka, 1935] in that the spaces between the groups of closely positioned characters made the characters in these groups appear to be correctly associated with each other. In other words, the spaces gave younger children visual cues as to which characters formed words. It is possible that interword spacing showed fewer advantages with older children than younger children with respect to reading performance because the older children in the experiment found the text too easy to understand. They may have anticipated some words and thus did not profit from the additional visual cues offered by interword spacing.

This experiment had two limitations. First, only two age groups (ages 7 to 8 years and ages 10 to 11 years) were included in the research. If the experiment is repeated with children outside these age groups, different results may be obtained. As some researchers have suggested, younger children are still developing their reading skills, so are more likely than older children to be affected by typographic variables [Hughes and Wilkins, 2000, 2002; Reynolds and Walker, 2004]. Second, the study only used a small number of interword spacing arrangements. It may be found that interword spacing that is larger than a character wide is more beneficial to Taiwanese children than fully-spaced interspacing.

This study contributes to the limited body of work that relates to children reading text with different sized interword spacing arrangements on tablet computers. The findings of this experiment should be useful to instructional designers, typographers and child educators creating reading materials for Taiwanese children.

Acknowledgment

This experiment was kindly supported by a grant from the Ministry of Science and Technology in Taiwan (contract number: MOST103-2410-H-415-047).

References

Bai, X.J., Liang, F.F., Blythe, H.I., Zang, C.L., Yan, G.L., and Liversedge, S.P. (2013). Interword spacing effects on the acquisition of new vocabulary for readers of Chinese as a second language, *J. Res. Read., 36*(S1), pp. S4-S7.
Bassetti, B. (2009). Effects of adding interword spacing on Chinese reading: a comparison of Chinese native readers and English readers of Chinese as a second language, *Appl. Psycholinguistics, 30*(4), pp.757-775.

Bernard, M., Chaparro, B. S., Mills, M. M., and Halcomb, C. G. (2002). Examining children's reading performance and preference for different computer-displayed text, *Behav. Inform. Technol., 21*(2), pp.87-96.

Bernard, M., Fernandez, M., and Hull, S. (2002). The effects of line length on children and adults' online reading performance. *Usability News, 4*(2). Retrieved from http://usabilitynews.org/the-effects-of-line-length-on-children-and-adults-online-reading-performance/

Bernard, M., Chaparro, B. S., Mills, M. M., and Halcomb, C. G. (2003). Comparing the effects of text size and format on the readability of computer-displayed Times New Roman and Arial text, *Int. J. Hum-Comput. St., 59*, pp. 823-835.

Chi, C. F., Cai, D., and You, M. (2003). Applying image descriptors to the assessment of legibility in Chinese characters, *Ergon., 46*(8), pp. 825-841.

Hsu, S., and Huang, K. (2000a). Interword spacing in Chinese text layout. *Percept. Motor Skill, 90*(2), pp. 355-365.

Hsu, S., and Huang, K. (2000b). Effects of word spacing on reading Chinese text from a video display terminal, *Percept. Motor Skill, 90*(1), pp. 81-92.

Hughes, L. E., and Wilkins, A. J. (2000). Typography in children's reading schemes may be suboptimal: evidence from measures of reading rat, *J. Res. Read., 23*(3), pp. 314-324.

Hughes, L. E., and Wilkins, A. J. (2002). Reading at a distance: implications for the design of text in children's bog books, *Bri. J. Educ. Psychol., 72*, pp. 213-226.

Inhoff, A. W., Liu, W., Wang, J., and Fu, D. (1997) Hanyu juzi yuedu zhong de yandong yu kongjian xinxi de yunyong (Eye movements and the use of spacing information in reading Chinese sentences), eds. Peng, D., "Hanyu renzhi yanjiu (Cognitive research on the Chinese language)," (Shandong Jiaoyu Chubanshe Press, Taiwan). pp. 296-312.

Koffka, K. (1935) *Principles of Gestalt Psychology.* (Harcourt Publishing, New York).

Li, X., Rayner, K., and Cave, K. R. (2009). On the segmentation of Chinese words during reading, *Cognitive Psychol., 58*, pp. 525-552.

Liu, I. M., Chuang, C. J., and Wu, J. T. (1987). Guiding rules for the computational analyses of Chinese words and proposition, *Chinese J. Psychol., 29*, pp. 51-61. (In Chinese)

Liu, I. M., Ye, J. S., Wang, L. H., and Chang, Y. K. (1974). Effects of arranging Chinese words as units on reading efficiency, *Acta Psychologica Twaiwanica, 16*, pp. 25-32.

Nielsen, J. (2010). Children's websites: Usability issues in designing for kids. Retrieved from http://www.nngroup.com/articles/childrens-websites-usability-issues/

Reynolds, L., and Walker, S. (2004). You can't see what the words say: word spacing and letter spacing in children's reading books, *J. Res. Read., 27*(1), pp. 87-98.

Wang, P. Y., Wang, H. F., and Liu, Y. C. (2013). Elementary students' reading behaviors of e-books with different adaptive designs, *J. Educ. Media Libr. Sci., 51*(2), pp. 267-291.

Wertheimer, M. (1923) Laws of organization in perceptual forms (Untersuchungen zur Lehre von der Gestalt), II Psychologische Forschung, eds. Ellis, W. D., *A sourcebook of Gestalt psychology*, (Routledge, London) pp. 310-350.

Wilkins, A., Cleave, R. Grayson, N. and Wilson, L. (2009). Typography for children may be inappropriately designed, *J. Res. Read., 32*(4), pp. 402-412.

Yao,Y. (2011). Interword spacing effects on reading Mandarin Chinese as a second language, *Writ. Syst. Res., 3*(1), pp. 23-40.

Yu, B., Zhang, W., Jing, Q., Peng, R., Zhang, G., and Simon, H. (1985). STM capacity for Chinese and English language materials, *Mem. & Cogn., 13*(3), pp. 202-207.

Chapter 7

Elements of Chinese
typeface design

Xiaoqing Lu and Ting Tang

This chapter briefly introduces the modern Chinese typeface based on classification, in-cluding its distinguishing features, different usages, and representative typefaces of the different styles. The complexity of the Chinese typeface, particularly in terms of the large quantity of Chinese characters, makes the Chinese typeface designs more difficult to devel-op than those of other typefaces. In general, the workflow of Chinese typeface design in-cludes three important phases, namely, formation of originality, development of the design specification, and implementation of the entire plan. Some particular challenges related to the development of the Chinese typeface are discussed, such as achieving the ideal visual balance of a character by adjusting the size, width, position, and density of its strokes; aligning the centers of the strokes and avoiding collision; and evaluating the effects of the different components on the layout of characters. To guarantee a consistent style, typefaces in different languages, when used simultaneously on one page, also need modification or redesign.

1.1 Introduction

In this chapter, we briefly introduce the modern Chinese typeface based on classification, including its distinguishing features, different usages, and representative typefaces of the different styles, such as Song, Hei, Fang Song, and Kai. The main part of this chapter describes the workflow involved in the Chinese typeface design. The complexity of the Chinese typeface, particularly in terms of the large quantity of Chinese characters, makes the Chinese typeface designs more difficult to develop than those of other typefaces. In general, the approach includes three important phases, namely, formation of originality, development of the design specification, and implementation of the entire plan. Moreover, several particular chal-lenges related to the development of the Chinese typeface are discussed, such as achieving the ideal visual balance of a character by adjusting the size, width, position, and density of its strokes; aligning the centers of the

109

strokes and avoiding collision; and evaluating the effects of the different components on the layout of characters. With the rapid international integration arising from the exchange of views, products, and services all over the world, more content needs to be published simultaneously in different languages. To guarantee a consistent style, characters or typefaces in different languages should be modified or redesigned at the stroke level.

1.2 Background information

1.2.1 *Basic concepts*

The Chinese writing system is drastically different from Latin-based languages [Bathrobe, n.d.; Wikipedia, 2015]. A Chinese character generally represents one syllable of spoken Chinese, and may be a word on its own or a part of a polysyllabic word. All of them are glyphs whose components depict objects or represent abstract notions. Each Chinese character stands as a discrete unit, a self-contained form within an imaginary square box. A line of Chinese text is not separated by spaces into individual words, but only interrupted by punctuation marks. Before we provide details on the design of the Chinese typeface, understanding the important underlying concepts relative to Chinese characters is necessary.

1.2.1.1 *Centroid*

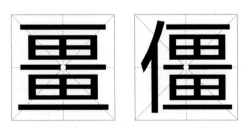

Figure 1: Centroids of Jiang (畺) and Jiang (僵).

The alignment of English letters and words relies on a baseline. However, aside from a baseline, the centroid of each character serves an important function in Chinese character alignment. Figure 1 shows the difference between the centroids of two characters. The horizontal orientation is not the only direction in which Chinese texts are typeset. The layouts of such texts frequently require arrangement in the vertical orientation. The centroids of characters should not be displaced in a horizontal line while being capable of shifting left or right in a vertical line.

The centroid of a Chinese character depends on its geometric attributes, as well as on its structure. Taking characters '畺' (jiang) and '僵' (jiang) for example, the centroid of character '畺' and the center of character '畺' coincide because the structure of the former is bilaterally symmetric both in the up–down and left–right directions. However, the structure of character '僵' is asymmetric, given that its left part, which has sparse strokes, and its right part, which has dense strokes, endow increased weight on the right part compared to the left part in terms of visual effect. Consequently, the centroid of character '僵' slightly deviates to the left of the center of its right part '畺'.

1.2.1.2 *Body frame and surface frame*

There are two important concepts relative to the size of Chinese characters: Body Frame (BF) and Surface Frame (SF). In a Chinese font, each character is fitted into its own space container, which is square shaped and allows the characters to be set neatly into rows. Typeface designers call such a square BF, shown in grey in Figure 2, reminding themselves not to allow any stroke to exceed the borders of a BF. BF is generally fixed for a certain font. SF, however, is the bounding box of a character, shown in dotted line in Figure 2. SFs vary from character to character in one font, but the differences among most SFs are slight. Neither BF nor SF can be seen in an accomplished typeface. They are just adopted by designers to ensure those characters of a same font appear to be the same size in terms of human visual perception.

Figure 2: Two Spring (春) characters from different fonts with same BF and different SF.

1.2.1.3   *ZhongGong*

ZhongGong (中宫), a special concept for Chinese typeface design, literally means central palace. However it references more than just the central part of a character, it depicts the density of a character. Shown as Figure 3, the two graphs can be seen as the same character with different layouts of central strokes. A character with tight ZhongGong (left) exhibits more strokes arranged near the center, whereas those strokes stretch outside in a character with loose ZhongGong (right).

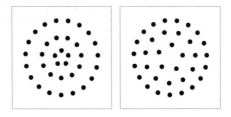

Figure 3: Same character with tight ZhongGong (left) and loose ZhongGong (right).

1.2.2   *Typeface category*

Chinese characters comprise perhaps the oldest surviving writing system in the world and have existed for 8,000 years. Chinese typefaces have four major styles: Song, Hei, FangSong, and Kai, which intrinsically link the history of Chinese script. More new typefaces have been developed from other traditional scripts, such as seal, clerical, and cursive scripts, based on the handwritings of famous calligraphers and from innovations in modern art. As a result, Chinese characters have a variety of typefaces [Founder Type; Hanyi fonts; ZhongYi; DynaComware].

1.2.2.1   *Song (宋)*

Song, also called Ming in Japan, is a distinctive printed style of regular script with a long history dating back to the Song Dynasty. The Song style, as shown in Figure 4, is widely used in Chinese books, newspapers, and magazines. The most striking feature of Song is the triangle at the end of each single horizontal stroke. Such design can be perfectly exhibited in traditional printed documents with high resolution. However, when such style is used for small computer displays or smartphones, most triangles are often rendered as a single dot, thus disturbing the original style. Moreover, the horizontal strokes in the Song style are thin, whereas vertical strokes are thick. The characters in the Song style exhibit geometrical regularity.

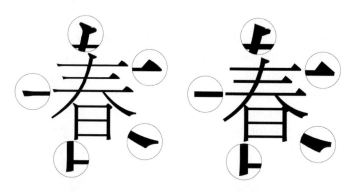

Figure 4: Examples of Song: (left) traditional Song (FangZhengBaoSong, 方正报宋); (right) modern Song (FangZhengBoYaFangKanSong, 方正博雅方刊宋).

1.2.2.2 *Hei (黑)*

Hei is known as the East Asian gothic style typeface, as shown in Figure 5, akin to the Sans-serif styles of Western typography. This style is commonly used in headlines, signs, and videos. Hei generally lacks decorations and has strokes of even thickness. Strokes in the classic Hei style have squared ends. However, new Hei styles tend to adopt rounded line ends and corners. Hei typefaces have low contrast, large counters, and frame-filling glyphs. Thus, these typefaces can be highly legible in low resolution.

黑鹿定外掉

黑鹿定外掉

Figure 5: Examples of Hei: (top) FangZhengLanTingHei (方正兰亭黑); (bottom) Microsoft YaHei (微软雅黑).

1.2.2.3 *FangSong (仿宋)*

FangSong is also called Imitation Song, which suggests that the former shares several main characteristics with the latter, particularly in terms of geometrical regularity in structure. However, FangSong, as shown in Figure 6 and Figure 7, has several distinctive differences from the Song style. The strokes in FangSong are relatively thin, whereas the stroke width variation between horizontal and vertical strokes is very low. Moreover, major horizontal strokes in a character are not absolutely horizontal but rather slant up slightly from left to right. Finally, the beginnings of strokes have slant serifs, and the intersections have sharp corners.

FangSong was created for book publishing and is currently being used for the typesetting of formal documents.

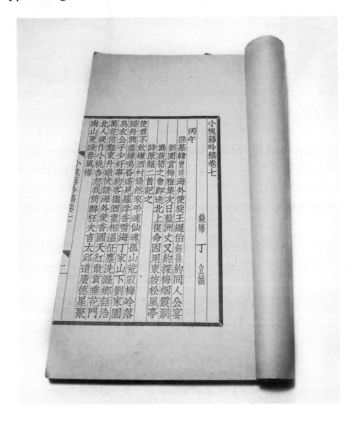

Figure 6: Collection of poems, *Xiao Huai Yi Yin Gao* (小槐簃吟稿), printed in the Ju Zhen Fang Song (聚珍仿宋) typeface in the early 1920s.

更迹透流破多

更迹透流破多

更迹透流破多

更迹透流破多

Figure 7: Examples of FangSong: (first row) HuaWenFangSong (STFangsong)
(华文仿宋); (second row) FangZhengFangSong (方正仿宋); (third row)
FangZhengKeBenFangSong (方正刻本仿宋); (fourth row) FangZhengJuZhenXinFang
(方正聚珍新仿).

1.2.2.4 *Kai (*楷*)*

Kai or KaiShu, also commonly known as regular script or standard script,
is the newest Chinese calligraphy style and is thus the most commonly used
in modern writings and publications. Figure 8 illustrates four examples of
Kai. This regular script is the most easily recognized, such that it is usually
introduced to children and beginners learning the Chinese language. Kai
has inherited many of the characteristics of neatly written text. Each stroke
is independent and is placed carefully in clear order. Every end of the
strokes shows how a brush is put down on and lifted from paper.

中国人这支笔

中国人这支笔

中国人这支笔

中国人这支笔

Figure 8: Examples of Kai: (first row) FangZhengKaiTi (方正楷体); (second row)
FangZhengBeiWeiKaiShu (方正北魏楷书); (third row) FangZhengDaWeiTi (方正大魏
体); (fourth row) FangZhengSongKeBenXiuKai (方正宋刻本秀楷).

1.3 Chinese typeface design

Compared with Latin letters or Arabic numerals, Chinese characters are significantly more difficult to design for several reasons. First, significantly more Chinese characters exist. Approximately six thousand Chinese characters are meant for daily use, and 47,000 more characters exist in the Kang-Xi Chinese dictionary. This significant number of characters results in a very large reference database and a time-consuming design process. Second, the structure of Chinese characters is considerably more complex than that of Latin letters and Arabic numbers. Chinese characters often have more than 10 strokes and intersection points, thus increasing the complexity of structure stability and consistency in the expression of all characters.

Although the designs of Chinese typefaces and English typefaces share many common concepts, theories, and methods [Bringhurst, 1992; White, 2004], the complexity of Chinese typefaces, especially in terms of the large quantity of Chinese characters, makes achieving a perfect design for all characters in one typeface impossible for a single designer. On average, designing one Chinese font, which includes 6,763 Chinese characters defined in the national standard (GB2312), takes approximately three human years to complete. To accomplish the task of designing one font, a design team, typically comprising one senior designer, two intermediate designers, five general designers, and one inspector, work together for three to five months.

The manner of developing the originality of a certain font is of little consequence because a company will still select one senior typeface designer to take charge of the specification when the former decides to develop the font. In general, the experienced designer works with two intermediate designers to prepare the specification. In addition, one of them will be responsible for the direction and management of the successive font development. Five or more general designers design all the individual characters based on the specification. The inspector ensures the quality and style of the newly designed characters.

1.3.1   *Design workflow of Chinese typefaces*

Designing a Chinese typeface generally has three phases: 'formation of originality,' 'development of design specification,' and 'implementation of entire plan.'

1.3.1.1   *Formation of originality*

Every new typeface has a unique source of inspiration. For example, a modern opera house designed by French architects inspired the Fang-ZhengJunHei font (方正俊黑体); traditional signboards of local shops inspired the FangZhengSongYan font (方正颜宋体); and the FangZheng-JianZhi font (方正剪纸体) exhibits the essence of paper cutting, one of the most popular folk traditions in Chinese decorative art. Summarizing a general theory for stimulating inspiration is difficult because the originality involved in typeface design is diverse. However, the attributes of a typeface are based on three elements of typeface design: structure, stroke, and width. Structure includes the size and position of a typeface, as well as the centroid, which is drawn in auxiliary lines. Strokes, such as dots, horizontals, verticals, rises, press downs, and throwaways, are the main parts of Chinese characters and are expressed using vertex-based contours. The width of strokes varies according to different typeface styles.

1.3.1.2   *Development of design specification*

Perfectly designing a single character is easy. However, ensuring consistency in structure and style across all characters in one typeface is difficult. Theoretically, the best way to maintain consistency is for one designer to accomplish all character designs. However, three or four years are needed before a designer accomplishes his plans because more than 6,000 Chinese characters exist in one font. In modern typeface companies, multiple designers commonly collaborate at different levels to shorten the development cycle. However, this strategy also increases the risk of inconsistency. Design specifications are usually required for designing typefaces.

Comprehensive instructions regarding the design concept of new typefaces are essential for executing the thoughts of designers. Comprehensive instructions also enable many designers to accomplish a design through a

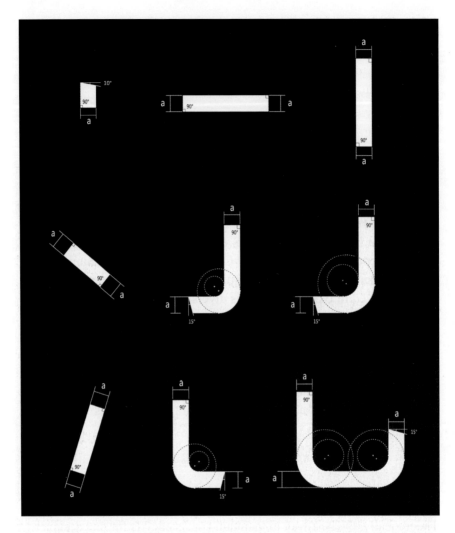

Figure 9: Specification example for Chinese typeface design (FangZhengJunHei, 方正俊黑) showing sample strokes (provided by Shaobo Li).

collaborative effort. Several or even dozens of sample characters in a spec-ification are inadequate for collaboration. The quantity of design samples depends on an in-depth analysis of the structure of character sets and the similarities among the characters. On the basis of years of experience, most font design companies agreed that Chinese characters have approximately 500 common radicals when almost all characters in a typeface are decom-posed. Feasible instructions should obviously contain sufficient sample characters that cover all these components while including as many deformations and combinations as possible. The number of characters should be at least 500. Using these sample characters in a specification, as shown in Figures 9 and 10, other cooperating designers could easily understand the design idea of a new typeface and consequently create other characters in the same style with common components and relatively minimal effort in terms of rearrangement.

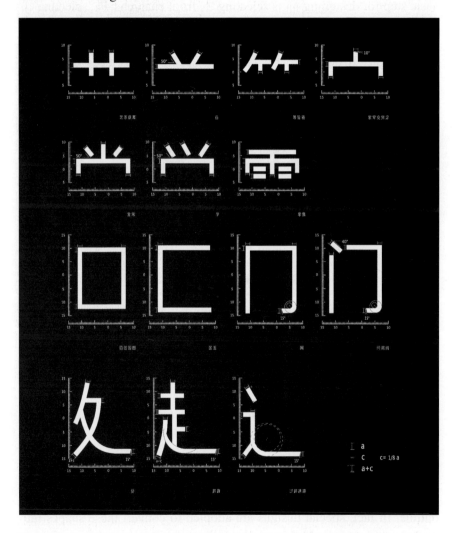

Figure 10: Specification example for same Chinese typeface design as Figure 9 (FangZhengJunHei, 方正俊黑) showing sample components (provided by Shaobo Li).

1.3.1.3 *Implementation of entire plan*

Using the sample characters, designers can construct new characters in the same style with common components. For example, 捅 (tong) consists of two main components: 木 (mu) on the left and 甬 (yong) on the right. The component 木 can be found in several sample characters, such as 横 (heng). The component 甬 can be found in the sample character 桶. The basic step for designing 捅 is selecting 木 from character 横, selecting 甬 from 桶, and then combining them.

Figure 11 shows a simplified illustration. However, this procedure is not simple. To achieve perfect or even acceptable typefaces, designers have to solve many challenging problems, some of which are discussed in the following sections.

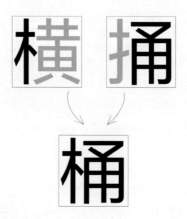

Figure 11: Design of new characters on the basis of previously designed characters according to their specifications.

1.3.2 *Special problems in Chinese typeface design*

1.3.2.1 *Visual balance: size*

Chinese characters are square shaped, as in the case of 国 (guo), 图 (tu), and 口 (kou). However, most Chinese characters do not possess a square outline. In fact, special designs are adopted to convert these shapes into approximate squares. Moreover, the outline of some characters, such as 卜 (pu), are rectangular. In 上 (shang), the outline is nearly triangular, and in

今 (jin), the outline is diamond-shaped. The differences among the various character shapes give rise to a challenge in character size uniformity.

Assigning the same size to the occupied area of all characters would not produce visual similarity. For example, 今 appears to be slightly larger than 口 if they are designed with the same occupied area. An illustration is given in Figure 12.

Figure 12: Two characters with the same occupied area appear different in size: (left) a diamond and a square with the same area; (middle and right) are 今 and 口 with the same occupied areas.

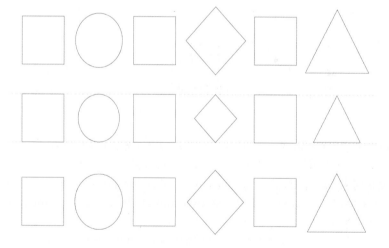

Figure 13: Different sizes of shapes and their visual effects: (top) shapes with the same area; (middle) shapes with the same height; (bottom) shapes with the same visual size.

Figure 13 clearly shows the differences in the details of the square, the diamond, and the triangle. A triangle or a diamond with the same area as a square appears slightly larger than the latter (Figure 13, top). However, a triangle or a diamond with the same height as a square appears slightly smaller than the latter (Figure 13, middle). To make these characters appear to have the same height, designers attempt to identify the most suitable sizes for different characters.

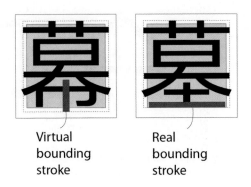

Virtual
bounding
stroke

Real
bounding
stroke

Figure 14: Virtual bounding stroke and real bounding stroke.

1.3.2.2 *Visual balance: bounding strokes*

Most outside strokes of a character contribute to forming the bounding box and are thus called bounding strokes. These strokes can be divided into two categories according to their joint type with the corresponding border. A stroke that joins a border with a point (a tip of the stroke) is called a virtual bounding stroke (Figure 14, left), whereas one that joins a border with a line (one edge of the stroke) is called a real bounding stroke (Figure 14, right). Different bounding strokes have different visual effects relative to character size. To make two similar characters look the same in size, different designs are adopted for virtual and real bounding strokes. Figure 14 shows that the tip of virtual bounding strokes is designed to overstep the bound of the occupied area slightly. The edge of a real bounding stroke is kept inside the area.

1.3.2.3 *Visual balance: density of stroke*

The perception of the visual size of a character is influenced by another subjective factor, that is, the density of character strokes. Characters that consist of more strokes should generally appear larger than characters that consist of fewer strokes. For example, if 口 (kou) and 整 (zheng) are designed to be similar in SF size (Figure 15, top), the character 整 looks more compact and smaller than 口. To achieve visual balance among the characters with different stroke densities, the SF of a complicated character is often adjusted carefully to appear larger, as shown in Figure 15, bottom.

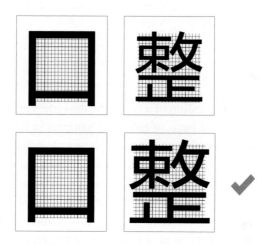

Figure 15: Characters with different stroke densities: (top) 口 and 整 that are similar in SF size; (bottom) SF of 整 is enlarged.

1.3.2.4 *Center alignment*

Properly and effectively aligning the center of components ensures a good set of characters. Two basic rules can be summarized as follows: centers of components in an up–down-structured character should be aligned vertically, whereas those of components in a left–right-structured character should align horizontally. For more complicated characters, such as up–middle–down, left–middle–right, whole surround, half surround, and nested structures, more local alignments are set on the basis of hierarchical character decomposition, as shown in Figure 16. For example, the character 楼 (lou) can be divided into left and right parts in the first level. Then, the right part can be divided into upper and lower components. Thus, these two levels between corresponding components should be aligned differently.

Figure 16: Examples of centroid alignment. (Top) four characters are askew, according to a professional's view, as some components are not aligned. The reference lines joining two centroids should be vertical or horizontal; (bottom) the centroids of corresponding characters are aligned.

1.3.2.5 *Collision avoidance*

Following the specification of a typeface, designers create most characters in this typeface on the basis of reference samples in the specification or by borrowing some components of the finished characters. Collision avoidance is a notable occurrence in this process. Given that the components are from different characters, their adoption for constructing new characters may cause some strokes to connect or even overlap. Figure 17 shows that a horizontal stroke in 木 joins another horizontal stroke in 黄 (huang). Such unexpected connection not only damages the structure of characters but also hampers legibility. Consequently, the length and position of the strokes should be adjusted to achieve a harmonious layout.

Figure 17: Example of collision avoidance: (left) 木 is joined with 黄; (right) two components are separated by adjusting the length and position of a horizontal stroke.

1.3.2.6 *Effects of stroke width on visual balance*

Stroke width is an important factor that influences the visual perception of size and stability. Adopting one solid width when designing all characters in one typeface is not feasible. For example, if the same stroke width is used for 膏 (gao) and 口 (Figure 18), 膏 looks obviously heavier than 口 because the former contains more strokes and possesses a more complicated structure. To harmonize these characters visually, they should be adjusted to the appropriate solid stroke width.

The length of a stroke affects visual perception relative to the width of the stroke. Figure 19 illustrates this situation. Among the three lines with the same width, the longest line always appears thinner than the two other lines. Conversely, the shortest line appears the thickest.

Figure 18: Characters 膏 and 口 with the same stroke width.

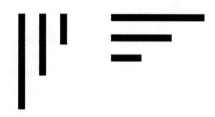

Figure 19: Strokes with same width and different length.

The Wundt Fick illusion [Fick, 1851] indicates the relation between the position of a stroke and the corresponding visual perception of length. Figure 20 shows that although all the lines in each of the four examples have the same length and width, the vertical lines in the first two (on the left) appear longer than the horizontal lines to which they are connected. Meanwhile, the horizontal lines in the last two examples appear longer than the vertical lines.

Figure 20: Examples of Wundt Fick illusion.

All of the foregoing observations highlight the necessity for adjusting strokes. An experienced designer usually spends considerable time adjusting stroke widths individually to balance complicated characters with multiple strokes visually. Figure 21 shows 膏 and 口 in the FangZheng-LanTingHei (方正兰亭黑) typeface. Some adjustments to the stroke width in these characters can only be observed after careful examination.

Figure 21: Sample characters with adjustment of stroke width.

1.3.2.7 *Effect of component size on character structure*

Traditional Chinese calligraphy has rules regarding character structure [Sun I Vision Design, 2011]. For example, having a tight upper loose lower, tight left loose right, and tight inside loose outside are valuable for designing modern typefaces. Identical components that appear in a single character are a good example. The sizes of duplicated components should be adjusted because their visual sizes are influenced by their positions in the structure of a character. A concise interpretation that consists of two identical squares is illustrated in Figure 22.

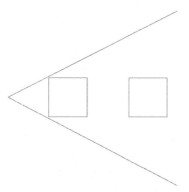

Figure 22: Two identical squares look different in size.

The left square near an acute angle appears slightly larger than that on the right. Considering that Chinese text is read from left to right, experienced designers are inclined to adopt components with different sizes to achieve a more stable structure. Four Pin (品) characters obtained from different typefaces that consist of three identical components of 口 are shown in Figure 23. Most 口 components at the lower left are designed to be smaller than their neighbors on the right on the basis of the rule 'tight left loose right.' In particular, the width of a 口 component at the lower left (labeled as b in Figure 23) is generally designed to be shorter than the width of a 口 component at the lower right (labeled as b or c in Figure 23) for many typefaces. Such fine adjustments fit the visual illusions caused by component positions and stabilize character structure.

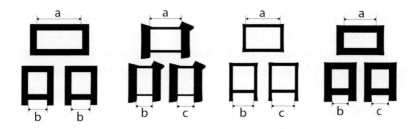

Figure 23: Sample Pin (品) characters with same components in different typefaces: (left) FangZhengLanTingHei (方正兰亭黑); (second from left) FangZhengZhunYaSong (方正准雅宋); (third from left) FangZhengXiDengXian (方正细等线); (right) FangzhengHei (方正黑体). The widths of three 口 components in each 品 character are labeled as a, b and c when they are not equal in a character.

1.4 Harmony between different languages

As a result of globalization, articles now commonly contain several languages. Selecting typefaces originally designed for different languages, coordinating their different styles, and designing a harmonious layout across diverse cultures are intractable problems.

1.4.1 *Uniform stroke styles*

Some accepted recommendations could achieve a harmonious combination of Chinese and English text. These recommendations include Chinese Hei for Sans-serif English typefaces and Chinese Song for serif English typefaces. Such suggestions are obviously insufficient for professional designers. To accomplish high-level work, typeface designers are required to perform highly specific modifications or even to create new typefaces. For example, the Hewlett–Packard company launched a market strategy, 'The Computer is Personal Again,' in 2006. It was necessary to design a series of advertisements about the same content but in different languages. In the Chinese version of this advertisement, the stroke style of every Chinese character references the structure of the corresponding letters in the English advertisement.

1.4.2 *Coordinating the sizes of typefaces in different languages*

When Chinese and English typefaces with the same typeface size are used, the typefaces appear inharmonious in size. Chinese and English typefaces adopt different methods for describing the size of typeface. Both typeface size and ZhongGong affect the visual size of Chinese typefaces. For English typefaces, x-height is the most important feature for depicting the visual size of letters [Kobayashi, 2005]. To achieve high accuracy when coordinating the sizes of typefaces combining different languages, the interior of the typefaces should be adjusted.

1.4.3 *Unification of stroke width*

Assigning the same weight to different typefaces in one paragraph is a common method for achieving a smooth and unified layout. However, when the typefaces are from different languages, the layout effect is not always satisfied because the weights of these typefaces may have different meanings. To identify more alternative weights, designers tend to select typeface families to match other language typefaces in terms of size. Figure 24 shows examples of characters from the Helvetica family with the Chinese font FangZhengYuHei (方正悠黑). Helvetica Neue 65 in Figure 24 (left) appears too dark, such that English letters protrude from the paragraph. Helvetica Neue 45 in Figure 24 (middle) appears too light. In Figure 24 (right) the English typeface redesigned on the basis of Helvetica is suitable for FangZhengYuHei (方正悠黑).

PostScript 字形描述技术是用美国 Adobe 公司的 PostScript 页面描述语言来描述字形的一种技术。CID 字库是美国 Adobe 公司发表的最新字库格式，所有字形描述都采用 PostScript Type 1 格式，它具有易扩充、速度快、兼容性好、简便、灵活等特点，这种标准格式保证了跨平台的高质量输出。

PostScript 字形描述技术是用美国 Adobe 公司的 PostScript 页面描述语言来描述字形的一种技术。CID 字库是美国 Adobe 公司发表的最新字库格式，所有字形描述都采用 PostScript Type 1 格式，它具有易扩充、速度快、兼容性好、简便、灵活等特点，这种标准格式保证了跨平台的高质量输出。

PostScript 字形描述技术是用美国 Adobe 公司的 PostScript 页面描述语言来描述字形的一种技术。CID 字库是美国 Adobe 公司发表的最新字库格式，所有字形描述都采用 PostScript Type 1 格式，它具有易扩充、速度快、兼容性好、简便、灵活等特点，这种标准格式保证了跨平台的高质量输出。

Figure 24: Combination of Chinese and English fonts with different stroke widths.

References

Bathrobe (n.d.) Bathrobe's East Asian Writing Systems http://www.cjvlang.com/Writing/writchin/index.html, accessed on 27 May 2015

Bringhurst, R. (1992) *The elements of typographic style*, (Hartley & Marks, Canada)

DynaComware (n.d.) http://www.dynacw.cn/, accessed on 27 May 2015

Fick, A. (1851) *Da errone quodam optic asymmetria bulbi effecto*. (Marburg, Koch, Dissertation).

Founder Type, Beijing Founder Electronics Co. Ltd, (n.d.) http://www.founder-type.com.cn/, accessed on 27 May 2015

Hanyi fonts (n.d.) http://www.hanyi.com.cn, accessed on 27 May 2015

Kobayashi, A. (2005) *Latin typeface: the background and use*, (Bijutsu Shuppansha)

Sun I Vision Design, (2011) *Type Design Guide Book*, (Science Press, China Science Publishing & Media Ltd.).

White, A.W. (2004) *Thinking in type: the practical philosophy of typography*, (Allworth Press).

Wikipedia (2015) Written Chinese http://en.wikipedia.org/wiki/Written_Chinese, accessed on 27 May 2015

ZhongYi Electronic Ltd.(n.d.)http://www.china-e.com.cn, accessed on 27 May 2015

Chapter 8

Optimizing type for use in specific media

Eben Sorkin

This chapter describes optimizing type for specific media. It draws upon the author's perspective and experience as a type designer. The chapter lists information to be gathered before beginning an optimization process and some ways to evaluate and apply that information to optimize type. Examples of problems to be overcome using optimization as well as examples in which an optimization process ceases to be relevant are also reviewed. Both printed type and type rendered to screen are considered. Some of the ways in which optimization for type could be approached in the future for computer rendered text are also discussed.

1.1 Introduction

This chapter examines the principles and methods used to optimize type for specific media known to the author, who has been a professional type designer since 2010. The material presented reflects his experience and thinking on the subject.

The most celebrated type designs are often notable at least in part because they were designed for a specific media[a] and thus are a particularly good fit to the task they were designed for.

Type optimization is a process motivated either by anticipation of a problem or in response to an observed problem. A more sophisticated motivation for optimization is to create continuity of the printed result of a font across two or more kinds of differing media and or printing methods.[b] This requires making a font with versions or 'grades' optimized to a specific process.

---

[a] An incomplete set of typefaces that fit this description include: Freight by Joshua Darden 2005, Verdana by Matthew Carter 1996, Georgia by Matthew Carter 1993, Bell Centennial by Matthew Carter 1975–78

[b] Mercury Text by Hoefler & Frere-Jones, 1996

When thinking about optimization for specific media it is necessary to avoid considering media in isolation. Instead I recommend considering a set of factors and their interactions.

1.2   Factors relevant to optimizing

1.   Distance at which the font will be read
2.   Physical size at which the font will be reproduced
3.   Kind/s of media to optimize for
4.   Technology used to reproduce the font
5.   Formal characteristics of the font
6.   Angle of view
7.   Readers of the font

By gathering information about these factors, the relevant design considerations for optimizing are described. The more complete and precise the information is, the more it becomes possible to make deliberate and appropriate type design choices when optimizing a font.

Although the ideal is a full and detailed set of information, as a practical matter I have found it is not always possible to collect a complete set or to be completely certain about all the information. It is desirable therefore to maintain an awareness of how definite the information about each factor is to avoid over- or under-emphasizing that factor in the design process.

Thinking in terms of perception is a way to hold these factors together. The point of any optimization is to compensate for distortion in the way the font will be perceived by a reader. The factors listed are a list of considerations that may have an impact on a reader's perception. Distortion matters when it changes the clarity and utility of fonts. Fonts are tools and optimizations are there to make them better tools. Distortion can also alter the feeling or expression that the font brings to a text. It is only when a change to a font's design allows a type to restore or improve utility and/or expression that we can claim optimization has taken place.

For scientists who are using type for experimental purposes, being aware of how and why type may be optimized is also valuable because it can help them to better control experimental variables. A side benefit of this awareness is that it can also help make these same experiments more relevant and useful for type designers and typographers.

1.3 Visual angle: physical size and reading distance

Once the information is gathered the next problem is making practical use of it. What relationships should you begin with? Perhaps the most dominant relationship among the factors is the visual angle. This term refers to the size the font will be on the retina inside the eye when it is read. The question of what the visual angle of a font is for optimizing can be resolved by looking at the relationship of the first two factors in our list: the physical size at which the font is reproduced and the range of distances from which the font will be read. A large visual angle permits clearer and more nuanced perception. A small visual angle is more challenging because fonts are more likely to be subject either to deficiencies in font reproduction or in our own ability to see and read them – or both.

An identical font of the same physical size read from different distances has a different visual angle (Figure 1).

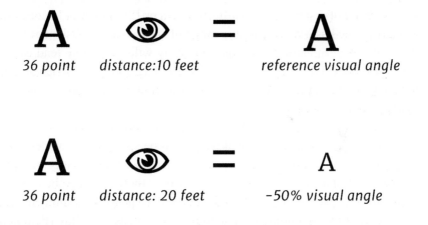

Figure 1 : Distance changes the visual angle.

That same font reproduced twice, once twice as large as the other, can have an equivalent visual angle provided the viewing distance is twice as far away for the font whose size is twice as large (Figure 2).

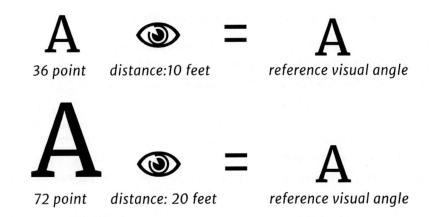

Figure 2: Different physical sizes can have equivalent visual angles with distance.

Some optimizations will be fairly simple when it comes to the reading distances we should anticipate. For example fonts intended for books, maps, magazines and other printed matter tend to be read from a fairly narrow range of distances: typically 30-40 cm or 12-16 inches. In contrast, a smart phone has a more variable range of likely reading distances from the eye. A sign in an airport or on a highway will need to be read easily from an even wider range of distances. With a larger range of visual angles it is practical to test from a set of the most likely reading distances as well as at the possible extremes.

Regardless of the physical size at which they are reproduced, when the visual angle is smaller, fonts tend to need to be spaced more widely and use lower stroke contrast. This tendency can be seen historically in Latin which makes it a cultural convention. However there may also be reasons to do with the maximum acuity of the human eye possibly combined with the effects of the psychological phenomena known as crowding [Pelli and Tillman, 2008]. If crowding is involved then the extra space given to fonts at smaller visual angles will be helping to correctly group the features we detect and combine to recognize glyphs. Fonts that will be read at larger visual angles often employ glyph widths that are relatively less wide and spacing that is tighter. However the need for this appears to be less given the large range of solutions seen for designs at large sizes. Depending on the style of the design it may also fall to a designer to make the details of the design more nuanced or subtle at a large visual angle or more heavy, substantial or brutal in the case of small visual angles.

1.4   Output: font reproduction technology and media

As was the case with visual angle, we will need to again mix two factors from our list. In this case we will consider media and the technology used to reproduce the font together. The character of kinds of media and kinds of imaging technologies only become apparent and relevant when they are brought together and output is created. This output and patterns of recurring problems seen in it can be evaluated and then corrected in the design of a font. It is this need for specificity that makes optimizing practical in the face of the overwhelming number of potential mixtures of media and technologies for reproducing fonts.

Although we have established a practical way of managing the sheer diversity of media and font reproducing technology let us nevertheless briefly examine the diversity of both possible media and font reproduction technologies.

When we think of media itself our first idea will likely be a physical material such as paper, film, plastic, foil or some other surface onto which a font can be printed. These forms of media offer a dauntingly large range of variation in characteristics. Some media will soak up ink a great deal, some very little and still others are impermeable requiring ink, toner or paint to dry on its surface. Some media have a rough texture and others are very smooth. Media can also be matte or shiny. Media can also exhibit a broad range of hues and degrees of brightness, thickness and even transparency. This is just a partial listing of characteristics. Each of these characteristics in turn makes a specific form of media either more or less suitable for another specific font reproduction technology.

Through applying cut vinyl, embossing, de-bossing, staining, sandblasting, cutting with lasers or carving, a font can be applied to surfaces less likely to come to mind as media, such as wood, stone, concrete and metal (see Figures 3-6).

Media can include the side of an aircraft, a building or ocean-going ship. As with the previous more conventional examples the technology must be well matched to the characteristics of the material it will be applied to.

Figure 3: Sand blasted and painted stone in the East Boston branch library sidewalk.

Figure 4: Letters designed by Lida Lopes-Cardozo; digitised by Eben Sorkin; laser-cut for Will Hill at Cambridge School of Art. Photo: Will Hill.

Figure 5: Palau de la Música Catalana, Barcelona, Spain.

Figure 6: Two story tall letters on the Facebook campus, Menlo Park, CA.

The sky becomes medium when airplanes 'print' dot matrix style in the sky with dots of smoke (Figure 7).

Figure 7: Sky as seen from Golden Gate Park San Francisco, CA.

For output to inspire the effort of optimization the output must contain a problem that needs to be corrected. Figure 8 demonstrates an obvious problem from a relatively crude reproduction technology.

Figure 8: detail, YMCA Billboard, East Boston MA.

Figure 9: YMCA billboard seen at typical viewing distance. The white arrow points to the area seen in detail in Figure 8.

Problems that are sufficiently minor in the context of their normal use will not inspire optimization. The roughness seen in Figure 8 is no longer visible in Figure 9.

Type designers who are testing their designs will overcome the limitations of a poor laser printer by using a similar method. They will output their designs at a large size and step back from the page until the image of the text is at the appropriate visual angle.

Clearly we can see that the more severe the output problem, the greater the size and scale required to overcome it. The scenario most likely to inspire optimization is the opposite: physically small text. Reproduction at small sizes is much more likely to exhibit and suffer from deficiencies when output. With small text a greater distance may make the problem even worse by making the text harder to read. If the text is instead brought closer to the eye then the deficiencies in reproduction become more obvious.

Compare the degree of distortion in Figure 10 and Figure 11. Both are distorted but the details are kept more intact in the '5' in Figure 11 which is physically larger.

Figure 10: Text seen on the side of a cardboard box of laser printer paper.

Figure 11: Taken from the same source as Figure 10.

Digital fonts and reading

Figure 12: AE shown with and without ink traps made in rounding UFO. The AE glyph is from the Sorkin Type Co. font family Fjalla.

Type which will be set in or on media that exhibit 'ink gain' will tend to show an expansion of the shape of glyphs through the bleeding and or expansion of ink on the surface of the media. This kind of distortion can be partially compensated for. For example the white spaces where strokes join can be designed so that corners are cut into more deeply.[c] This feature is sometimes called an 'ink trap' or 'light window'. Frederik Berlaen's tool 'Rounding UFO' has a function for programmatically adding this feature (see Figure 12).

In addition to ink traps the shape of the letter itself can also be made somewhat smaller to allow for the degree of gain or expansion that is anticipated.

Features of glyphs which are close together can be made to be farther apart for example between the base letter and a diacritic mark (Figure 13).

Figure 13: The 'a' glyph on the right has its diacritic mark raised. Sample from the author's Merriweather font family.

---

[c] See: Bell Centennial by Matthew Carter 1975–78, Galfra by Ladislas Mandel 1975-1981.

Slow changes in curves look circular whereas fast changes in direction appear sharper and have a shape that is more triangular or boxy. Ink gain can alter the character of a curve making the direction of a curve appear more gradual or slow. To compensate for anticipated ink gain, curves can be made more abrupt or sharper (Figure 14).

Sea Sea
Sea Sea

Figure 14: The upper two words without and with blur to simulate ink gain. The lower example is a modified set of shapes designed to resist the effects of ink gain. Words set in Merriweather and a modified Merriweather.

Figure 15: Ink gain in cutting into letter shapes.

With reversed or white 'knock out' type the ink gain cuts into the glyph shape rather than expanding it (Figure 15).

The process called 'halation' is where light shines through glyphs which are illuminated or which are reflective. This is quite similar to ink gain as a problem in that glyph shapes seem to expand.

Outputs that erode glyph shapes present a different problem. One solution is to build up the corners that are likely to be rounded by the erosion. The resulting studs or spikes will erode back to the desired shape. Again, the program 'UFO rounded' has a method for generating these features (Figure 16).

Figure 16: Basic AE shape on the left one with spikes on the right to resist visual erosions.

A limit in the resolution of the technology, ink gain, and irregularity in the media being used can each contribute to a reduction in the ability to reproduce fine detail. These kinds of problems require font designs in which the thin parts of glyphs are made heavier or in some cases the fine parts of the design must be removed.

1.4.1 *Dynamic type on screens*

The range of variation of screens and projection is not as large as we observe in static media but it is still very large and changing rapidly. At the time of writing there are an increasing range of manufactured goods which have historically not featured screens but which are beginning to make screens crucial to their basic use. Examples of this change include thermostats, cars and wrist watches (see for example Figure 17).

Figure 17: In 2014 Audi presented a screen based dashboard or instrument cluster. http://www.audi.com/com/brand/en/vorsprung_durch_technik/content/2014/03/audi-virtual-cockpit.html.

More familiar use of screens includes phones, tablets, computers, tele-visions, VR goggles and the cinema.

Screens vary in the detail they can offer and in their reflectivity and contrast in the case of e-paper screens, or in their luminance and contrast as is the case with CRT, AMOLED, LCD and LED screens. Screen resolution has made a great deal of progress in the last decade. For instance early e-paper screens in 2009 had much lower contrast and resolution than they do in 2015. E-paper is useful in bright reading conditions because it does not need to emit a light that is brighter than is in the environment for the image to be perceived. Instead it reflects environmental light in a manner similar to paper. In contrast, laptops and smart phones use light emitting technologies.

Unlike paper which will vary in effective resolution mostly depending on printing technology, screens have an inherent maximum resolution. Software combined with the video cards that control screens are the equivalent to font reproduction technology relevant to screens.

Very low resolution screens tend to require font designs that are simpler and grid oriented in both their construction and spacing. At the lowest resolutions the most pressing problems to solve are basic and critical. For instance we will want to avoid part of the glyph needed for easy recognition disappearing (see Figure 18).

Figure 18: The Author's font Merriweather rendered in Wordpad at 8pt on Windows XP. The top example has no hints and the example below is using the TTFAutohinter. In addition preserving the shape of the letters the TTFAutohint makes the text rendering software use anti-aliasing which produces the grey pixels seen in the lower example.

Although the software which renders text to screen is critical, the font itself may also contain software to help it render well. The software in the fonts is referred to as 'hints'. These hints supplement the local text rendering software. When they are used they influence the reproduction of the font's image on screen by temporarily altering the outlines of glyphs and sometimes also the spacing of the font. Hints can be considered a form of font optimization in part because they can be used to improve the appearance of a font on screens but also because for a given use they are effectively altering the shapes of glyphs for that use.

Hinting is powerful but it works better when the shapes found in fonts have been altered to get optimal results. For example in early versions of TTFAutohint if the height of overshoots and undershoots was made consistent fewer errors in rendering would result. In conventional type design this would not normally be done because it conflicts with the need for optical rather than geometric regularity in the font's design.

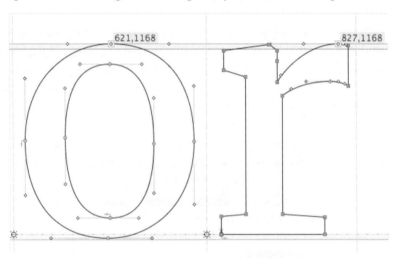

Figure 19: Glyphs 'o' and 'r' showing the height of overshoot from the author's font typeface Merriweather. Image taken from Fontlab Studio 5.

Optically based overshoots vary in height based on the degree to which a shape is pointed or sharp rather than flat. The sharper the shape the more it should overshoot in order to appear to be visually even (Figure 19).

Many of the characteristics that help optimize a font for low resolution screens are held in common with optimizing a font for use at small optical sizes: wider spacing, lower contrast, heavier details and heavier weight. As screen resolution increases type designers have greater freedom in choosing forms and spacing. Historically fonts that have been made specifically for screens will choose a horizontal or vertical[d] shape rather than diagonal when this is possible.

As of the time of writing screen resolutions that have paper-like detail at typical reading distances have been released for smart phones, laptops and desktops. The iPhone 5 for instance has a pixel density of 325+ pixels per inch or 'ppi'. One of the highest densities known to this author at this time is an astonishing 2098 ppi almost 6.5 times higher.[e]

In the same way that distance and the optical size that results from it can sometimes effectively make differences in printing technology less relevant, differences in rendering software are becoming similarly less perceptible as screen resolutions rise. Better screen resolution means less optimization is necessary for the new high resolution screens as a form of media.

Fonts that were made for low and medium resolution screen use can sometimes look out of place in very high resolution environments. They can be optimized to perform better in high resolution environments by adapting their shapes for larger optical sizes. What is the practical impact?

Microsoft implemented a font family for Windows 8 called Sitka. Sitka comes in six optical versions for each style in the family. Users can select optical sizes for themselves. However the Windows OS also has the novel capability of automatically choosing an optical version of Sitka for the user.

Nick Sherman has taken this idea further by proposing a new font format which instead of presenting or switching automatically between a handful of static instances could instead be made to continuously adapt to conditions like a responsive web site. This kind of font format would in theory make a very broad range of continuous adaptive optimization for screen and or other media possible.[f]

---

[d] A good example of this is the lower bowl of the two story 'g' which John Berry mentions on page 9 of 'Now Read This' a booklet made in 2004 to promote fonts made for the then new Clear Type technology in Windows XP.

[e] http://www.androidauthority.com/worlds-highest-ppi-display-2098ppi-oled-display-sony-254182/

[f] http://alistapart.com/blog/post/variable-fonts-for-responsive-design

1.5 Formal characteristics of the font

There are a large number of observable formal characteristics or design variables found in font designs. When a type is optimized it is these characteristics that will be adjusted.

The more ubiquitous the characteristics within the design the greater its value is likely to be. Weight, contrast, width, slant, and spacing are all examples of characteristics found across an entire font. A font with high contrast or a strong slant is much more likely to need adjustment for media than a design with low or medium slant or contrast.[g] The adjustment needed is likely to be a reduction in contrast or slant. Very thin or heavy fonts are more likely to need adjusting than middle weights. Similarly middle widths are less likely to need optimizing than wide or narrow ones.

Some formal characteristics are tied to parts of glyphs. These parts many not occur in every glyph but are instead scattered across the glyphs found in the font. Examples include stems, joins, bowls, and terminals. The frequency that a characteristic has in the script being designed matters a great deal. For example in the Latin script stems are fairly common. However in Cyrillic they dominate. In Greek stems are relatively uncommon and round or bowl shapes dominate. Some scripts such as Chinese and Devanagari have a high proportion of glyphs with a high stoke density and therefore have a large number of joins. Any attempt at optimization should take these script-specific tendencies into account.

Some characteristics are only present in sub-sections of the typeface. Their importance to an optimization process can depend on how the font being optimized will be used. For example, because the lower case tends to predominate in most but not all uses of type the characteristic of this group tends to be quite important to the optimization process. However an all caps use would negate their importance altogether.

---

[g] Distortion applied to low contrast glyphs is less likely to be noticed than when it is applied to high contrast ones. Stronger slants are more likely to render poorly on low resolution screens.

1.6 Angle of view

The perspective of the reader should also be considered. A sign for drivers painted on to the surface of a road is an example of optimizing for this factor. In this case the letters are stretched vertically to make them easier to read for drivers while approaching the sign which is printed on the road. See Figures 20 and 21.

Figure 20: 'Stop' sign for drivers. Note the very thick top stroke on the T.

Figure 21: A similar sign for drivers on a street in Hong Kong.

A street sign that needs to be visible from several angles can benefit from the use of large counters and wider than normal letters. People
viewing the sign from a position directly in front of the sign will be able
to easily tolerate somewhat wider letters while people who see it from an
angle on the left or right sides will benefit from the resistance that wider
letters have to compression. Spacing the letters more widely will also help.
See Figure 22.

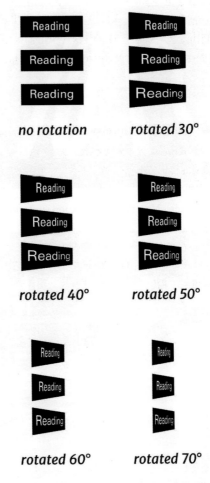

Figure 22: This is a mock up of an imaginary street sign. A compressed style is used on
top; a regular style is used in the middle and a wide style is used on the bottom. The signs
have been rotated and given perspective. This set of examples show that compressed
letterforms have greater problems of legibility than wide ones as the viewing angle moves
increasingly away from centered view. The sign uses the type family Univers.

1.7 The reader

When thinking about optimizing for media it is necessary to also think about who the reader might be. It is a mistake for instance to simply assume a single kind of reader who is an adult, and an expert reader and who has perfect vision. Getting some insight into the readership a font is intended for can help you know how to optimize your font. Reading ability can vary for reasons of age, education, interest, and so on. For example we now know that a young reader will benefit from wider than normal word spaces (Pelli and Tillman, 2008). Readers with lower or reduced acuity including older readers will benefit from texts set at larger sizes.

1.8 Conclusion

Type is most effectively designed for media when a range of additional information is available. Relatively complete and precise information makes it possible to ground design choices in actual reading circumstances and in the needs of the readers.

References

Pelli, D. G. and Tillman, K. A. (2008). The uncrowded window of object recognition. *Nature Neuroscience*, 11(10), pp. 1129-35.

Chapter 9

'Harmonised type design' revisited

Titus Nemeth

In 1993 Charles Bigelow and Kris Holmes published *The design of a Unicode font*. It was one of the first scholarly discussions of type design for multiple scripts, and likely coined the term harmonised design. Bigelow and Holmes defined the concept thus: 'By "harmonization", we mean that the basic weights and alignments of disparate alphabets are regularized and tuned to work together, so that their inessential differences are minimized, but their essential, meaningful differences preserved.' In 1993 the introduction of the Unicode standard provided the technological background which allowed this novel approach as fonts could now contain many thousands of characters. And just as Unicode aspired to be the single, universal encoding standard of the world, now it became tangible to create typefaces with unified typographic representations of many of the world's scripts. *Harmonised type design* was soon widely embraced, copied and promoted, and was received with little, if any, critique. Bigelow and Holmes' assertion that 'harmonization seems like a desirable goal' appears to have been a view which was widely shared in the trade, and *harmonisation* became an established concept. This article revisits the notion of *harmonised type design* 20 years after its inception. It critically assesses the origin of the concept, identifies its parallels to modernist design ideas, and queries its applicability in different typographic scenarios. Some limits of the concept of *harmonised type design* are discussed and different interpretations of designing type for multiple scripts are briefly mentioned.

1.1 Introduction

In 1993 Charles Bigelow and Kris Holmes published 'The design of a Unicode font' [1993], an account of the development of the Lucida Sans Unicode typeface. Based on the older Lucida Sans design, the suffix 'Unicode' identified concept and aspiration of the new typeface, both rooted in the historical circumstances of its development.

With the maturing of personal computers in the early 1990s, the need for standards compliance and cross-platform compatibility became increasingly apparent, and the Unicode Standard was conceived as the universal encoding scheme that should facilitate seamless international document exchange.[a] Developed by leading technology companies in the USA, it was only concerned with the encoding of characters; its definitions deliberately eschewed questions of appearance and – at least in principle – made no assumptions about the form of text thus encoded. But as Unicode aspired to provide an encoding standard for all languages of the world, it raised novel questions about typographic design. Although fonts could now technically contain characters for scripts as diverse as Arabic and Thai, there had hardly been any consideration about the aesthetic, cultural and practical implications of such border-crossing typefaces. Whereas commercially successful Latin typefaces had been extended to Cyrillic and Greek, barely any designs ventured beyond the relative familiarity (and similarity) of these European scripts.

Against this background, and commissioned by Microsoft as a demonstration of the new technology, Bigelow and Holmes conceived Lucida Sans Unicode. Its express purpose was 'to provide a standardized set of glyphs that could be used as a default core font for different operating systems and languages' [Bigelow and Holmes, 1993, p. 291] in one, visually unified design. Bigelow and Holmes thus coined the term, and to a large extent also the concept of harmonised design'.[b] As the type's reference to Unicode implied, the aspiration for this design approach went well beyond the familiar realm of European scripts. When the first version of Lucida Sans Unicode was released in 1993, it contained Latin, Cyrillic, Greek and Hebrew characters, and the designers planned the addition of Arabic, Armenian, Devanagari and other Indian scripts.

With the advent of the World Wide Web in the mid-1990s, internationalisation of computing and document exchange rapidly rose to unprecedented importance, and so did typefaces which included characters for multiple scripts, often in one 'harmonised design'. To be sure, not all, and likely a minority of such types would have consciously followed Lucida Sans Unicode as model, or the design principles articulated by Bigelow and

---

[a] For details of its history see Unicode, Inc [2009].

[b] Note that the term had been used before, albeit for a different purpose. When Jan Tschichold's Sabon type was first published, it was described as 'the first harmonized type', circumscribing its conceptual basis as a design for the main then current composition techniques: linecasting, Monotype composition and hand-composition. See Dreyfus [1994].

Holmes.[c] Nonetheless, as the first of its kind, accompanied by a substantial descriptive text, Lucida Sans Unicode marks an historic milestone.

Twenty years on, this article proposes to revisit the notions first articulated by Bigelow and Holmes in the light of applied multi-script typography. In order to arrive at more general observations, most examples shown here predate the concept of harmonisation, providing an historically longer, and technologically more diverse perspective. Indeed, this perspective is part of the argument, which identifies connections between typographic technology and harmonised design. In line with this perspective is the emphasis on applied typography, rather than type design, as the argument is less about *how* type designers have addressed harmonisation, than *where* and *whether* harmonisation is a useful approach.In conclusion, the paper briefly reviews some aspects of design practices which evolved in the wake of Lucida Sans Unicode.

1.2   What is harmonisation in type design?

When Bigelow and Holmes began their Lucida Sans Unicode project, a unified design approach to a typeface covering multiple scripts was a novel proposition. Neither the conceptual, nor the practical implications and limits had been explored, and the two designers saw the project as a test bed for the concept of harmonisation. In their words, the idea meant 'that the basic weights and alignments of disparate alphabets are regularized and tuned to work together, so that their inessential differences are minimized, but their essential, meaningful differences preserved.' [Bigelow and Holmes, 1993, p. 292][d] According to Bigelow and Holmes, through this approach 'the "noise" of insignificant design artefacts and historical accidents is filtered out, leaving the "signal" of significant character features amplified in comparison.' Thus, it was assumed that the principle of harmonisation could benefit the transmission of information, or in other words improve legibility. Furthermore, practical and aesthetic considerations were advanced in favour of harmonisation: 'Within a harmonized font, when text changes from Latin to Cyrillic, or from Greek to Hebrew,

---

[c] More recently, the term 'matchmaking' has frequently been used for a similar design approach. Semantically, the active 'making' of the match may indeed be an appropriate description of the process.

[d] The next three quotes are from the same source.

or when mathematical expressions or other symbols are introduced into text, the visual size, weight, and rhythm of the characters should not appear to change, should not jar or distract the reader, but the basic character shapes should nevertheless be distinctive and immediately recognizable.'

The case for harmonisation as seen by Bigelow and Holmes can therefore be divided into two parts: (1) the amplification of the 'signal' for improved legibility, and (2) the regularisation for aesthetic and practical reasons. The first part of the argument relies on the concept of 'signal' and 'noise', yet lacks further evidence or justification of the assumed advantages. Indeed, Bigelow and Holmes are conscious of the potential drawbacks in this approach, for 'if [harmonisation] erases distinctive differences between scripts, it increases the possibility of confusion. In this view, the attempt to filter out unwanted noise may instead remove significant portions of the signal and distort what remains, thus decreasing the signal and adding noise.' In other words, if signals which are different and ought to be different are rendered similarly, their distinctiveness becomes blurred. Indeed, one needs to look no further than to highly modular (and thus regular) typefaces such as ITC Avant Garde, to appreciate that generally speaking, more uniformity reduces, rather than improves the transmission of information. It follows, that the 'signal' and 'noise' argument does not provide a convincing rationale by itself, leaving the case for harmonisation primarily down to aesthetic and practical reasons.

Although the relevance of such considerations is undeniable for typography, perhaps the scientific semblance of the argument for harmonisation appears somewhat lessened from this perspective. If regularity, then, is at the heart of the argument, the concept is firmly embedded in typographic practice, and it may be useful to consider it within a wider historical frame. For as Robin Kinross points out, the visions of 'universal' types have 'cropped up repeatedly, encouraged by the standardization that is inherent in printing.' [Kinross, 2002a, p. 233]

1.3 Harmonisation as an extension of modernism

Regular, systematic and therefore *rational* approaches to typography and the making of type have a long history. Kinross's *Modern typography* [2004], perhaps the most comprehensive discussion of the subject, traces the origins of rational and regulating approaches to typography back to the turn from the seventeenth to the eighteenth century and the making of the 'romain du roi' type. It was conceived at the drawing board, a feature which made James Mosley observe that it 'can be claimed to mark the beginning of the concept of "type design", a process in which the form of the alphabet for a printing type is determined independently of its means of production.' [1997, p. 5] This approach to the making of type received much mockery from practitioners for its unworldly attitude, most clearly apparent in overly regularised letterforms and the improbable demands of precision from the punchcutter.[e]

Whereas the 'romain du roi' may be seen as an early precursor, notions of rationally planned type became a recurring theme only in the twentieth century. As Kinross reminds us [2002a], related concepts of 'universal' aspirations can be traced from the emergence of an articulate modernity in the 1920s and 30s, to the late 1960s, up to the beginnings of digital typography, often with explicit references to technological progress. Herbert Bayer's alphabet for the Bauhaus (1926) and Jan Tschichold's letterforms for Walter Porstmann's new orthography (1930) were but the most radical instances of an approach to type design which was based on, and derived legitimacy from its rational, constructed and systematic principles. During the same era, one also finds the first successful application of similar, albeit tamed, ideas to a commercially viable type in Paul Renner's Futura (1927). After the rupture of the Second World War, Adrian Frutiger's milestone Univers (1954) stands out as perhaps the most convincing combination of aspirations to regularity, systematic planning, and conventional letterforms.[f] As is apparent from this incomplete listing, a history of rational approaches to type design would go well beyond the scope of this chapter.[g]

---

[e] As Mosley points out, another less discussed achievement of the committee was the establishment of a systematic measurement of type sizes and proportions. The 'Calibres de toutes les sortes et grandeurs de lettres' defined a rationally planned and regular sequence of related type sizes, as well as the principal proportions of the alphabet: capital and ascender height, x-height and descender height. For Mosley, this system is a likely and uncredited precursor to the point systems of Fournier and Didot, endowing the designers of the 'romain du roi' with great historical importance; nonetheless, he also grants that the academicians 'can possibly be charged with some lack of appreciation of the practical realities of the crafts that they attempted to explore and codify.' [Mosley, 1997, p. 14].

[f] For a critical contemporary appraisal of Univers see Froshaug [2000a].

[g] For discussions of the evolution of the notion of typeface families see Kinross [2002b], Bil'ak [2008] and recently Ulrich [2014].

Yet even a superficial glance at the more recent history shows how resilient and ultimately successful notions of rational planning and systematisation in type design have become. From Frutiger's Univers to Otl Eicher's Rotis (1988), Lucas de Groot's Thesis (1994) and Peter Bil'ak's Greta Sans (2012), to name but a few widely celebrated examples, the elements which are considered part of a typeface (family) have been expanding in unprecedented ways and gave birth to what may be called type 'systems'. Indeed, the trend of type-system-design, which assembles ever-more historically unrelated styles under an umbrella name and concept, may be seen as one of the defining characteristics of current practice.

Arguably, from this perspective Bigelow and Holmes's notion of harmonised design, relating to the regularised treatment of different scripts, may be seen as part of a wider phenomenon. If the rationally planned, systematically organised and stylistically regularised design of type is a defining feature of contemporary practice, the extension of this trend to non-Latin scripts was bound to arise with increasing internationalisation. Indeed, for designers with western background and/or education, the reasoning for harmonisation would be compelling. It strikes a chord with an audience which has been accustomed and trained to think in grids and design systems, which has embraced typefaces for their perceived 'universal' and allegedly 'neutral' qualities, and which, by and large, has been anchored deeply in Latin-centric typography.

With the benefit of the historical perspective, it even appears as if the case for harmonisation was perceived as self-evident, for little justification was provided in its favour. Bigelow and Holmes's summary that 'harmonization seems like a desirable goal' [1993, p. 292] may be applicable in the specific context of the Lucida Sans Unicode project, but calls for further scrutiny if taken as a more general design principle. In order to better identify the reasons for the apparent need of harmonised design, it may be useful to consider different typographic scenarios and query the applicability of the notions proposed by Bigelow and Holmes.

1.4 Where do we need harmonised type?

For the purpose of this discussion, one can distinguish two broad categories of multilingual texts in which two or more different scripts are likely to appear together. In the first category, the bulk of the text is written in one script and the other script(s) only appears in a complementary role, as in the archetypal case of the bilingual dictionary. Other examples of this category, which for the present discussion are called 'mixed settings', can be found in related kinds of documents such as those created for language training, linguistic analysis and generally scholarly texts.

The second suggested category, despite its acknowledged breadth, assembles all forms of parallel translations in which, at least in principle, all languages and scripts should be of equal standing and relevance. From literary texts to public signage, instruction manuals, package inserts and government forms, a range of vastly different kinds of texts fall into this definition; and notwithstanding their diversity, it is fair to assume that where texts have been translated and are presented together, the readers of all languages are considered as being equally important. Thus, it should follow that the presentation of their respective languages in type is also given equal importance.

1.4.1 *Mixed settings*

It is easy to think of practical constraints of documents with mixed settings which can be eased by harmonised type. Especially in cases where economical setting is at a premium such as dictionaries, more regularisation facilitates space efficient typography. Indeed, the different use of Cartesian space by different scripts appears as one of the most challenging factors in all kinds of multi-script settings.

The letterforms of Arabic, for example, have distinctive features which are distributed over the entire y-axis, making any regularised horizontal alignments difficult. As letters fuse with other letters according to their context, the positions of distinctive features frequently change. Moreover, a broader range of proportions is typical of the Arabic script, with some letterforms being tall and narrow, others flat and wide; critically, not only the proportions are diverse, but also the respective sizes and it is not uncommon for one letterform to appear many times as big as another. As a result, the Arabic alphabet is often described (at least by western observers) as appearing smaller than its Latin counterpart, for if the biggest Arabic letters are equalised with the biggest Latin letters, the small Arabic letterforms are diminishing. So where both scripts appear in the same line of text, obvious practical problems arise for the typographer: if one uses an Arabic body size equal to the Latin, it looks small; but if a larger body is chosen so that the Arabic appears similar in size, alignment and setting of the matter are more complicated.

Here, one is reminded of Anthony Froshaug's dictum that 'typography is a grid' [2000b], which concisely (albeit unwittingly) summarises both the primary difficulty of multi-script composition, and the fundamental Latin bias of typography. For as the reader would have gauged by now, the principal reaction to the conundrum of diverse uses of vertical space has rarely been to treat every script according to its own characteristics. More common is the attempt to standardise the proportions in a way more akin to those of the Latin script – as indeed proposed by harmonised design. Thus, letterforms, irrespective of their size and proportions (not to mention the script's morphographic rules which define how letters are assembled in words and sentences), are modified according to the basic module of the typographic grid: a rectangle whose regular height allows the assembly of letters into lines and paragraphs. The advantages of such an approach for the typographer (or historically the compositor) are readily apparent, and establish the link to the precursors of harmonisation. Standardised type sizes – think of the 'romain du roi' – with regularised faces enable the mixing of different scripts with insouciance, and therefore greatly facilitate composition while economising space. In this perspective, the case for harmonisation appears as one strongly informed by practical constraints and needs.[h]

Despite the argument's apparent seductive power, a review of actual practice reveals that the regularity and uniformity it aspires to has not always and everywhere been equally coveted.[i]

A striking example of a different approach can be found in A.F.L. Beeston's *Written Arabic* (Figure 1), a concise language teaching booklet

---

[h] Here, one should bear in mind that many of these constraints originated from the Latin script and frequently constitute less than ideal conditions for scripts with different characteristics.

[i] The following examples were chosen for their exemplary qualities within the confines of this paper. Self-evidently, they can only provide a snapshot of the virtually unlimited body of multi-script settings, yet it is hoped they will illustrate the main lines of the argument. All figures except figure 4 and 5 show items from the author's collection. Figure 4 and 5 show an item from the collection of the National Library of Australia, Canberra, Bib ID 1534032, which is gratefully acknowledged.

158

Digital fonts and reading

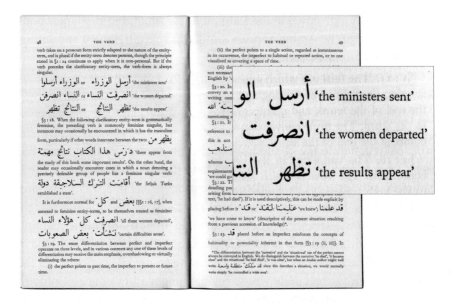

Figure 1: A.F.L. Beeston (1968) *Written Arabic*, Cambridge University Press. Reduced to 35% linear detail enlargement in box.

published in 1968 by Cambridge University Press, and printed by Stephen Austin and Sons in Hertford, UK. Here, a clear typographic editorial voice is apparent, prioritising function and pedagogic usefulness in an uncompromising way. The Arabic type follows conventional proportions and styling, suitably so for a document aimed at beginners who are likely to be most familiar with handwritten letterforms. The large size used for the script tables at the beginning of the text facilitates easy recognition of letters and deciphering of words, and demonstrates with great clarity the joining of letters. Yet the emphasis on the usability for the reader is most apparent in the main text. The interspersed Arabic words are set in a size of unapologetic irreverence for the Latin type, boldly emphasising convenience for the reader (a novice language learner), over abstract design aspirations. Half-way through the booklet the size of the Arabic is drastically reduced, consistent with the functional attitude, as by now the reader can be expected to be more familiar with the script.

It goes without saying that available typefaces and sizes would have influenced the typographic choices of *Written Arabic*, and that more finely graded types could have improved the appearance of some paragraphs. Nonetheless, its approach to multi-script typography remains refreshingly unencumbered by the *Systemzwang*[j] of regularised design systems, while producing a highly readable and at times attractive document. Moreover, *Written Arabic* is not unique in its approach.

Another instructive example is found in *The M.E.C.A.S. Grammar of Modern Literary Arabic,*[k] published in 1965 by Khayats in Beirut, Lebanon, and printed by the Heidelberg Press in the same city (Figure 2).

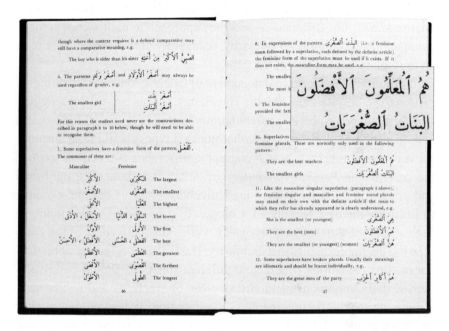

Figure 2: The Middle East Centre for Arab Studies (1965) *The M.E.C.A.S. Grammar of Modern Literary Arabic*, Beirut: Khayats. Reduced to 35% linear, detail enlargement in box.

As in the setting of *Written Arabic*, there is little apparent concern for regularity, and there is no attempt to disguise the differences between Arabic and Latin. Both scripts are given their appropriate size and space. Yet whereas in *Written Arabic* the setting does not suggest planning according to the text's characteristics, and the Arabic sometimes sits awkwardly within the Latin text, the *M.E.C.A.S. Grammar* exhibits a more balanced

[j] This German term could be translated as 'system coercion', and denotes the inherent self-replicating power of a system, or the system's tendency to impose its principles.

[k] The Middle East Centre for Arab Studies was an institution in the Lebanon, run by the British Foreign Office. It aspired to train British public servants in all aspects of the Arab world, and therefore attained a reputation as a 'spy school'. See Craig [1998].

composition. Here, undoubtedly due to the place of publication where mixed Arabic and Latin texts are common, the combination of the scripts appears to have been planned from the outset. Because the English text is set with ample interlinear space, it allows for the comfortable insertion of Arabic words and phrases without changes of density. The Latin type size is pleasant for continuous reading, whereas the Arabic's larger size aids the quick perception of letters and small vowel marks for learners. Overall, the *M.E.C.A.S. Grammar's* generous approach to multi-script composition achieves a high level of clarity, readability and elegance, making it an exemplary publication of the genre.

To return to the archetypal document of category one, also in bilingual dictionaries, despite their specific constraints, the successful combination of different types without apparent harmonisation is common. Indeed, it is here that the functionality of non-harmonised types should least surprise, for it is the dictionary where typographic difference is a central tenet of the design. The *Persian Vocabulary* by A.K.S. Lambton, first published and printed in 1954 by Cambridge University Press, is but one example to illustrate the case (Figure 3). Composed in hot-metal with Monotype Series 507, the Persian lacks elegance, yet its distinctiveness to the Latin type is a desirable quality in a dictionary. Here, as in most typographic scenarios, text categories which have different functions should be visually demarcated. Notions of hierarchy, degrees of emphasis and textual-navigation all depend on typographic differentiation. Indeed, a large part of the typographer's job is to visualise the unlikeness of the many diverse elements a text may contain, to design difference by the judicious application of unmistakably distinct typographic treatments to the text. Against this background, the applicability of harmonisation to type used in mixed settings could be questioned for its inherent risk of blurring differences.

1.4.2 *Parallel settings*

In parallel settings, the rigidity of the typographic grid is much alleviated. The technical constraints of mixed settings which prescribe regularity along the y-axis do not apply, providing greater flexibility in the treatment of different scripts.[1] This flexibility is apparent from the first complex typo-

---

[1] In print publications which have two languages on facing pages, shine-through from

graphic multi-script documents, the polyglot bibles. Their makeup demonstrates how characteristics of different languages are better served by typographic flexibility, than rigid regularity.

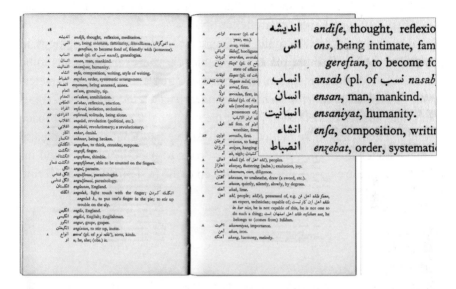

Figure 3: Lambton, A.K.S. (1969) *Persian Vocabulary*, Cambridge University Press, first published in 1954, this edition is the fourth reprint in offset. Reduced to 35% linear, with detail enlargement in box.

A multilingual *tour de force* like Thomas Roycroft's 1650s polyglot bible, which assembles nine languages in one parallel text edition, is a case in point (Figure 4). Here, no uniform baseline grid is possible, as the different founts are all cast on different bodies. Arabic, Persian and Syriac are set with noticeably greater interlinear space than Amharic, Greek, Hebrew and Latin, in order to accommodate for the vowels above and below the letters (Figure 5).[m] Thus, the sizes of the text areas are chosen so as to maintain the synchronisation between languages, a difficult task which is remarkably well handled. Occasionally the width and arrangement of columns also changes, showing flexibility from spread to spread to accommodate for changing text lengths. To be sure, this does not mean

---

recto to verso may remain an issue, but not an insurmountable one.

[m] In this particular Arabic fount, the common diacritic dots, which should be part of the letter, are cast and set separately like the discretionary vowel marks, contributing to the poor legibility of the type.

that the composition of every language is ideal, as much depends on the quality of the type and the skill of the printer, which would have varied from script to script.[n] Yet the approach of these progenitors of all multi-script typography shows that parallel settings do not necessarily require regularity, but may benefit from flexibility.

Indeed, the different lengths of languages make *irregular* settings in multi-script editions more plausible. Arabic text, for example, tends to be shorter than its English equivalent. It follows, that although the characteristics of the script call for greater interlinear space, and possibly a larger body size, the script's efficiency along the x-axis balances the overall space requirements. Thus, bilingual editions of Arabic and English may actually achieve better text synchronisation from page to page if type size and interlinear space are *not* identical, but chosen to the best effect of each script.

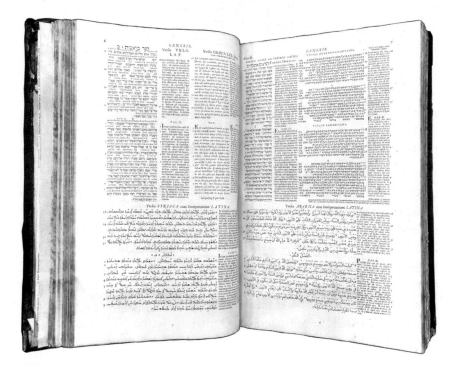

Figure 4: Walton, B. ed. (1657) *Biblia sacra polyglotta*, 6 vols., vol.1, Reduced to 20% linear.

---

[n] In the event, the Arabic type is so incompetent as to be virtually unreadable.

Figure 5: Detail of figure 4.

Parallel settings that follow a similar approach are common wherever emphasis is laid on the smoothest reading experience, rather than design dogma. The iconic Loeb Classical Library, first published by Harvard University Press in 1912, is but one of the most celebrated cases – albeit only for the relatively unproblematic pairing of Greek and Latin.°

A convincing Arabic-French example from the nineteenth century is found in the *Histoire de Chems-Eddine et de Nour-Eddine*, (Figure 6) first published by Hachette in Paris in 1853, and printed at the Imprimerie Impériale. Its spreads are organised into four text blocks of different proportions, accommodating the original Arabic (in Maghrebi orthography), a French translation, a literal translation as well as a transliteration. With simple means every text category is differentiated, maintaining proportions and spatial relationships that combine to a harmonious whole. The individual type choices merit particular attention. The original text is set

° A recently initiated series by the same publisher extends the editorial idea of the Loeb Library to Indian literature. The Murty Classical Library of India, designed by Rathna Ramanathan of M9 Design in London, is a collection of parallel bilingual editions, pairing the major literary languages of India with English translations. Here, a combination of newly commissioned Indian types and existing Latin and Arabic types are used in a typographic approach that embraces variety over regularity.

in an Arabic type with stylistic references to Maghrebi scribal culture; the French translation and, on a smaller body, the literal translation, are set in a typical contemporary roman type; and the transliteration is distinguished with an italic fount. These choices suggest a search for appropriateness and authenticity *within* the cultural framework of each respective language, rather than a uniform, regularised aesthetic for all. Thus, the type used for the French translation makes no attempt to imitate the Arabic, and vice-versa, there is no apparent dilution of the characteristics of the Arabic script to conform to those of Latin.[p] Indeed, as the reading of each text category is bound to differ, the question as to why they should be stylistically regularised begs to be asked.

Figure 6: Cherbonneau, M. (1853) *Histoire de Chems-Eddine et de Nour-Eddine*, Hachette, Paris. Reduced to 35% linear, detail enlargement in box.

Similar cases abound before the 1980s and the digital revolution. Ironically, with hindsight it appears as if analogue typographic processes sometimes provided more flexibility, and were less prone to *Systemzwang* than the computer-based systems current for the last thirty to forty years. Even in the restrictive (and today little-understood) technology of hot-metal

---

[p] Note that this is to be seen within the typographic context which implicitly imposes paradigms and techniques that arose from the Latin script, and thus prescribes non-Arabic features by definition.

composition, exemplary cases of multi-script typography can be found. Some publications coming from Lebanon in the period from independence (1943) to civil war (1975), its short-lived golden era of Arabic printing, testify to the quality pre-digital composition could achieve.

Like the aforementioned *M.E.C.A.S. Grammar,* the *Anthologie bilingue de la littérature arabe contemporaine* illustrates this point (Figure 7). A collection of Arabic literature with accompanying French translations, this volume was published and printed in 1961 by the Imprimérie Catholique in Beirut. The book is composed in the original hot-metal version of Monotype Series 549, a type that became genre-defining for high-quality Arabic book typography, and a Latin type of no lesser pedigree: Monotype Baskerville. For both languages, thus, a type of proven quality was chosen and set in the point size and with the appropriate leading required for the parallel setting;[q] consistent with this approach is the flexibility of the type area, which is allowed to vary slightly in height for language synchronisation. The resulting book provides an agreeable reading experience for each language on its own terms, with indubitable aesthetic qualities.

Although only a small selection (which could easily be expanded on), the above examples demonstrate that parallel editions do not require, and may in fact gain from thoughtful type mixing, rather than regularity as sought in harmonised design. Moreover, the natural contrast of different scripts not only offers aesthetic qualities, but may, when handled sensibly, provide tangible practical advantages in composition. In document design, the case for harmonised type design relies, thus, on a strong aesthetic preference for stylistic homogeneity.

Yet, as the category of parallel settings is defined in the present context, it entails numerous other applications with requirements different to those for continuous reading. Often, these uses are more recent and have no historical examples to draw from. In the following section, a brief glance beyond document design is therefore combined with some considerations of current practice in multi-script typography and type design.

---

[q] Arguably, the Arabic could have benefited from more leading, which could have been balanced by a reduction of the body size, yet the limited range of founts available in hot-metal may not have allowed this.

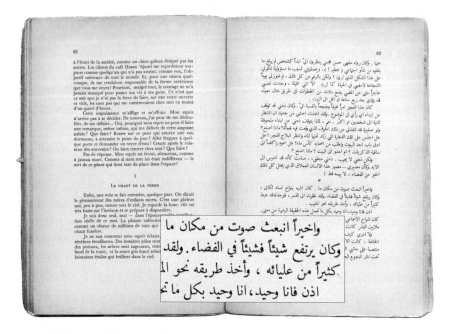

Figure 7: Monteil, V. (1961) *Anthologie bilingue de la littérature arabe contemporaine*, Imprimerie Catholique, Beirut. Reduced to 35% linear, detail enlargement in box.

1.5   Other applications and current practice

International airports provide a typical case of multi-script typography outside the domain of document design.[r] Especially in the recently emerged travel hubs in the Arabian Gulf and Asia, signage frequently incorporates two or more scripts.[s]

Bangkok's Suvarnabhumi airport (Figure 8) provides an interesting case, with many signs featuring Chinese, Latin and Thai scripts.[t] Their typographic treatment is instructive, for here scripts with fundamentally

---

[r] Bigelow and Holmes [1993, 293] name the signage of air travel as a factor which contributed to the familiarity of sans serif type around the world, influencing their stylistic choice in the Lucida Sans Unicode project.

[s] At the time of writing, none of the traditional western hubs in London, New York, Amsterdam, Paris or Frankfurt seem to provide any non-Latin signage.

[t] Beyond the overall impression, for this assessment the author relies on the judgements of colleagues familiar with Chinese and Thai scripts.

Figure 8: Signage at Bangkok's international Suvarnabhumi airport, photographs taken by the author in July 2014.

different characteristics meet: a bicameral alphabet, a unicameral abugida, and a logographic script are combined in what appears as a harmonious, yet not overly regularised configuration. Thai, the primary language, is set above Chinese and Latin, with ample space for vowels and tone marks above and below the characters. Its apparent size is slightly larger than the two additional scripts (justifiably so in Thailand), yet does not overpower Chinese and Latin which comfortably share the same vertical space without undue distortion of their respective proportions. Stylistically, Latin and Thai are set in matching low-contrast types, with the Chinese somewhat set apart by its more modulated design, yet to no apparent functional disadvantage. Potentially, here a harmonised design approach could contribute to a more balanced image, aligning the Chinese stylistically more closely with the two other scripts. Conversely, in a harmonised type vertical proportions would likely be more restrained, and thus run counter to the successful use of space achieved through type mixing in this example.

Unfortunately, the successful examples of parallel settings in signage are in the minority. Especially in the Gulf states, where multi-script settings are the norm, the quantity of poor examples far outnumbers the convincing cases.

At Abu Dhabi airport (Figure 9), a custom Arabic typeface designed to imitate some characteristics of Frutiger is representative of an approach to multi-script design which can be summarised under the term 'Latinisation'.[u] Here, proportions and characteristics of the Latin script are imposed on Arabic letterforms to the detriment of their legibility. Elements below the baseline, which are significantly more frequent and important in Arabic than in Latin, are diminished to match the descender depth, whereas tall letterforms are reduced, artificially creating an x-height where there is none in the Arabic script.

Figure 9: Signage at Abu Dhabi's international airport, photograph taken by the author in September 2013.

If in Abu Dhabi design dogma arguably overrides functionality, by contrast the concept for the signage at Dubai's airport is not readily apparent (Figure 10). Advertisers Naskh bold, a high-contrast Letraset rubdown lettering design conceived by Mourad and Arlette Boutros in the late 1970s, is paired with bold Helvetica, suggesting little concern for stylistic compatibility or legibility. Perhaps, it may also indicate uncritical reliance on marketing claims, for according to Boutros, Advertisers Naskh was designed 'to work in perfect harmony with Helvetica', and that 'the addition of linked straight lines to match the Latin baseline level is designed to achieve harmony when used alongside a Latin equivalent typeface such

---

[u] Judging from Bigelow and Holmes's definition of harmonised design, the signage at Abu Dhabi airport would not find their approval.

as Garamond, Palatino and Times Roman' [Boutros, 2014]. Here, one is strikingly reminded of the flexibility of harmonisation as a concept for commercial exploitation, and its success on this level is undeniable.

Figure 10: Signage at Dubai's international airport, photograph taken by the author in October 2012.

Indeed, in recent years, harmonised design has been adopted and promoted most vocally for marketing purposes, albeit rarely with reference to this term, or its originators. Foundries have recognised the potential market for non-Latin variants of their best-selling typefaces, and released a flurry of so-called 'extensions' to existing Latin designs. DIN, Frutiger, Helvetica, Palatino and Univers, just to name the most prolific company in this context, Monotype, all received their Arabic version, borrowing stylistic properties and – importantly – brand-recognisability from the Latin model. Whether a non-Latin extension to a design carrying decades worth of use can truly embody the same notions and associations in a different typographic culture is open to debate, although this question is rarely raised. How such extensions are undertaken is another consideration which merits attention.

When Bigelow and Holmes proposed the concept of harmonised design, they were acutely aware of the potential for homogenisation it entailed. They tried to avoid it by a conscious and deliberate attempt to learn and embrace 'the basic rules of each non-Latin alphabet on its own terms' [Bigelow and Holmes, 1993, p. 299][v] Thus, regularisation was attempted, but only up to a certain point which, according to the knowledge and sensibilities of the designers, stopped short of compromising the integrity of the script for 'Latinate notions'.[w] Bigelow and Holmes drew the line in the

---

[v] The next three references are from the same source.

[w] The question remains as to how and where the line between (desired) harmonisation and

design of the Hebrew characters thus: rather than imposing a 'strict Latin model', they tested different alignments, and chose the (unaligned) height between Latin capitals and minuscules for the Hebrew letters. Moreover, the designers maintained the conventional contrast of Hebrew letters in which horizontal strokes are thicker than verticals – the opposite of the Latin model – yet 'weighted the Hebrew characters to have visual "presence" equivalent to that of the Latin.'

Whereas Bigelow and Holmes's suggested approach appears as a sensible midway, negotiating script integrity and typographic constraints, more recently some harmonised designs disregard such caution. For example Boutros's Tanseek type distorts the proportions of Arabic letterforms to fit the Latin x-height, and the bold weights of Nadine Chahine's Frutiger Arabic feature the contrast of the Latin model, with vertical strokes thicker than horizontals.[x] Whether such decisions are truly successful in attaining formal harmony, and indeed what this harmony represents could only be discussed on a case-by-case basis, which goes beyond the scope of this chapter.

Yet, it is worth mentioning that different approaches to designing type for multi-script typography can be found in other quarters. Adobe, among others, is going a different path in its expanding catalogue of non-Latin type. Rather than extending renowned typefaces with other scripts, following a narrowly defined stylistic model and brand, most of its non-Latin designs are independently conceived as original typefaces. Designs like Adobe Arabic, Hebrew, Thai and Devanagari feature Latin glyph complements which are loosely reflecting style, apparent size and colour of the non-Latins, yet as their generic names suggest there is no pretence of direct translatability of a specific design from one script to the other. Here, it appears as if an approach was taken that prioritises design integrity, providing typefaces which can stand on their own without deference to existing Latin models, implicitly encouraging the added flexibility type mixing can provide.

(undesired) homogenisation should be drawn, and one would likely get different answers from different practitioners.

[x] Conversely, the brand Frutiger thus denotes on one hand a conventional Latin design, while on the other it features an Arabic design with inverted stroke contrast, a stylistic form not found in the œuvre of Adrian Frutiger.

1.6 Concluding remarks

As the discussion of multi-script scenarios demonstrates, the case for harmonised type design is not as self-evident as Bigelow and Holmes suggested in 1993. Undoubtedly, there are specialised applications in which pragmatic considerations and technical constraints make notions of harmonised design applicable. A typical example would be the original context of the Lucida Sans Unicode project, a type designed for a graphical user interface which for technical convenience needed to adhere to a shared set of vertical metrics, and for branding purposes to a unified visual language.[y]

The fact remains that harmonisation overwhelmingly takes characteristics, concepts, proportions and aesthetic notions of the Latin typographic world for granted, and seeks to adapt other scripts to these existing paradigms. Froshaug's observation that 'typography is a grid' remains remarkably accurate in today's digital environment, where the rectangular module still dominates design thinking and practice. And as has been argued above, regular, rectangular modules are – despite their appeal to a certain form of rationality – not as successful for most scripts, as they are for Latin.

At any rate, harmonised design in its various guises is here to stay, if only for commercial convenience. As Kinross noted [2002a], the dream of the universal typeface which could achieve 'a world of purified communication, of meaning unencumbered by the obstacles of form' through rational planning, has been a recurring one. And the observation that 'like all dreams – especially recurring ones – it seems to say a good deal about the dreamer' remains equally true in the realm of multi-script typography.

Acknowledgements

The author would like to thank Jacob Cawthorne and Ben Mitchell for their observations about the Chinese and Thai signage at Bangkok's Suvarnabhumi airport and the reviewers for their helpful observations and suggestions.

---

[y] Note that actual script mixing is rare in a GUI as a language change commonly affects all its elements. Moreover, the question whether a certain western aesthetic conveys the same notions in a different cultural context remains to be answered, but goes beyond the scope of this chapter.

References

Bigelow, C. and Holmes, K. (1993). The design of a Unicode font, *Electronic Publishing*, 6(3), pp. 289–305.

Bil'ak, P. (2008) Family planning, or how type families work, https://www.typotheque.com/articles/type_families (accessed September 9, 2014), first published in *CAP & Design*, November 2007 (in Swedish).

Boutros™ Arabic Typography (2014) "Boutros Advertisers Naskh", http://www.boutrosfonts.com/spip.php?article23 (accessed September 9, 2014).

Craig, J. (1998) *Shemlan: a history of the Middle East Centre for Arab Studies*, (Macmillan, Basingstoke).

Dreyfus, J. (1994) *Into Print: Selected Writings on Printing History, Typography and Book Production*, "Jan Tschichold's Sabon: The first 'Harmonized' Type," (The British Library, London) pp. 190–197, first published as "Sabon: the first 'harmonized' type" in the *Penrose Annual*, 61, London, 1968.

Froshaug, A. (2000a) *Anthony Froshaug: Typography & texts / Documents of a life*, ed. Kinross, R., "Univers," (Hyphen Press, London) pp. 174–176.

Froshaug, A. (2000b) *Anthony Froshaug: Typography & texts / Documents of a life*, ed. Kinross, R., "Typography is a grid," (Hyphen Press, London) pp. 187–190.

Kinross, R. (2002a) *Unjustified texts: perspectives on typography*, "Universal faces, ideal characters" (Hyphen Press, London) pp. 233–245, first published in *Baseline*, no. 6, 1985.

Kinross, R. (2002b) *Unjustified texts: perspectives on typography*, "What is a typeface?" (Hyphen Press, London) pp. 113–130, first published in *Baseline*, 7, 1986, pp. 14–18,

Kinross, R. (2004), *Modern typography*, 2nd Ed. (Hyphen Press, London).

Mosley, J. (1997). French academicians and modern typography: designing new types in the 1690s, *Typography Papers*, 2, pp. 5–29.

Ulrich, F. (2014) *From compressed light to extended ultra: Visual systems in type designs*, http://next.fontshop.com/content/from-compressed-light-to-extended-ultra/ (accessed September 17, 2014).

Unicode, Inc. (2009) *History of Unicode*, 'Chronology of Unicode Version 1.0,' http://www.unicode.org/history/versionone.html (accessed September 9, 2014).

Chapter 10

Using pattern languages in typographic design

Rob McKaughan

Pattern languages, a design method created by Christopher Alexander for architecture, have enjoyed popularity in several fields including software and interaction design. These fields have found that pattern languages improve communication and documentation, particularly in multi-discipline teams. Patterns help designers break down complex problems and better understand the relationships of design elements. Patterns bridge disciplines by documenting the relevant knowledge from several fields as applied to solving a single problem. Finally, the creation of a pattern language is an opportunity to make explicit the assumptions and wisdom of skilled typographic practice. This chapter reviews the progress of pattern languages in the architecture, software, and interaction design fields to understand how typeface design might benefit from using a pattern language. To illustrate the use of patterns for typeface design, this chapter includes a pattern language for designing newspaper typefaces.

1.1 Introduction

Everyone knows how to sing the blues. 'I hate to see that evening sun go down / Because my baby, he's gone left this town.' [Handy, 1914]. 'I used to have plenty of money, the finest clothes in town / but bad luck and trouble overtaken me, bound to get me down.' [Hopkins, 1994]. In a sense, all blues songs are the same. The music is built around a twelve bar melody and a common chord progression. The lyrics tell stories primarily of bad luck, bad lovers, and bad habits. Yet, this seemingly limited language of the blues is one of the richest genres of American music and has given birth to Rock and Roll and many other forms of popular music.

Blues musicians rarely start a song from scratch. The tradition of the blues provides a language of tried-and-true musical, lyrical, and narrative patterns that musicians can use to tell their stories in new ways. That language of patterns forms a solid foundation upon which artists can build expressive work.

In the 1960s, architect Christopher Alexander observed another language of patterns: 'Every place is given its character by certain patterns of events that keep happening there.' [Alexander, 1979]. He also observed that 'there is a fundamental inner connection between each pattern of events, and the pattern of space in which it happens.' [Alexander, 1979]. The architectural features of a place form these patterns in space, which in turn interact with the events and thus the character of the place. From this insight, Alexander created a new design approach for architecture by collecting these patterns into what he called a pattern language.

Each pattern in a pattern language is a rule of thumb abstracted from existing proven designs. More specifically, a pattern is a description of a problem and its solution in a particular context. These patterns are not recipes; they balance concrete physical descriptions while abstracting the pattern's concepts for use in other designs. The patterns focus on the characteristics of the product, and not the process used by the designer [Tidwell, 2005]. They also include a clear description of why the pattern works well, with lots of examples. These patterns can then help practitioners, from novices to master architects, to create appropriate designs.

For example, one of the patterns in Alexander's *A pattern language* [Alexander, 1977] describes the problem that people naturally abandon rooms with one window for rooms with light coming from multiple directions. To create rooms people enjoy remaining in, the pattern's solution recommends that architects build every room to have at least two walls facing the outdoors. This pattern, aptly named **light on two sides of every room** (pattern names appear in bold throughout this chapter), describes only the relationships of windows to walls and their impact on people. It does not prescribe particular floor plans, window treatments, or specific implementations. While this pattern might be something a master architect would know intuitively to build, a novice or a student might not. The intention of the pattern is to give any practitioner a good solution for this problem, as well as an understanding of why the solution works.

Pattern languages have enjoyed great popularity in other design fields, particularly in software engineering and interaction design. Practitioners in these fields have found that pattern languages provide a common language amongst designers and members of other disciplines [Erikson, 2000; Beck *et al.*, 2002]. Patterns capture and disseminate knowledge [Beck *et al.*, 2002], helping novice designers become productive more quickly [Chung *et al.,* 2004], and aiding experienced designers working in new areas [Kotula, 1996]. Patterns also help design in a complex problem space. The methodology of applying patterns provides a systematic design process, and it can identify gaps in the design brief or specification [Coplien in Beck *et al.*, 2002]. Finally, thinking with patterns causes designers to work at a level of abstraction, removing the project-specific details, to see the essence of the design [Kotula, 1996].

Typography, like the fields mentioned above, is similarly concerned with complex, multilayered problem spaces. Consider the layout of a simple paragraph: legibility and economy do battle to set line spacing, column width, and type size; all of which are also influenced by page size, layout, editorial tone, and typeface choice. Laying out a paragraph requires balancing many variables. Typeface design is similarly complex. Consider the variety of newspaper typefaces such as those in Figure 1. Each letter represents many design choices – some stylistic, others practical thanks to the difficulties of printing legibly at small sizes with cheap paper and ink. All of these choices interact with each other. For example, the small sizes of newspaper text dictate certain letterform proportions, however the stylistic choice of a humanist axis over a Didone axis can make typefaces of the same proportions appear larger [Carter, 1971]. Thus a mindful stylistic choice can help address a practical issue. Just as easily, a stylist choice can create new problems.

shape shape shape shape

Figure 1: Four typefaces for newspapers; from left to right: Times New Roman, Nimrod, Zócalo Text, and Swift Neue, all set at 26 point to more easily view differences in features, proportions, and the modulation of the width of strokes.

To make these choices quickly, it is helpful for designers to clearly understand the nuances of problems they are trying to solve, and how their solutions interact to improve or to diminish the overall design. Clearly documenting the choices and interactions in designs makes them easier to re-use, speeding up the design process in future projects, as well as providing a means of sharing good solutions with the entire community, creating a common language. The documentation also becomes a source of training for junior designers. It also is an opportunity to document hidden or forgotten assumptions, as well as to integrate the increasingly diverse fields of knowledge required to design documents and typefaces well.

Pattern languages have proven to be adept at solving these problems in several different design fields. They have the potential to be quite valuable. This chapter explores these possibilities through an example of a pattern language for newspaper typography and typeface design.

1.2   Pattern languages

The structure of pattern languages provides much of their practical value. Essentially, a pattern language is a collection of design rules of thumb captured from existing, proven designs. Each pattern describes a problem context and a suitable solution. The problem description lists all the design constraints that occur in the given context, including those constraints created by related patterns. These constraints are always expressed in physical terms [Alexander, 1979]. This physical specificity makes patterns specific in application, therefore concrete and actionable. It also makes patterns easy for novices to grasp.

A well-written problem description does more than define the context, it implicitly defines the applicability of the given pattern. Every problem has multiple solutions, therefore, multiple patterns that could apply. Designers carefully consider the design constraints for a project, and select only those patterns with contexts that are relevant to the problem at hand [Corfman, 1998]. This makes design choices and the impact of those choices explicit and deliberate.

Having clearly defined the problem space, a pattern must give a solution. A pattern's solution describes the physical attributes and relationships that resolve the constraints in the given context. Here again, physical descriptions keep patterns concrete and actionable, but there is an element of abstraction: solutions focus primarily on the relationships amongst elements, not on single elements [Tidwell, 2005]. Also, they describe only the relevant details of the solution, not a complete implementation. This abstraction enables individual patterns to be broadly applicable. Solutions may also make use of other patterns, specifying the relationships between them. This helps break up complex problems into smaller ones and focuses designers on the interplay of elements throughout the design.

A unique feature of pattern languages is that patterns clearly describe the rationale behind each solution including the design tradeoffs and their consequences. Dearden and Finlay [2006] note that patterns 'capture insights about the design that can inform even an experienced designer; explaining not only how a problem can be solved but also why a design choice is appropriate to a particular context.'

Patterns naturally become a conversational language because each pattern contains a unique name that is easy to remember and use [Meszaros and Doble, 1998]. The pattern names become a lexicon, and the specificity of the pattern descriptions lends precision to this lexicon. Pattern languages therefore are design languages facilitating communication amongst designers [Dearden and Finlay, 2006] and teams [Borchers, 2000].

Most importantly, each pattern includes several examples from real world designs. As Kohls and Uttecht [2009] point out, 'There is one section in most documented patterns that we consider as indispensable: the examples section. ... Only experience with multiple examples helps identify relevant variables.'

The structure of patterns generalizes good designs while retaining an element of concreteness [Bayle *et al.*, 1998]. This dual nature prevents patterns from being prescriptive. Instead, they describe design spaces more than specific designs [Buschmann *et al.*, 2007]. Because patterns are not overly specific, they enable variety in implementation. For example, Alexander's **Entrance transition** pattern suggests using architectural features to give multiple cues of a transition from public to private place. The pattern does not prescribe a specific ground plan, but lists several patterns as options: **Garden wall**, **Tapestry of light and dark**, **Trellised walk**, etc. The designer can choose any of these, as well as choose how they want to realise each option that they choose. The actual design created from patterns is always an adaptation of design principles to a specific situation.

1.3 An illustrative example

At first glance, pattern languages can seem quite abstract. In practice, pattern languages are most easily understood through example. This section will use a pattern language for newspapers [McKaughan, 2011] to illustrate the possibilities pattern languages have for typographic or typeface design. We start by painting an overall picture of the pattern language by naming several of the patterns and describing how they work in concert.

Next, we go into more detail by listing the complete specification of one of those patterns. This is followed by a discussion which walks through that pattern in detail, highlighting the pattern structure and practical benefits.

1.3.1 *A pattern language for news*

Consider the front page of a newspaper. The brand is instantly recognizable from the overall layout and typeface choices, even before we recognize the publication logo. The weights and styles help readers navigate the page to find an article, and the text of that article is set so that it is easy to read, while packing in as much text as possible to save printing costs. The page demonstrates a number of problems and choices: some are conventions for newspapers, some reveal the brand, and some solve material necessities of the print medium. These problems and choices operate at many different levels, from overall layout to the length of serifs, and all interact to form a unified whole.

This pattern language attacks these problems by first identifying broad issues such as branding, then proceeds through increasingly more detailed patterns all the way down to the level of letterform design.

Returning to the newspaper front page: A pattern called **news typographic design** outlines the overall typographic requirements of newspapers – issues of brand, editorial feel, printing economy, etc. – and points towards general purpose patterns to maintain **typographic identity**, using a **variegated typeface family** composed of many styles, with an optional **complementary sans-serif**. The newspaper would have to employ a **reading typeface** and an **economic text setting** to give readers a comfortable reading experience while remaining within cost constraints.

News typographic design also takes advantage of genre-specific patterns such as **newspaper text proportions** and **headline typefaces**, which outline the requirements for the design of a newspaper typeface. These patterns lead to more detailed patterns for designing a typeface in this context with **dark-printing letterforms** with **malleable joins**, **economic widths**, and **large apparent size**. Media-specific patterns that describe typefaces for **low-resolution screens** or **sturdiness for stereotyping** help adapt a design to a particular medium.

The above patterns work together to set the design requirements for a newspaper. A few additional patterns can give the designer flexibility for related publications. For example, to design the Sunday magazine supplement for a newspaper, a designer might replace **economic text setting** and **newspaper text proportions** with a **luxurious text setting** and **book text proportions**, while still employing the rest of the newspaper's patterns. The result would be a much more open, magazine-like layout appropriate for a lazy Sunday morning read, while still adhering to the overall design of the publication. The magazine supplement would therefore function alongside the newspaper as a complementary member of the publication's family.

1.3.2 *Example pattern: newspaper text proportions*

The following is the complete specification for the pattern, **newspaper text proportions**, mentioned in the previous section. It illustrates typographic patterns in more detail, particularly in the way that patterns specify relationships and employ other patterns to establish problem contexts and to solve them. A discussion of this pattern's construction follows the pattern.

1.3.2.1 *Problem context*

Morison eloquently described the context of newspaper typefaces:

> The problem in designing a newspaper type is to secure the maximum size of letter on the smallest size of body with the least waste of space between letters and words; while also preserving the right relation between the appearance of the letters and the length of the line to which they are set, and to increase, if possible the ease of switching the eyes from the extreme right to the extreme left of the line [Morison, 1956].

Newspaper text proportions also derives its context from the **reading typeface** and **legible economic text setting**: news type in a **legible economic text setting** is often set at 8–10 point, set with 1–2 points of leading or even set solid (line height is the type size itself with no extra space between lines), with measures of typically 12ems accommodating 4–6 words. To balance economy and readability, the setting will have just enough interlinear space to be adequate for reading. The grey of text blocks set in this manner must balance with other elements of the **news**

typographic design. The speed of news production prevents editors from fine-tuning all these parameters for each page.

1.3.2.2 *Solution*

Use proportions that provide sufficient interlinear space to read easily when set solid. Letter widths should be narrow enough to fit an average of six words in the given measure while still being easy to read.

1.3.2.3 *Rationale*

Economy and readability are the two primary, opposing forces in newspaper proportions. Economy drives increasing the number of lines per column-inch and characters per line, driving type to be set solid, and increasing the character density of each line.

Readability requires sufficient interlinear space to allow the eye to easily track from the end of a line to the beginning of the next. Meanwhile, a reader's perception of readability demands type that appears large.

Therefore, a balance must be struck: proportions to allow solid setting with readable interlinear space, while also having a high character density, without appearing crowded or dark, all while remaining readable.

1.3.2.4 *Implementation*

A news typeface must have the greatest possible size and clearness of impression [Morison, 1932]. It must appear equally readable and have a comparable size to typefaces previously used by the publication.

Use proportions that are oblong, not square, [Hutt, 1960] and that have **economic widths** to fit the appropriate number of words per line. Use sufficiently high ascenders so that good interlinear spacing is built into the design [Morison, 1956]. Shortening descenders can create extra space. The proportions of these extenders must balance with the x-height so that letters have **large apparent size**. Figures 2 and 3 demonstrate this balance of extenders, x-height, and interlinear space.

Adjust serif dimensions to give the appropriate grey on the page. Serifs should taper because halation causes straight serifs to lose apparent length [Dawson and Farey, 2002].

Stock markets worldwide closed this evening with no gains and no losses amidst news that today is just another day, like every day. In response, the Securities and Exchange Commissioned released a statement that, "The numbers just aren't changing. There's no point in watching them all day. Investors should go home and get a life."

Industry pundits claim that someone forgot to turn the crank that winds up NASDAQ. Meanwhile, Twitter was ablaze with dis-

Stock markets worldwide closed this evening with no gains and no losses amidst news that today is just another day, like every day. In response, the Securities and Exchange Commissioned released a statement that, "The numbers just aren't changing. There's no point in watching them all day. Investors should go home and get a life."

Industry pundits claim that someone forgot to turn the crank that winds up NASDAQ. Meanwhile, Twitter was ablaze with discussions vabout BitCoin, but nobody really

Figure 2: These text settings show the balance of vertical and horizontal proportions in a news context. Both columns are set on an 8-point baseline grid. The right column is set in a newspaper typeface, Nimrod, at 8-point. The left column is set in Hoefler Text, and has been scaled to match Nimrod's x-height, thus both columns should have equal legibility. The left column is harder to read, though because its ascenders and descenders break up the interlinear space, often causing collisions as in the case of the letter g on the second line, making the text hard to scan.

Stock markets worldwide closed this evening with no gains and no losses amidst news that today is just another day, like every day. In response, the Securities and Exchange Commissioned released a statement that, "The numbers just aren't changing. There's no point in watching them all day. Investors should go home and get a life."

Industry pundits claim that someone forgot to turn the crank that winds up NASDAQ. Meanwhile, Twitter was ablaze with discussions about BitCoin, but nobody really understood what they were talking about, nor what it had to do about anything. Traders at the New York Stock Exchange

Stock markets worldwide closed this evening with no gains and no losses amidst news that today is just another day, like every day. In response, the Securities and Exchange Commissioned released a statement that, "The numbers just aren't changing. There's no point in watching them all day. Investors should go home and get a life."

Industry pundits claim that someone forgot to turn the crank that winds up NASDAQ. Meanwhile, Twitter was ablaze with discussions about BitCoin, but nobody really un-

Figure 3: These settings continue the illustration: The right column is set in Nimrod 8-point exactly as in figure 2. The left column is set in Mrs. Eaves, also at 8-point, set solid. Its small x-height and proportionately narrow letters pack in more text than Nimrod and with plenty of interlinear space. However, the very small letters are difficult to read and are off-putting. Taking figures 2 and 3 together, we see that for news settings, the x-height must be large enough for readability, ascenders and descenders moderate for interlinear space, and widths narrow enough for the necessary text density. It is easy to see that Nimrod was designed for this environment whereas Hoefler Text and Mrs. Eaves were not.

1.3.2.5 *Pitfalls*

Often designers believe that page economy requires a condensed typeface, however this is not always the case. The contemporary news writing
style tends towards short paragraphs, leaving much whitespace following
the last line of each paragraph. Walter Tracy and Allen Hutt found that
when setting English text in this writing style, a wider (or less condensed)
letterform has little or no effect on the column length [Hutt, 1973]. The
whitespace on the last line of a paragraph absorbs the extra space used by
the wider letters. The proportions of a news typeface, therefore, need not
be highly condensed to be economic. This effect varies with language and
editorial style.

1.3.2.6 *Related patterns*

This pattern contributes to the economy of a **legible economic text setting**.

1.3.3 *Discussion: the anatomy of a pattern*

The first section of the pattern sets up the context of the pattern it attempts
to solve (e.g. Morison's quote), and identifies any constraints the context
identifies (e.g. 8–9pt text size, set solid). The pattern explicitly lists the
source of these constraints (e.g. the **legible economic text setting** pattern)
so that designers understand the relationship between those sources and
the solution to this problem, and thus how to adapt changes in one to the
other. It also identifies environmental requirements, such as the editor's
lack of time for fine-tuning, so that hard requirements are clear.

The solution section provides a concise statement of the solution to the
problem in terms of relationships to other entities. Specifying relationships
(e.g. relating letter proportion to line spacing requirements) creates a concrete solution that enables designers to adapt the solution to the particular
document, while still being abstract enough to apply to other documents.

The rationale for this solution immediately follows. This rationale
is one of the unique factors of patterns as it not only explains why the
solution works, but abstracts the solution so it is broadly applicable. The
implementation section contains the concrete details on how to implement
the solution, including examples wherever possible. This gives the practical side of the pattern. In a way the rationale and implementation are

yin-yang complements: the abstract and the practical. As described above, this attribute enables patterns to be both actionable and broadly applicable.

This pattern language contains a unique section not found in pattern languages used in other fields: the pitfalls' section. This section captures an important body of knowledge that often differentiates experts from novices: the knowledge of what does not work. The pitfalls' section documents common misunderstandings, misinterpretations, or easy mistakes one can make in implementing the solution to this context. The hope is to improve a practitioner's efficiency by warning them about known bad ideas. Reiners *et al.* [2011] employed a similar idea as an Anti-pattern-attribute in their software pattern language framework.

The pattern concludes with references to other patterns. This explicitly identifies the other patterns to which this pattern contributes a part of the solution (e.g. this pattern helps solve a **legible economic text setting**), as well as other patterns this pattern depends on.

1.4 Possibilities for pattern languages in typographic design

There are many ways pattern languages can be useful in typographic design. This section focuses on three key opportunities: solving complex problems simply, combining knowledge from related fields, and making unstated assumptions explicit.

1.4.1 *Solving complex problems simply*

Typeface design and typographic layout require solutions to problems that are multilayered and have many variables to balance. For example, the layout of a paragraph depends not only on the column width and the overall page layout, but also on the design of the typeface used for the text, especially letterform proportions. For example, the proportions of newspaper typefaces enable them to work with much less line spacing than the designs of book typefaces do. Meanwhile, printing costs can encourage editors to increase the density of text on the page, and thus to reduce the type size used in a paragraph. That type size influences the overall impression that a page of text gives. Choosing how to lay out a paragraph of text requires balancing all of these factors and considering the implications on broad and minute design requirements.

The structure of a pattern language lends itself well to solving these multi-layered typographic problems. Individual patterns can address different levels of scope in the design, from overall layout to fine letterform features like the design of serifs or the joins between strokes within a letter. Each pattern solves an aspect of the overall design brief, and also explicitly interacts with other patterns to solve larger, more complex problems. This interaction helps maintain the coherence through all levels of the design so that the sum of design choices creates a consistent document whole.

For example, consider the following patterns for newspaper layout and typeface design. An **economic text setting** for newspapers requires very high text density and the ability to justify text evenly in narrow columns. To accomplish this, it is helpful to be able to slightly widen and condense letters automatically in software to fit text well in the given space; however, this manipulation can distort letterforms. Typefaces designed with **malleable joins**, in which strokes join at ninety-degree angles, survive this treatment without distortion. Thus, **malleable joins** are a great advantage in this sort of environment, and so the **economic text setting** pattern will explicitly call for them. Similarly, an **economic text setting** is essential for newspapers, so a broad pattern documenting the **news typographic design** might call for a medium-scale pattern like **economic text setting** to meet its cost and preference requirements. Designers may likewise employ other patterns to solve other aspects of the design. All of these patterns work together, explicitly and implicitly, to satisfy the requirements of the publication at all levels of the design.

As mentioned previously, the structure of patterns can help manage the complexity of a design. The relationships identified by patterns help designers understand the relationships between design elements [Bayle *et al.*, 1998]. Designers can use this understanding to break down problems and to reflect on the impact of changes to a design. In a study by Dearden *et al.,* [2002] 'experienced designers indicated that the language had supported their design activity, in one case highlighting elements that would otherwise have been missed.' Coplien concurred: 'Once in a while, a pattern will solve a problem that seems like it should be in requirements, but the requirement is found to be missing.' [Coplien in Beck *et al.*, 2002]. Saponas *et al.* [2006] concluded that patterns enable designers to eliminate more issues early in the design process. Designers using patterns can therefore produce initial prototype designs that are more robust and better suited to project requirements.

Patterns break complex problems down into a set of relationships between elements. These relationships, in turn, identify free and invariant variables. This enables designers to be expressive (explicitly by free variables), while still reliably addressing document needs (invariant variables). For example, while **news typographic design** and **economic text setting** define typeface proportions, and while **malleable joins** define one letterform feature, the style of the typeface is left undefined. Style, therefore, is a free variable, while the proportions and join structure are invariant. The patterns clarify the designers understanding by making the tradeoffs and relationships between variables explicit, thus making design choices easier and clearer to make. In this way, patterns become good food for design thought for each project.

This property of patterns, that of breaking down complex problems into clear relationships, makes them quite useful in education and in improving the contribution of novice designers. In a study using pattern languages for web site design, Dearden *et al.* [2002] observed that the process of using patterns 'enabled novice users with no experience of web design to participate in the design of a website.' Chung *et al.* [2004] found that patterns helped novices produce ideas and communicate them easily, avoiding problems early in the design process. Tidwell [1999] points out that it is difficult for novice designers to keep in mind all the myriad design principles they should apply. Because patterns encapsulate these principles, a pattern language helps novices use good principles effectively in their designs.

1.4.2 *Combining knowledge*

Typographic design is increasingly a multidiscipline effort. Designers work with software developers, industrial designers, project managers, web designers, cognitive psychologists, and, of course, clients. Written properly, pattern languages are understandable by people in different disciplines. Patterns can bridge the communication gap between disciplines [Schmidt, 1995]. If written well enough for readers outside the problem domain, patterns can help people in a multidisciplinary team understand each other better [Borchers, 2000].

Much more interesting, however, is the potential pattern languages have to integrate knowledge from diverse fields. Authorship of typeface design patterns need not be limited to typeface designers. Patterns can encapsulate the diverse knowledge areas needed for typeface design: cognitive psychology, graphic design, typographic design, printing processes, engineering, etc.

In doing so, patterns can relate issues from multiple fields to each other, and to place them in a specific, relevant context. For example, consider a pattern about condensed letter proportions. That pattern could include typeface design knowledge on making condensed types, knowledge from cognitive psychology on crowding and the legibility of narrow letters, and engineering recommendations on print or screen rendering of these forms. Designers would not have to interpret each field separately and synthesize their own theory to apply to their projects. Instead, the pattern language would provide a common, multi-disciplined understanding. Such a common understanding would be very valuable in typeface design because designers must forge their own multi-disciplined ideas, invariably leading to disagreement amongst designers.

1.4.3 *Making assumptions explicit*

The preceding sections outline the practical advantages to pattern languages. There is also an important philosophical impact that pattern languages can have on typography as a discipline: the creation of a pattern language is an opportunity to make assumptions explicit.

The typographic discipline boasts over five hundred years of traditions. Over time, conventions have formed, in part due to technical restrictions such as the size of a printing press, economic issues such as the cost of paper and materials, issues of legibility, and also due to a craftsman's mindful intuition for solving these problems. What was economic necessity later becomes convention and even later becomes invariant truth even though the necessity or technology the assumption was based on has faded. Few have attempted to revisit typographic conventions and practice to determine which assumptions are outdated, which are still applicable, and, more importantly, which have never been explicitly stated before.

Writing a pattern language is an act of deep reflection. One has to agree on what good design is, and more importantly, what contributes to making a particular design good: i.e. what specific relationships exist that can generate new, equally good designs, repeatedly and reliably. To do this requires getting to the root of why those relationships work and, along the way, which typographic principles are valid and why. Creating a pattern language can thus help clarify the theoretical basis of typography.

A pattern language could also help clarify cases of simple disagreement. The canon of typography includes many opinions that are unverified and taken as fact, often resulting in confusing or contradictory information. For example, in 'The Evolution of Times New Roman,' [1973] John Dreyfus asserts that for serifs to hold up through the stereotyping process, serifs should be thin and tapered like those of Perpetua. Allen Hutt writes in 'Walter Tracy, type designer' [1973] that serifs should be blunt, as Jubilee's serifs are, to survive the same process. Two equally respected authors, writing in the same year, are in direct contradiction, without any further literature to resolve the debate. Design patterns must be specific to be useful, requiring clarity be brought to these murky waters.

1.5   Alternatives to pattern languages

The pattern language is not the first system created to document design knowledge. Among those systems that the information design and interaction design fields have looked into are guidelines, style guides, and genres. It is worth considering their relative advantages and disadvantages with respect to typography.

Relative to style guides, patterns appear to be an improvement. Style guides focus on a single publication or a particular implementation environment. Patterns, on the other hand, abstract away the particular implementation environment and thus apply to many situations. This abstraction can be helpful when designers must adapt to circumstances not anticipated by a style guide. Patterns also identify the context in which they are applicable [Dearden and Finlay, 2006], which provides guidance as to which patterns are most appropriate for a given problem. Borchers [2000] found patterns superior due to 'their standard format, hierarchical networking, inclusion of examples, and discussion of problem context as well as solution.'

Compared to guidelines, patterns are both more general and use examples that are more specific [Dearden and Finlay, 2006], enabling patterns to be more universally applicable as well as actionable. In interaction design, Granlund *et al.* found that guidelines omit basic UI design knowledge:

> The major forces influencing design: the user, the context, and the task, are missing from guidelines. Design rationale is missing, too. Patterns capture and document all of this important knowledge [Granlund *et al.*, 2001].

The difference between guidelines and pattern languages is more subtle than the above. Unlike guidelines, patterns are generative, informing designers about design options at each point in the design process, while providing an easy way to capture options already explored [Borchers, 2000].

Document genre analysis was formulated by Delin, Bateman, and Allen based on the work of Waller and Twyman. This framework analyzes the content, rhetoric, layout, navigation, and linguistic structure of documents to find the common relationships in these structures. From this commonality, one can study how document genres form and evolve over time [Delin *et al.*, 2002].

Waller *et al.* [2012] describe three key differences between patterns and genres: firstly, genres use existing names, names that users of documents might use, to describe structures and genres. A pattern language, on the other hand, is an exercise for practitioners in naming the underlying structures in their work. Secondly, genres describe conventions; whereas patterns follow underlying insights into the strategies or behaviors of those who use created works. Finally, Genres, by definition, describe genre [Delin *et al.*, 2002], whereas patterns are specifically intended to cross genre boundaries. In fact, as Tidwell [1999] points out, patterns can even cross disciplines.

There may be a further distinction: genres were initially formulated as an analysis technique to study how documents coalesce into genres [Delin *et al.*, 2002]. Pattern languages, however, were created for practice, specifically to empower ordinary people to improve the quality of architecture in their lives [Alexander, 1979]. Both frameworks operate in the space of design relationships, but they were conceived for different users and purposes. Patterns and genres differ in that genres form a descriptive framework focused on genres as seen by users of documents, whereas patterns form a design framework focused on creators. That said, it is likely that both frameworks can be used for either analysis or practice – indeed they can be quite complementary, with pattern makers finding inspiration in genre analyses and vice versa.

1.6 Conclusions

Christopher Alexander's pattern languages have enjoyed success as a design methodology in the software engineering, interaction design, and other fields. In these fields, pattern languages provided a design vernacular, helping improve communications and documentation. The inter-related, generative nature of patterns enabled them to solve complex problems, producing designs whose elements work together as a whole, integrated design. This structure also helped designers better understand the relationships of design elements. By encapsulating knowledge of good designs, pattern languages helped train novice designers and helped expert designers work in unfamiliar domains. Pattern languages also integrated knowledge from different disciplines, giving designers coherent multi-disciplined design guidance.

Pattern languages will be very useful for typographic design. Waller *et al.* [2012] concur and go on to describe a program of developing a corpus of document patterns informed by and informing document genre analysis. This substantial effort will be worthwhile in documenting an explicit understanding of the patterns, assumptions, and practices in document design.

Pattern languages also have many other helpful attributes: documenting typographic patterns is an opportunity to combine knowledge from reading science, typographic design, and engineering into a single, coherent knowledge base. The organized complexity of pattern languages will help designers understand and manage the many mutually dependent variables in typeface and document design. The natural design language arising out of patterns will help refine the typographic lexicon and will enable designers to document more easily their design tradeoffs – issues infrequently discussed in typographic literature. This documentation will help train novice and experienced designers alike to work in new areas. Finally, all these benefits can apply equally to typeface design and typographic design. The typographic community would profit from creating a pattern language for both.

References

Alexander, C. (1979). *The timeless way of building*. (Oxford University Press, New York).

Alexander, C., Ishikawa, S., Silverstein, M., Jacobson, M., Fiksdahl-King, I., & Angel, S. (1977). *A pattern language: towns, buildings, construction*. Later printing. (Oxford University Press, New York).

Bayle, E., Bellamy, R., Casaday, G., Erickson, T., Fincher, S., Grinter, B., *et al.* (1998). Putting it all together: towards a pattern language for interaction design: A CHI 97 workshop, *ACM SIGCHI Bulletin*, *30*(1), pp. 17–23. doi:10.1.1.35.3561

Beck, K., Crocker, R., Meszaros, G., Coplien, J. O., Dominick, L., Paulisch, F., & Vlissides, J. (2002). Industrial experience with design patterns, *ICSE '96 Proceedings of the 18th international conference on Software engineering,* (IEEE Computer Society, Washington, D.C.) pp. 103–114.

Borchers, J. (2000). Interaction design patterns: twelve theses, *CHI2000 Patterns workshop* (Vol. 2, p. 3). The Hague. doi:10.1.1.35.3561

Buschmann, F., Henney, K., & Schmidt, D. C. (2007). *Pattern-oriented software architecture: On patterns and pattern languages* (Vol. 5). (John Wiley & Sons, Chichester).

Carter, M. (1971). Olympian: a new type for papers. *Interpresgrafik*, 7, pp. 42–47.

Chung, E. S., Hong, J. I., Lin, J., Prabaker, M. K., Landay, J. A., & Liu, A. L. (2004). Development and evaluation of emerging design patterns for ubiquitous computing. In *Proceedings of the 5th conference on Designing interactive systems: processes, practices, methods, and techniques,* (ACM: Cambridge Massachusetts) pp. 233–242. doi:10.1145/1013115.1013148

Corfman, R. (1998). An overview of patterns. In L. Rising (Ed.), *The patterns handbook: techniques, strategies, and applications* (Cambridge University Press: Cambridge) pp. 19–30.

Dawson, R., & Farey, D. (2002). The Times vernacular 2002.

Dearden, A., & Finlay, J. (2006). Pattern languages in HCI: a critical review. *Human–Computer Interaction*, *21*(1), pp. 49–102.

Dearden, A., Finlay, J., Allgar, L., & McManus, B. (2002). Evaluating pattern languages in participatory design. In *CHI'02 extended abstracts on Human factors in computing systems*, pp. 664–665.

Delin, J., Bateman, J., & Allen, P. (2002). A model of genre in document layout.

Information Design Journal, 11(1), pp. 54–66.

Dreyfus, J. (1973). The evolution of Times New Roman. *Penrose Annual, 66*, pp. 165–174.

Erickson, T. (2000). Lingua francas for design: sacred places and pattern languages. In *Proceedings of Designing Interactive Systems*, (ACM Press: Brooklyn, NY), pp. 357-368. http://www.visi.com/~snowfall/ LinguaFranca_DIS2000.html.

Granlund, A., Lafreniere, D., & Carr, D. A. (2001). A pattern-supported approach to the user interface design process. In *Proceedings of HCI International* (Vol. 1) pp. 282–286. doi:10.1.1.20.7928

Handy, W.C. (1914, original publishing) St. Louis blues. Blues standard.

Hopkins, S. L. (1994) Sinner's prayer. Performed by Eric Clapton on *From the cradle*, compact disc.

Hutt, A. (1960). *Newspaper design*. (Oxford University Press, London).

Hutt, A. (1973). Walter Tracy, type designer. *Penrose Annual, 66*, pp. 101–115.

Kohls, C., & Uttecht, J.-G. (2009). Lessons learnt in mining and writing design patterns for educational interactive graphics. *Computers in Human Behavior, 25*, pp. 1040–1055. doi:10.1016/j.chb.2009.01.004

Kotula, J. (1996). Discovering patterns: an industry report. *Software: practice and experience, 26*(11), pp. 1261–1276.

McKaughan, R. (2011). *Towards a pattern language for typeface design*. Masters dissertation. University of Reading.

Meszaros, G., & Doble, J. (1998). A pattern language for pattern writing. *Pattern Languages of Program Design, 3*, pp. 529–574.

Morison, S. (1956). *Interlinear space or "leading" in typographical composition*. (unpublished). MS Add.9812/B3/21.2. Cambridge University Library Stanley Morison Archives.

Morison, S. (anonymous). (1932). *Printing the Times; a record of the changes introduced in the issue for October 3, 1932*. (Printing House Square, London).

Reiners, R., Astrova, I., & Zimmermann, A. (2011). Introducing new Pattern Language Concepts and an Extended Pattern Structure for Ubiquitous Computing Application Design Support. In *PATTERNS 2011, The Third International Conferences on Pervasive Patterns and Applications*, pp. 61–66.

Saponas, T. S., Prabaker, M. K., Abowd, G. D., & Landay, J. A. (2006). The impact of pre-patterns on the design of digital home applications. In *Proceed-*

ings of the 6th conference on Designing Interactive systems, (ACM: University Park, Pennsylvania) pp. 189–198. doi:10.1145/1142405.1142436

Schmidt, D. C., Fayad, M., & Johnson, R. E. (1995). Software patterns. *Communications of the ACM, 38*(10), pp. 37–39. doi:10.1145/236156.236164

Tidwell, J. (2005). *Designing interfaces: patterns for effective interaction design.* (O'Reilly Media, Sebastapol, California).

Tidwell, J. 1999. *Common Ground: A Pattern Language for Human-Computer Interface Design.* Available online: http://www.mit.edu/~jtidwell/common_ground.html.

Waller, R., Delin, J., & Thomas, M. (2012). Towards a pattern language approach to document description. *Discours. Revue de Linguistique, Psycholinguistique et Informatique,* (10). Retrieved from http://discours.revues.org/8673

Chapter 11

How does expertise contribute to the recognition of Latin and Chinese characters?

Mary C. Dyson, Keith Tam, Clare Leake, Brian Kwok

Are characters in writing systems (e.g. Latin or Chinese) perceived in the same way as objects or do we process characters in a different way? Previous research [Gauthier *et al.*, 2006] has suggested that readers familiar with a writing system are able to take advantage of the stylistic regularities in typefaces, whereas those without this expertise cannot. The experiments described in this chapter explore whether a different form of expertise, acquired through design training, also affects our perception of unfamiliar characters, meaningless shapes if we cannot read the script. A comparison was made of Chinese bilinguals and English monolinguals and those with and without design expertise. All participants were asked to discriminate between strings of characters in both Latin and Chinese and in different typefaces. The results reveal that non-designers are more susceptible to interference from incongruent font information than designers, particularly in an unfamiliar, or less familiar, writing system. However, design expertise appears to facilitate the abstraction of the character shapes from the stylistic variations. These results were found in UK students and not the more fluent bilingual students in Hong Kong suggesting the need for further exploration of the effects of different types and levels of expertise on character recognition.

1.1 Introduction

The extent to which character recognition is regarded as a form of object recognition, as opposed to a more specialized activity, varies. For some researchers, the logical starting point is to consider letters and words as objects [e.g. Majaj *et al.*, 2002; Pelli *et al.*, 2006; Pelli and Tillman, 2007]. In recognizing an object, such as a chair, we disregard variations in style or orientation or viewpoint. Similarly, in reading, variation in characters due to font or size needs to be ignored to identify the character.

Various studies, summarized in Sanocki and Dyson [2012], have shown that characters presented in mixed fonts, rather than a single font, are recognized less efficiently, even though the font is irrelevant. Sanocki [1987] termed this a 'font-regularity' effect and described the process whereby the perceptual system can become tuned to a particular font over time and a set of font parameters are developed.

Gauthier *et al.*, [2006] extended the research to compare font tuning effects between Chinese-English bilinguals, familiar with Chinese characters and the Latin alphabet, and non-Chinese who had no experience with Chinese characters but were familiar with the Latin alphabet. They found evidence for font tuning only when participants were familiar with the writing system, from which Gauthier *et al.* conclude that expert readers perceive letters in a different manner from shapes, i.e. taking advantage of font regularity. These results support an account of the perceptual system becoming tuned to typical font regularities through experience with the writing system.

The degree to which Chinese characters are processed holistically has been studied with non-Chinese and Chinese readers [Hsiao and Cottrell, 2009; Wong *et al.*, 2012]. These studies have drawn parallels with holistic processing of faces, which is regarded as an indicator of expertise in face recognition. One explanation for the link between expertise and holistic processing is that perceptual expertise involves fine-level discrimination between similar objects (e.g. recognizing individual faces) and holistic processing is developed as an optimal strategy for such discrimination [Richler *et al.*, 2011].

However, the relationship between reading expertise in Chinese and holistic processing may not be straightforward. Wong *et al.* [2012] found evidence of holistic processing of Chinese characters by experts in reading Chinese and novices. The similar results for experts and novices are explained by introducing two origins for holistic processing: experts allocate their attention to appropriate aspects of the stimulus; novices are inefficient in their processing [Wong *et al.*, 2012]. In contrast, Hsiao and Cottrell [2009] found holistic processing only in novices and conclude that the nature of processing is stimulus and task dependent, and does not relate only to visual expertise.

There is some evidence that typeface expertise, through design training, also develops a strategy of holistic processing which aids Latin typeface identification [Dyson and Stott, 2012]. Designers may therefore develop perceptual abilities which are qualitatively different from non-designers, and from the processes used in normal reading where identification of characters, rather than typefaces, is required.

The manner of processing Chinese characters is likely to depend on reading expertise as configural information, the relationship between features, is not important for recognizing Chinese characters [Ge *et al.*, 2006]; a Chinese reader identifies individual stroke patterns, whilst a non-Chinese reader may process the character as a whole [Hsiao and Cottrell, 2009]. However, despite the differences in character shape and alphabetic versus non-alphabetic writing system, Wong *et al.* [2012] do not propose two different types of reading expertise for Latin and Chinese.

A widely used method to explore holistic processing of faces, extended to words [Wong *et al.*, 2011], is the composite matching task which requires matching, or discrimination, of two stimuli whilst also presenting an irrelevant part. This part may be congruent with the target response (e.g. both same) or incongruent (e.g. targets are the same but irrelevant parts are different). One way of measuring holistic processing is the advantage for congruent conditions compared to incongruent, indicating that attention has been directed to all parts, not just the target.

With reading expertise, we can identify characters by ignoring font variation to reveal the basic shapes. However, a study by Lewis and Walker [1989] found that reaction times to words are slower if the perceptual qualities of the font are inconsistent with the meaning of the word (incongruent condition), e.g. the word 'heavy' in a 'light' font. This indicates an intrusion of the irrelevant font dimension.

In order to further explore the way in which characters are processed by experts (in reading) and to extend this to look at the contribution of typeface expertise, the following research questions were both addressed in two experiments:

- Do designers demonstrate font tuning in a writing system they cannot read?

- Does congruency between letter identity and font influence performance?

1.2 Method

1.2.1 *Experimental design*

Two experiments were conducted: one in the UK (Experiment 1) and one in Hong Kong (Experiment 2) involving Chinese and non-Chinese readers, with and without design training. All participants were presented with both Chinese and Latin characters, consequently non-Chinese readers were responding to characters in a writing system they could not read, i.e. no reading expertise (see Table 1).

1.2.2 *Participants*

Participants were volunteers from the University of Reading, UK (Experiment 1) and Hong Kong Polytechnic University, Hong Kong (Experiment 2). In Experiment 1, the non-Chinese-reading designers were twelve Masters students or final year BA students from the Department of Typography & Graphic Communication. The non-Chinese-reading non-designers were twelve students without any significant design education. The Chinese non-designer participants were twelve English as second language (ESL) students who (apart from one) had grown up in China and started learning English in primary or at the beginning of secondary school. Most had only been in England one or two months and were studying summer courses to improve their English before starting a Masters. It was not possible to recruit a group of Chinese-reading designers within the University of Reading. As students in Hong Kong are all bi-lingual, in Experiment 2 there were just two groups: non-designers (N=12) and designers (N=12). All of the participants were undergraduate students from the Hong Kong Polytechnic University. The designers were recruited from the School of Design, from the BA (Hons) in Design programme. The non-designers were recruited from other departments of the university.

It was made clear to participants in both experiments that their participation and the results were not part of any assessment on their programmes. The research project received ethical review according to the procedures specified by the University of Reading Research Ethics Committee and was given a favorable ethical opinion for conduct; participants in Hong Kong gave their informed consent.

Table 1: Summary of participant categories and their characteristics.

	Non-Chinese readers (monolinguals)		Chinese readers (bilingual)	
	Non-designers **N=12** **UK (Expt 1)**	**Designers** **N=12** **UK (Expt 1)**	**Non-designers** **N=24 UK+HK** **(Expt 1 & 2)**	**Designers** **N=12** **HK (Expt 2)**
Latin fonts	Reading expertise	Reading & typeface expertise	Reading expertise	Reading & typeface expertise
Chinese fonts	No reading expertise	No reading expertise but typeface expertise	Reading expertise	Reading & typeface expertise

1.2.3 *Material*

The experiments used a discrimination task where two character strings were judged as either containing the same characters or different characters. The order of characters was jumbled from one string to the next. The characters strings were in the same font or a different font. This resulted in pairs of letter strings that were either congruent in terms of characters and font (i.e. same characters in the same font or different characters in different fonts) or incongruent (i.e. same characters in two different fonts or different characters in the same font). Figure 1a and 1b illustrate examples of Latin character strings.

btov vobt
audk dkua
waxi isaw
axrp pxry

btov **vobt**
audk dkua
waxi isaw
axrp **pxry**

Figure 1a (left): congruent strings, Figure 1b (right): incongruent strings.

The Latin characters used two fonts: Berthold Bodoni and Stempel Garamond. These fonts have similar x-heights, which removes the problem of adjusting point size to have the same apparent size [Beier and Dyson, 2014]. Different x-heights are illustrated in Figure 2.

Figure 2: Times New Roman (left) has a smaller x-height than Verdana (right) and hence appears smaller visually even when set at the same point size.

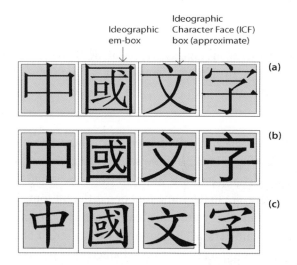

Figure 3: The grey boxes indicate the approximate Ideographic Character Face (ICF) boxes of three typefaces: (a) STSong Regular, (b) STHeiti Light and (c) Biao Kai Ti. Also known as 'average character face', the ICF box specifies the approximate bounding box of the full-width ideographic characters in a Chinese font. Fonts (a) and (b) appear similar in size when set at the same point size because the ICF boxes of these two fonts are of similar sizes. Font (c) appears to be smaller compared with (a) and (b) because its ICF box is smaller.

Chinese characters do not have x-heights, but because the 'Ideographic Character Face' (ICF) boxes vary, sizes might appear slightly different, but not as much as variation from x-heights in Latin fonts (see Figure 3).

The Chinese fonts differed between the UK and HK to extend the range of fonts tested. In the UK, the two Chinese fonts were SimSun and SimHei and in Hong Kong, STXihei and STSong (see Figure 4). SimHei and STXihei belong to the Heiti category of Chinese typefaces with minimal stroke modulations and can be considered equivalents to sans serif Latin fonts. SimSun and STSong are similar to seriffed Latin fonts in that they have marked stroke modulations and have serif-like terminals. These fonts share similar proportions and their appearing sizes are similar. They were chosen because they contain all of the characters that were needed for the study in both Traditional and Simplified versions.

内复考	阿 愛 安	内复考	阿 愛 安	wpti	**wpti**
SimSun	STSong	SimHei	STXihei	Garamond	Bodoni
UK	HK	UK	HK	UK, HK	UK, HK

Figure 4: Example fonts used in two experiments, shown at 50% point size.

Pilot work explored the characteristics of the character strings across the two writing systems, to achieve a level of difficulty for the Chinese material that was appropriate for both non-Chinese and Chinese participants. Initially four characters were tested, as this number showed evidence of font tuning in a previous study with Latin fonts [Dyson, 2014]. However, this number was found to be too difficult for the average non-Chinese reader and the Chinese strings were reduced to three characters, whilst retaining four Latin characters. We decided that three characters would not be too great a deviation from the four used in the Latin version because Chinese characters tend to be more complex in nature. The experimental procedure, adjusting the rate of presentation (see below), ensured that the Chinese version would not be too easy for Chinese readers. Latin fonts were presented in 36 point (in line with previous work) and Chinese in 24 point. Equating the average height of Chinese characters with the x-height of the two Latin fonts results in a size of around 18 points. This was increased to 24 point to cater for the difficulty experienced by non-Chinese readers.

Latin 4-character strings were created from 26 lowercase letters, randomly generated with no repeat characters per string, and meaningful combinations were removed. There were 400 same character and 400 different character strings from which items were selected at random for each participant. Trials (pairs of strings) were evenly split between same and different fonts, and same and different characters.

Given the vast number of Chinese characters (character sets for Traditional and Simplified Chinese fonts range from 6,000 to 13,000 characters), we decided to use the 581 most frequently used characters in publishing, mass media, and the Internet [Wang, 2006]. These were converted from Simplified to Traditional by the second author to create two sets. The 3-character strings were randomly generated and the same constraints applied as with Latin, i.e. no repeat character and no meaningful sequences.

1.2.4 *Procedure*

Experiment 1 was run on a Dell Latitude D820 laptop with a TFT-LCD of 8.7″ by 13.56″ and a diagonal of 15.4″, set to a resolution of 1280 × 800 (96dpi). Experiment 2 was run on a Dell Optiplex 755 computer, with a Dell 10.5″ by 18.75″ LCD monitor (21.5″ diagonal) attached to it, set to a resolution of 1280 × 800 (96dpi). E-Prime software controlled the timing and presentation of material, recorded responses, and provided feedback on the accuracy of responses.

Participants were shown two strings of 3 (Chinese) or 4 (Latin) characters, each followed by a mask made up of other letters (see Figures 5 and 6). The mask was used to halt the processing of the character string. The task was to determine whether the strings contained the same characters or different characters; where characters were different, just one character was changed. Participants responded by using a rating scale from 'sure same', 'same' to 'different' and 'sure different' using four keys on the keyboard ('A', 'S', 'K', 'L'). This scale allows the participant to adopt different criteria reflecting confidence in their decision. They were encouraged to use all four responses and received feedback on the accuracy of their response with either a green tick or a red cross. Although participants were told that the fonts would change they were told to ignore this.

To equate the level of difficulty across participants, the duration of strings was adjusted based on the results of two practice blocks. In the first practice block sets of strings were displayed at 4 different times. These times were set according to the difficulty of the specific task for the group of participants, i.e. non-Chinese readers started much slower for Chinese characters than Latin. The set where the participant had the most correct responses then determined the display time for the start of the next practice block. During this second practice block the display time was decreased using a staircase adjustment. This aimed to identify the duration for each participant that resulted in a performance level of around 75% (i.e. midway between chance and perfect performance).

In Experiment 1, non-Chinese readers started with Latin, and Chinese readers with Chinese, i.e. starting with the more familiar writing system. The Chinese readers were asked whether they were more familiar with Simplified or Traditional characters prior to the test and did the version containing those characters; all chose Simplified (most participants were

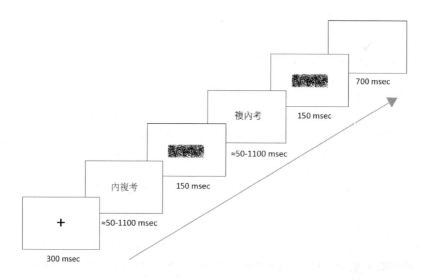

Figure 5: Sequence of screens for Chinese Traditional characters where font is the same but characters are different: correct response is different.

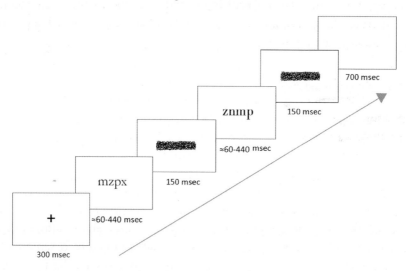

Figure 6: Sequence of screens for Latin characters where font and characters are different: correct response is different.

from mainland China). All Non-Chinese participants did the Simplified version because this was considered to be an easier task as characters are visually less complex. Their practice blocks were extended after pilot work indicated that the task was difficult and more practice would avoid results at chance level (i.e. guessing).

In Experiment 2, as participants were bilingual, half started with Latin and half with Chinese, and all Traditional characters.

Both experiments comprised the same number of 4 blocks of 48 trials in Latin and in Chinese characters.

1.3 Results

Accuracy of responses and reaction times (RT) were measured. A discrimination index p(A) was calculated to determine accuracy as this measures sensitivity and is independent of response bias. Scores range from 0.5 (chance performance) to 1.0 (perfect discrimination). Performance was compared on same and different fonts, and also congruent versus incongruent trials. All graphs include standard errors of the mean bars indicating the variability among participants.

1.3.1 *Experiment 1*

The three groups of participants were analyzed separately and the results are summarized below.

1.3.1.1 *Non-Chinese readers, designers*

An analysis of variance of the discrimination scores revealed a main effect of font tuning ($F(1,11)=10.44$, $p=0.008$, $\eta^2=.45$), and writing system ($F(1,11)=50.05$, $p<0.0001$, $\eta^2=.82$). As illustrated in Figure 7, same fonts are more accurate than different fonts; Latin characters are discriminated more accurately than Chinese, as would be expected.

The interaction between font tuning and writing system ($F(1,11)=3.65$, $p=0.08$, $\eta^2=.25$) was not significant, although the effect size is large. *Post hoc* comparisons using Student-Newman-Keuls of same versus different fonts in each writing system confirm that same fonts are more accurately discriminated than different fonts with Chinese characters ($p<0.05$), but not Latin.

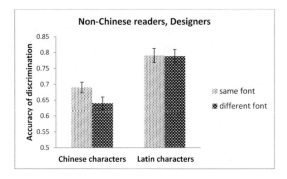

Figure 7: Average discrimination scores for two writing systems comparing same and different font pairs.

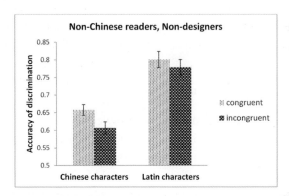

Figure 8: Average discrimination scores for two writing systems comparing congruent and incongruent font pairs.

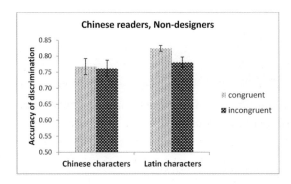

Figure 9: Average discrimination scores for two writing systems comparing congruent and incongruent font pairs.

Overall, Chinese characters, were responded to more quickly than Latin characters ($F1,11)=24.53$, $p=0.0004$, $\eta^2=.69$), but there were no differences in RT for same versus different fonts.

When analyzed in relation to congruence, no differences were found in accuracy or RT for congruent versus incongruent pairs.

1.3.1.2 *Non-Chinese readers, non-designers*

There were no significant differences between same and different font pairs in non-designers, but a main effect of congruency ($F(1,11)=6.78$, $p=0.025$, $\eta^2=.38$) and writing system ($F(1,11)=43.21$, $p<0.0001$, $\eta^2=.80$). The interaction between congruency and writing system is not significant ($F(1,11)=1.0$, $p=0.34$, $\eta^2=.08$). The results are shown in Figure 8. Unlike with designers, Chinese characters were not responded to more quickly than Latin.

1.3.1.3 *Chinese readers, non-designers*

There were no significant differences between same and different font pairs with Chinese non-designers, and no significant effects of congruency. However, the non-significant interaction between congruency and writing system has a large effect size ($F(1,11)=3.23$, $p=0.1$, $\eta^2=.23$) As shown in Figure 9, *post hoc* comparison of Latin characters reveal a significant difference between congruent and incongruent ($p=0.034$), not found in Chinese. There were no RT differences.

1.3.2 *Experiment 2*

1.3.2.1 *Chinese readers, designers*

There were no significant differences for accuracy or RT when comparing same and different fonts or congruency.

1.3.2.2 *Chinese readers, non-designers*

As with designers, there were also no significant differences.

1.3.3 Combining Experiments 1 and 2

Analyzing both experiments together, bilinguals (Hong Kong and UK participants) were more accurate than UK monolinguals, $(F(1,56)=27.87,$ $p<0.0001, \eta^2=.33)$ and Chinese characters were less accurately discriminated $(F(1,56)=45.99, p<0.0001, \eta^2=.45)$. As expected, these results were primarily due to less accurate performance by monolinguals with Chinese characters, resulting in a significant interaction between writing system and reading expertise $(F(1,56)=38.71, p<0.0001, \eta^2=.41)$.

An unanticipated outcome, illustrated in Figure 10, was a significant interaction between writing system and typeface expertise $(F(1,56)=5.70,$ $p=0.025, \eta^2=.09)$. There is a greater difference between the writing systems in non-designers.

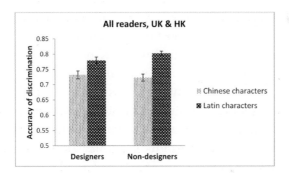

Figure 10: Average discrimination scores for designers and non-designers comparing two writing systems.

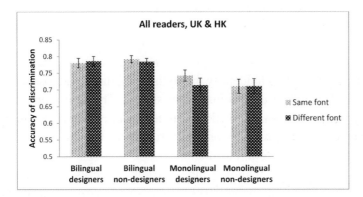

Figure 11: Average discrimination scores for designers and non-designers, according to reading expertise, comparing same and different font pairs.

There was also an interaction between font tuning, reading expertise, and typeface expertise ($F(1,56)=4.32, p=0.042$, $\eta^2=.07$) illustrated in Figure 11, which confirms the difference in outcomes between Experiments 1 and 2.

The RT results indicate that Latin characters are responded to more slowly ($F(1,56)=7.21$, $p<0.01$, $\eta^2=.11$) and there is an interaction between writing system and reading expertise with English monolinguals responding quicker to Chinese characters and slower to Latin, compared to bilinguals ($F(1,56)=27.3$, $p<0.0001$, $\eta^2=.33$).

1.4 Discussion

A clear distinction between the two locations emerges from comparing Experiments 1 and 2, with no effects of font tuning or congruency with Hong Kong participants. The most likely explanation is the level of bilingualism in Hong Kong, compared with UK participants. Although Chinese-reading participants in the UK were also familiar with English, their reading expertise is likely to have been less well developed than the Hong Kong students. Slower RT for English monolinguals reading Latin characters may simply be the result of the design of Experiment 1 as these participants completed the Latin part of the experiment first, and were therefore less familiar with the task.

The results from Experiment 1 suggest that differences may emerge when the writing system is less familiar. The two groups of non-Chinese readers processed Chinese characters in a different manner to Latin, presumably treating them as shapes, rather than meaningful characters. Of particular interest, however, is the font tuning effect found with designers who have no Chinese reading expertise. This suggests that their typeface expertise enables them to identify the stylistic regularities across same font trials which facilitate discrimination of shapes. The definition of expertise in letter perception, adopted by Gauthier et al., [2008], may therefore require refining to include not only expert readers, but also those who are expert in attending to font information.

The non-designers without Chinese reading expertise were also influenced by font information, but this served as interference when conflicting with the character information (incongruent condition). The characters may have been processed as a whole, as suggested by Hsiao and Cottrell [2009], with the most salient differences being between SimSun and SimHei. This may also explain the congruency effect for Chinese readers with ESL when viewing Latin characters. Although their discrimination of Latin characters is good, their unfamiliarity, relative to Chinese, may have resulted in interference from font characteristics.

The only difference in RT within these three groups was designers responding more quickly to Chinese characters than Latin, supporting the idea that Chinese fonts were processed in a different way to non-designers that increased the efficiency of the task.

The larger difference between the two writing systems in accuracy of discrimination for non-designers may reflect the attentional differences described above. As design training focuses on stylistic details of fonts, UK designers may have benefitted from attending to these aspects of Chinese characters, to compensate for lack of reading expertise, whereas attending to Latin fonts may have hindered character discrimination. In these circumstances, competing manners of expertise may misdirect attention to less appropriate aspects of the task.

1.5 Conclusion

The results confirm that designers can demonstrate font tuning in a writing system they cannot read, and congruency between letter identity and font influences performance of non-designers.

References

Beier, S. and Dyson, M. C. (2014). The influence of serifs on 'h' and 'i': useful knowledge from design-led scientific research. *Visible Lang.*, 47(3), pp. 74-95.

Dyson, M. C. (2014). *Applying psychological theory to typography: is how we perceive letterforms special?*, ed. Machin, D., "Visual Communication, " (De Gruyter Mouton, Berlin) pp. 215-242.

Dyson, M. C. and Stott, C. A. (2012). Characterizing typographic expertise: Do we process typefaces like faces? *Vis. Cogn.* 20(9), pp. 1082-1094.

Gauthier, I., Wong, A. C.-N., Hayward, W. G. and Cheung, O. S. (2006). Font tuning associated with expertise in letter perception. *Perception*, 35, pp. 541-559.

Ge, L. Z., Wang, Z., McCleery, J. P. and Lee, K. (2006). Activation of face expertise and the inversion effect. *Psychol. Sci.*, 17(1), pp. 12-16.

Hsiao, J. H. and Cottrell, G. W. (2009). Not all visual expertise is holistic, but it may be leftist: the case of Chinese character recognition, *Psychol. Sci.*, 20(4), pp. 455-463.

Lewis, C. and Walker, P. (1989). Typographic influences on reading. *Brit. J. Psychol.*, 80(2), pp. 241-257.

Majaj, N. J., Pelli, D. G., Kurshan, P. and Palomares, M. (2002). The role of spatial frequency channels in letter identification. *Vision Res.*, 42(9), pp. 1165-1184.

Pelli, D. G. and Tillman, K. A. (2007). Parts, wholes, and context in reading: a triple dissociation. *PLoS ONE*, 2(8), pp. e680.

Pelli, D. G., Burns, C. W., Farell, B. and Moore-Page, D. C. (2006). Feature detection and letter identification. *Vision Res.*, 46(28), pp. 4646–4674.

Richler, J. J., Cheung, O. S. and Gauthier, I. (2011). Holistic processing predicts face recognition. *Psychol. Sci.*, 22(4), pp. 464-471.

Sanocki, T. (1987). Visual knowledge underlying letter perception: font-specific schematic tuning. *J. Exp. Psychol. Human*, 13(2), pp. 267-278.

Sanocki, T. and Dyson, M. C. (2012). Letter processing and font information during reading: Beyond distinctiveness, where vision meets design. *Atten. Percept. Psycho.*, 74(1), pp. 132-145.

Wang, Y. Q. (2006). *Chinese characters 581* (The Language & Culture Press, Beijing).

Wong, A. C. N., Bukach, C. M., Hsiao, J., Greenspon, E., Ahern, E., Duan, Y. and Lui, K. F. H. (2012). Holistic processing as a hallmark of perceptual expertise for nonface categories including Chinese characters. *J. Vision*, 12(13), pp. 1-15.

Wong, A. C. N., Bukach, C. M., Yuen, C., Yang, L., Leung, S. and Greenspon, E. (2011). Holistic processing of words modulated by reading experience. *PLoS ONE*, 6(6), pp. e20753.

Chapter 12

Newspaper text

Lucie Lacava

This chapter examines the many factors to be considered in the selection of a text font for a newspaper. Following a brief look back at the history of newspapers, it explores the process of font selection, from the initial visual considerations, to the paper quality and the printing tests which are critical in determining whether the font is fit to print. The relationship between the personality of the font and the demographics of its future readership will also be explored. The central aim of this chapter is to show that, once carefully selected and tested, design must be used to further improve the readability of text. The correlation between the size of the font, the column width, and the hyphenation and justification greatly affect the readability or comprehension of the text. From theory to practice; two newspaper text case studies, one in English, the other in Arabic, will be discussed.

1.1 Introduction

When I first entered the world of newspapers back in the early 80s, the common mantra was that there were only a handful of newspaper text faces good enough to be used in newsprint. This statement no longer rings true since the last twenty years have been rather prolific in the creation of text fonts custom-designed for specific newspapers. Unfortunately, we may have reached the end of this era, since newspapers are no longer investing in advancing the quality of the print product alone, unless it is part of the big picture and benefits all of the new digital platforms.

Looking back at the history of news publications, it is difficult to pinpoint which text fonts were designed specifically for print, but certainly worth mentioning are: Century created for Century Magazine in 1894, and Ionic No. 5 introduced by Linotype, which made its first appearance in the Evening News of Newark, N.J. in 1926, and was soon adopted by 3,000 newspapers across the US after only 18 months [Anon, 1995].

It seems that we ought to give much credit to England for advancing the quality of typography in newspapers; The London Gazette, first published in Oxford in 1665, considered by many historians to be the first English newspaper [Andrlik, 2014], used Garamond as text font. It eventually made its way to the American colonies as the official newspaper published by his majesty King Charles II. Garamond, and the Old Style Galardes, became the most popular text fonts used in newspapers until the turn of the century. This is not surprising since it was considered to be among the most legible serif typefaces for use in print. Later in 1932, Times New Roman was developed for The Times of London. There is some controversy surrounding the origin of the design of Times New Roman. It may or may not have been the first text font commissioned specifically for usage in a newspaper. Either way, it is certainly the most famous, and worth a second look. Even though it promises to be a fascinating topic, we will not dwell on it in this chapter.

For reasons unrelated to its origins, Times New Roman continues to be one of the most popular, recognizable, and widely used text fonts today. Perpetuated by the fact that it has been made easily available as default in many operating systems such as Mac OS X, and MS Windows, teachers from senior school are known to have repeatedly asked that assignments be printed using none other than Times New Roman, as is the text in this book.

1.2 Fonts and demographics

By the 1900s, magazines were expensive to produce and distribute, but also the content was of interest mostly to a wealthy demographic. On the other hand, newspapers, whose readership was predominantly male, were accessible as a mass medium. Thirteen years after Times New Roman first appeared in The Times of London, Peggy Lang appraised its true worth in a periodical 'Times Roman: A Revaluation' [Lang, 1946]. Of particular interest in the article is her reference to the MEMORANDUM ON A PROPOSAL TO REVISE THE TYPOGRAPHY OF THE TIMES prepared in 1930 by Mr. Stanley Morison, which begins by describing the qualities of the proposed editorial text and heading fonts, and the nature of the reading public of THE TIMES back then.

'It cannot be denied that the approval of such readers will be found if it be shown that… the new typography is worthy of THE TIMES—masculine, English, direct, simple, not more novel than it behoveth to be novel, or more novel than logic is novel in newspaper typography and absolutely free from faddishness and frivolity.' [Lang, 1946]

One can deduce from the above excerpt the importance given to the reader and Morison's perception of how the institution, the quality of the content, and the typography must be functional, as opposed to ornate, and most importantly reflect a sense of national pride. Three generations later, all of these attributes still ring true in the selection of a newspaper font, except for the 'masculine' remark. Today's newspapers, unless aimed at a niche market, are designed to appeal to male and female alike. Lang continues to describe the painstakingly detailed process, which can serve as a template for future generations.

Today a serif font is universally used as newspaper text. The classic traits of a modern newspaper text typeface are: narrow width, increased x-height, small cap-height, open counters, robust serifs, reduced stroke contrast, and looser spacing.

I took part in a legibility study in 1990: a joint effort organized by The Poynter Institute, FL, and the Font Bureau, MA, where a number of text fonts using identical settings were printed on seven different newspaper presses at different institutions across the continent. The results were an eye opener for me since the same text could range from extremely legible to almost illegible from one newspaper to the next depending on paper quality, inking, and the printing process.

A great lesson learned from the above experience was to select a handful of potential text fonts and always run a series of print tests at the same location where they would be printed from. One should never assume that the latest release would fit the bill.

I had the opportunity and privilege to work with world renowned type designers on several occasions where I commissioned custom text fonts for specific newspaper projects. Among the most popular today would be Chronicle, originally designed by Hoefler & Frere-Jones for the Toronto Star. Chronicle Text has since evolved into four grades of Roman, which are progressively more robust to accommodate different degrees of inking on the presses.

A budget allotted for custom-designed newspaper text fonts is increasingly rare. Only for certain high profile redesigns or 'refresh' as we prefer calling them today, might a publisher agree to invest in an entire family custom-designed for a specific title. After all, type is in the DNA of the brand, as the logo alone does not make the brand.

1.3   Case Study 1: the Baltimore Sun redesign

The Baltimore Sun redesign of 2005 was one of those special projects. At the onset of the redesign it was agreed by the powers that be (and the redesign committee) that we would be commissioning custom fonts. I invited Jean François Porchez to propose a series of sketches for text and display typography. Porchez was a great fit since he had previously designed a series of extra condensed Didones, which had some affinities with the display faces in use at the time, and had designed text faces for *Le Monde* in France. It is always wise to carry over some distinctive visual elements from the previous design, and keep some familiarity with the old for the reader's sake and comfort. Furthermore I had seen Porchez speak at the Association Typographique Internationale (ATypI) conference in Vancouver, and was particularly interested in his theory on how the diagonal stress of the lower case round characters accelerated the reading of text. The mandate given to Porchez was to design a series of display Didones, and a matching text family.

Figure 1: Mencken headline, deck and text as it appeared on newsprint.

'Mencken is a Didone for the 21st Century' Jean François Porchez

Looking back at the first half of the 1900s, typographers in North America had adopted Bodoni as the universal style for newspaper headlines. Because of the high contrast between the thicks and thins Bodoni was considered to be one of the most beautiful and elegant fonts of all time, it combined aesthetic appeal with high legibility on newsprint. On the other hand, a modern newspaper text font must have even strokes; however, I personally welcome a little more contrast in the letterform. The inking on newsprint usually makes a text face appear bolder, and fuzzier. The contrast in the letter strokes would actually act as an inkwell, resulting in a sharper crisper appearance on paper. An inkwell (or inktrap) is usually found in type designed specifically for agate. A deeper or exaggerated angle is created where the strokes of a letter meet, allowing the ink to fill the triangle in between, resulting in a sharper corner after printing (Figure 2).

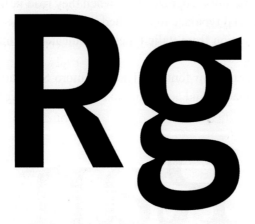

Figure 2: Amplitude, by Christian Schwartz.

Type designer Christian Schwartz explains below his inspiration behind Amplitude, and how inktraps work on newsprint.

'In [design] school, I often used Matthew Carter's Bell Centennial, originally designed for telephone directories, as a display face. I liked the striking and unique forms created by the 'ink traps', spaces carved out where strokes converged that would later be filled in by the expansion of ink on paper. Without these notches, forms would fill in to the point of illegibility. While I was working at Font Bureau, we had a lot of newspaper projects come through the studio, and

I got some hands-on experience with the specific demands of printing small type on absorbent paper. Amplitude is a reaction to these two factors, and is essentially an agate face drawn for display. However, the inktraps function as more than a stylistic quirk on paper, and keep the typeface legible on newsprint at all sizes.'
[Schwartz, n.d.]

My theory is that having a little more contrast between the strokes of a text font will have a similar effect to inktraps. Sharpness and extra contrast are qualities I look for in newspaper text faces.

When possible, it is preferable to keep text and display in the same serif family, resulting in a more harmonious transition, and a subtle but uniform look throughout (Figure 1).

Porchez named the new text font after Henry Louis Mencken (1880-1956), renowned American journalist, editor and columnist for The Sun, and known typophile. According to the London Daily Mail, 'Mencken ventured beyond the typewriter into the world of typography, because he felt Americans did not recognize irony when they read it, he proposed the creation of a special typeface to be called ironics, with the text slanting in the opposite direction from italic types, to indicate the author's humour.'
[ZeCraft, n.d.]

The previous custom fonts in The Baltimore Sun had been in place since the mid-nineties, and according to reader surveys were a main point

Figure 3: Sun text (top), Mencken text (bottom) occupies the same width but has a larger x-height resulting in improved legibility at smaller point sizes.

of dissatisfaction. Generally newspaper readers do not like to change their reading habits, and changing the text font of a newspaper is guaranteed to cause reaction. It is always recommended to make the text face bigger, or at least 'appear bigger' when replacing the text font. Porchez designed Mencken Text to be slightly more condensed than the previous text font, but with a larger x-height, and slightly bolder, making letter forms appear bigger and therefore more legible, without taking up valuable extra line space (Figure 3).

Porchez describes below what makes Mencken a good newspaper typeface. Of particular interest to me is his theory of the 'oblique axis' which I would describe as an aerodynamic design feature which accelerates the eye movement from one letter to the next, giving the text a gentle lift resulting in a faster read (Figure 4 and 5).

'Mencken Text ...is a low contrast Transitional-style typeface designed with an oblique axis, an emphasis on horizontals and possesses open counters. The Text family features more Didonesque [Didot is a typical french typeface from the end of 18th century] capitals to harmonise with the Head versions... ' [ZeCraft, n.d.]

'The first feature is probably a large x-height, strategies to cut small size with more open counters, reducing contrast in the distribution of weight, meanwhile increasing the features of the typeface in order to make key details still visible when very small...

...Based on my experience with Le Monde oblique typeface, I decided to change the main characteristics of Mencken for small sizes: the axis move to oblique, weight contrast is reduced, ending stroke opened (compare "e") to increase the legibility. Newspapers faces are a real challenge today. To fight the narrow effect in text face, the best is to play with proportions of the various letters: Increasing a bit some widths, reducing others, depending on the language you're working on. This way, you can lie to readers about the real general narrowness of a typeface, because of the variations in widths, you created a rhythm, a modulation who help to maintain a sort of fluidity, very important to read easily.'[a]

---

[a] Interview with Tim Ahrens, Questions Design, 27 January 2007

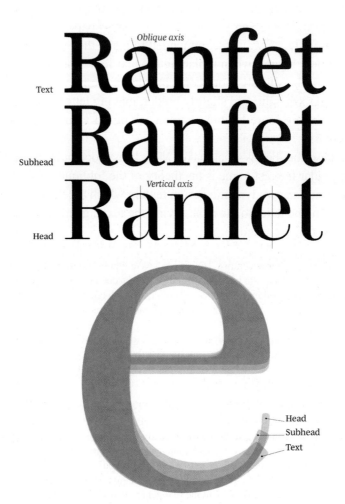

Figure 4: Characteristics are different depending on their size of use. Comparison of Mencken text and display.

Once the beta version of the text font has been tested and approved, then comes the designer's work of setting the right point size and leading based on the column width, followed by the 'h&j' or hyphenation and justification. Software programs such as InDesign and Quark Xpress allow for very sophisticated spacing features. Still, a designer will require several days if not weeks of adjusting by infinite decimals the space between the words and within the words, the 'm or the n width' of the indents, and the

Figure 5: The oblique axis of the text speeds up the eye movement; the large x-height increases legibility; and the didonesque affinities with the display offer a harmonious reading experience in the transition from headline to text.

leading, just to get the right even gray from the text. See Figure 6a and 6b for an example of the Baltimore Sun before and after the redesign.

Today, more broadsheet newspapers are moving to a narrower web width, and are adopting flush left or ragged text to fit the slimmer columns and avoid 'rivers'. Rivers are white space created by having wide gaps between words on multiple consecutive lines, when the type is set too big for the width of the column.

Other factors that can affect legibility are widows and orphans — single words found at the bottom of a paragraph or at the top of a column. These create unwanted white space. Too many consecutive hyphens at the end of lines within a column can also be annoying to the reader. Given the option, I prefer more hyphens versus bad word spacing; of course copy editing can remedy most of these issues.

Figure 6a: the Baltimore Sun: before.

Figure 6b: the Baltimore Sun: after.

1.4   Case Study 2: Al Ittihad redesign

The most challenging project in my career to date has to be Al Ittihad. This political daily newspaper is one of the leading and most highly regarded newspapers in the United Arab Emirates. Following the successful launch of The National in 2008, a startup based in Abu Dhabi, I was invited by the Editor to critique its sister paper Al Ittihad located a couple of floors up in the same building.

Al Ittihad is the oldest Arabic language newspaper in the Emirates. During my critique I said, among other things, that the headlines and text must have been difficult to read, no pun intended, since I had no knowledge of Arabic whatsoever. My observations were based on the fact that the headlines had been horizontally scaled, a technique used to squeeze more words per line, which has the negative effect of distorting the letterforms, while the text font seemed to be filling in at the counters, for example the bowls of letters resembling the lower case e in script. The Editor agreed with my critique and gave me the contract to redesign the entire paper including display and text fonts. The mandate was to redesign the oldest Arabic newspaper in the UAE, while respecting tradition.

First I had to take a crash course in Arabic type design, not literally, but had to do enough research to fully understand the different styles and their origins. I was lucky to have been introduced to Patrick Giasson, who worked for Monotype in London at the time.

I was immediately drawn to Kufi, for headlines, because of its geometric clean and modern appearance, (ironically, Kufic is one of the oldest Arabic styles) comparable to Futura or Helvetica. While the Naskh, a serif like font, seemed more appropriate for text.

Giasson explained through several sketches and email exchanges the differences between the various styles. For text settings and immersive reading, most publications in the Arabic language use modulated fonts, and predominantly in a simplified version of the Naskh style.

Other styles, particularly Kufi, are also in common usage, but in a different context. The geometric simplicity of the Kufi style conveys a contemporary, 'modern' essence. Therefore it is now quite commonly used for headlines in contemporary publishing (magazines rather than newspapers).

The text typeface which had been used by the newspaper up to that point was a very conventional design with very soft letter shapes and very modest counter shapes which tended to fill in even at normal text size. Its soft design and light weight gave it a weak presence on the page.

Submitting a text typeface with more open counter shapes and a more geometric flavour seemed logical and ideal; the new design improved legibility and had a sturdier presence on the page.

The more angular and clearly defined design of the characters also gave more tonality to the text while still striking a good balance between conventional design and a contemporary modulation.

Giving strong angularity to the characters achieved two goals, at the micro- and macro- levels. Firstly, the deeply incised counter shapes would act as ink traps at small sizes. Secondly, the angularity of the design would also echo and harmonise with the confident geometry and tapered finials of both the Headline typefaces and the Sections typeface.

In so doing a stylistic consistency could be kept in the typographic palette of the newspaper, from the largest elements of the Sections titles, through the Headlines and down to the smallest text settings.

During a process which lasted 14 months, we introduced four custom designed Arabic typefaces. These modern display faces form a strong link with the paper's Islamic heritage. The end result was greater legibility of the text, and an evolutionary redesign, acclaimed both inside and outside the newsroom.

Once the proposed text A was approved (Figure 7), Giasson made further adjustments to improve the text (Figure 8).

Since compact leading can result in clashes of small marks above tall ascending letters, shortened versions of tall letters with small marks were created to avoid the risk of collision with low descending letters from the line above. Creating a more regular global line height results in less disruption in reading flow. Giasson's horizontally compact design is space saving, allowing more words per line than a typical Arabic newspaper typeface.

In Arabic, several letters share the base shape and are only differentiated by dots' number and position. In Ittihad Text, markedly larger dots than average text typefaces offer clearer letter differentiation therefore increased legibility even at very small sizes such as finance/sports listings and agate (Figure 9).

فن الخط يحضر بتميز في طريق الحرير بالشارقة	فن الخط يحضر بتميز في طريق الحرير بالشارقة	فن الخط يحضر بتميز في طريق الحرير بالشارقة

يمثل مهرجان الفنون الإسلامية بالشارقة في دورته الحادية عشرة، والذي يحمل شعار على طريق الحرير والمقام في متحف الشارقة للفنون ومتحف الفن العربي المعاصر في الشارقة حاليا، عيدا للفنانين والخطاطين والمتذوقين للإبداع، وهذا المهرجان الدولي الذي انبثق عن مهرجان المرئي والمسموع، يحمل في ثناياه عمق الحضارة الأصيلة لشعوب سكنت في ثلاث قارات، وعلمت الإنسانية أبجدية الخط والكتابة والفنون، بحيث يجيء مهرجان على طريق الحرير كنافذة مفتوحة للتفاعل الثقافي والحضاري بين الفنانين العالميين على أرض الإمارات. ومن

يمثل مهرجان الفنون الإسلامية بالشارقة في دورته الحادية عشرة، والذي يحمل شعار على طريق الحرير والمقام في متحف الشارقة للفنون ومتحف الفن العربي المعاصر في الشارقة حاليا، عيدا للفنانين والخطاطين والمتذوقين للإبداع، وهذا المهرجان الدولي الذي انبثق عن مهرجان المرئي والمسموع، يحمل في ثناياه عمق الحضارة الأصيلة لشعوب سكنت في ثلاث قارات، وعلمت الإنسانية أبجدية الخط والكتابة والفنون، بحيث يجيء مهرجان على طريق الحرير كنافذة مفتوحة للتفاعل الثقافي والحضاري بين الفنانين العالميين على أرض الإمارات. ومن

يمثل مهرجان الفنون الإسلامية بالشارقة في دوره الحادية عشرة، والذي يحمل شعار على طريق الحرير والمقام في متحف الشارقة للفنون ومتحف الفن العربي المعاصر في الشارقة حاليا، عيدا للفنانين والخطاطين والمتذوقين للإبداع، وهذا المهرجان الدولي الذي انبثق عن مهرجان المرئي والمسموع، يحمل في ثناياه عمق الحضارة الأصيلة لشعوب سكنت في ثلاث قارات، وعلمت الإنسانية أبجدية الخط والكتابة والفنون، بحيث يجيء مهرجان على طريق الحرير كنافذة مفتوحة للتفاعل الثقافي والحضاري بين الفنانين العالميين على أرض الإمارات. ومن

Current font	Proposal A	Proposal B

Figure 7: Current and proposed text comparison. Proposal A was selected.

However, the narrow space-saving proportions of the characters of Ittihad Text + large dot size for increased legibility could result in potential dot collisions with other dots or base letters. To address this, Giasson reviewed all letter combinations.

Careful adjustment of dot position to ensure good legibility and avoid dot collisions were done via OpenType coding, i.e. automatic adjustment as the line is composed, so users do not need to make manual adjustments.

UAE newspapers use Latin numeral characters. The Latin numerals usually stand out from the Arabic text; in their usual structure, the weight distribution emphasizes the vertical strokes. Pen-derived Arabic scripts, such as Naskh, are modulated on a more horizontal stress. To remedy this, Giasson created numerals with weight emphasis on the horizontal strokes, to better blend/harmonize with the Arabic script (Figure 10).

Newspaper redesigns have the reputation of introducing white space to the detriment of the written word. The new Ittihad text did not require any additional editing or trimming of stories, while offering an improved reader experience.

◆ حين تحدّث أرسطو في كتابه "فن الشعر" عن الأجناس الأدبية فرّق بين الشعر الدرامي والشعر الغنائي، وأولى عناية فائقة للصنف الدرامي. أما الشعر الغنائي فسكت عنه لأن منتجَه أقل درجة من منتج الأشعار الدرامية، لا سيما أن الشاعر الذي يكتب قصيدة غنائية إنما يبرع في توليد المجازات والاستعارات لا غير. أما الشاعر الذي يكتب شعراً درامياً فإنه يبرع في صناعة الحكايات التي ينجزها "أشخاص فاعلون هم الأشخاص الذين يخلقهم الشاعر" ويدخلهم في صراع درامي مرير من شأنه أن يولّد لدى المتلقي انفعالي الشفقة والخوف، ويؤدّي إلى التطهير منهما في الآن نفسه. لهذا كله فصل أرسطو بين المأساة والملحمة والشعر الغنائي جازماً بأن المأساة جنس درامي يتولّى القول والفعل فيه الأشخاص الذين يخلقهم الشاعر. أما الملحمة فيتولى القول فيها الشاعر حيناً، والأشخاص الذين يخلقهم حيناً آخر. في حين أن الشعر الغنائي إنما يرد على لسان منتجه فهو الذي يتولّى القول ، ولا وجود فيه لحكاية وأشخاص فاعلين يتولون الفعل والقول. لذلك حين نقوم بتحديد مفهوم الغنائية وضبط الفوارق بين الشعر الغنائي، والشعر الدرامي، والشعر الملحمي، قصد رصد التحولات التي طرأت على الشعر الغنائي نتيجة التنافس بين الأجناس الأدبية، ندرك أن مفهوم القصيدة الغنائية في الثقافة العربية مفهوم مضلّل بالتمام والكلية. بل إنه مفهوم يحجب أكثر مما يكشف.

وهذا يعني أن الخطاب النقدي العربي المعاصر ظل يتعامل مع الشعر من خارجه ويتبنّى التصنيفات القديمة دون أن يقع التفطن إلى أن القصيدة التي توصف بكونها غنائية قد أثْرَت نسها بمنجزات العديد من الأجناس الأدبية والفنون والمعارف. لقد استفادت من التقنيات الروائية ومن السرد بصفة عامة. اغتذت ببعض التقنيات السينمائية، واستلهمت المسرح أيضاً. وهي إنما تستمد شعريتها من تخطّيها لمفهوم الغنائية. يكفي هنا مثلاً أن نتلفّت إلى تجربة محمد درويش، وهي تجربة كثيراً ما توصف بأنها تجربة غنائية محض، وسنبيّن أن نعت هذه التجربة بكونها تندرج ضمن النمط الغنائي إنما يمثّل إفقاراً لمنجزات صاحبها وحجباً لثراء تجربته. يكفي أن نعيد مساءلة فصيدة درويش وسنجد أنفسنا مرغمين على الاعتراف بالفضل لشاعر مضى مع الإيقاع حتى حتفه. إن قصيدة درويش قد عصفت بالحدود والضفاف الفاصلة بين الأجناس الأدبية وتمكنت من فتح آفاق لا عهد للشعر العربي بمثلها. لقد تمكنت من ابتناء قاعها الأسطوري وأثْرَت نفسها بالعناصر الدرامية فتخطّت الغنائية. وعمدت أحياناً أخرى إلى التوغل داخل رحاب معرفية، بموجبها، تماهى الشعري مع الفكري والمعرفي، وانفتح الشعر على الفلسفة وأسئلة الوجود، وكفّت الكتابة عن كونها مجرد إنشاء وتمرّس بالكلام لتصبح فعل وجود. ومعنى كونها فعل وجود أنها تنهض لتنازل قدراً لم يخترْه الشاعر لكنه اختار أن ينازله ويواجه عدمه الخاص.

Figure 8: Final text sample.

Figure 9: Larger dots offer clearer letter differentiation.

بلغت قيمة مشتريات الأجانب، غير العرب، من الأسهم أمس نحو 111,89 مليون درهم في حين بلغت قيمة مبيعاتهم نحو 79,94 مليون درهم. وبلغت قيمة مشتريات المستثمرين العرب، غير الخليجيين، نحو 119,62 مليون درهم وقيمة مبيعاتهم نحو 127,61 مليون درهم.

أما بالنسبة للمستثمرين الخليجيين، بلغت قيمة مشترياتهم 56,59 مليون درهم في حين بلغت قيمة مبيعاتهم نحو 36,32 مليون درهم خلال نفس الفترة. ونتيجة لهذه التطورات، بلغ إجمالي قيمة مشتريات الأجانب، غير الإماراتيين، من الأسهم نحو 288,09 مليون درهم لتشكل ما نسبته 52,19% من إجمالي قيمة المشتريات، في حين بلغ إجمالي قيمة مبيعاتهم نحو 243,87 مليون درهم لتشكل ما نسبته 44,18% من إجمالي قيمة المبيعات، ليبلغ بذلك صافي الاستثمار الأجنبي نحو 44,22 مليون درهم كمحصلة شراء.

أرقام — 0123456789

بلغت قيمة مشتريات الأجانب، غير العرب، من الأسهم أمس نحو 111,89 مليون درهم في حين بلغت قيمة مبيعاتهم نحو 79,94 مليون درهم. وبلغت قيمة مشتريات المستثمرين العرب، غير الخليجيين، نحو 119,62 مليون درهم وقيمة مبيعاتهم نحو 127,61 مليون درهم. أما بالنسبة للمستثمرين الخليجيين، بلغت قيمة مشترياتهم 56,59 مليون درهم في حين بلغت قيمة مبيعاتهم نحو 36,32 مليون درهم خلال نفس الفترة. ونتيجة لهذه التطورات، بلغ إجمالي قيمة مشتريات الأجانب، غير الإماراتيين، من الأسهم نحو 288,09 مليون درهم لتشكل ما نسبته 52,19% من إجمالي قيمة المشتريات، في حين بلغ إجمالي قيمة مبيعاتهم نحو 243,87 مليون درهم لتشكل ما نسبته 44,18% من إجمالي قيمة المبيعات، ليبلغ بذلك صافي الاستثمار الأجنبي نحو 44,22 مليون درهم كمحصلة شراء.

أرقام — 0123456789

بلغت قيمة مشتريات الأجانب، غير العرب، من الأسهم أمس نحو 111,89 مليون درهم في حين بلغت قيمة مبيعاتهم نحو 79,94 مليون درهم. وبلغت قيمة مشتريات المستثمرين العرب، غير الخليجيين، نحو 119,62 مليون درهم وقيمة مبيعاتهم نحو 127,61 مليون درهم.

أما بالنسبة للمستثمرين الخليجيين، بلغت قيمة مشترياتهم 56,59 مليون درهم في حين بلغت قيمة مبيعاتهم نحو 36,32 مليون درهم خلال نفس الفترة. ونتيجة لهذه التطورات، بلغ إجمالي قيمة مشتريات الأجانب، غير الإماراتيين، من الأسهم نحو 288,09 مليون درهم لتشكل ما نسبته 52,19% من إجمالي قيمة المشتريات، في حين بلغ إجمالي قيمة مبيعاتهم نحو 243,87 مليون درهم لتشكل ما نسبته 44,18% من إجمالي قيمة المبيعات، ليبلغ بذلك صافي الاستثمار الأجنبي نحو 44,22 مليون درهم كمحصلة شراء.

أرقام — 0123456789

Figure 10: Roman numerals harmonize with Arabic text.

1.5 Conclusion

Since writing this chapter, my faith in the creation and proliferation of new text faces for newspapers has been renewed. During the past few months I have been working on a newspaper project in South East Asia. Thanks to a generous budget, and the need for a common look and feel across all platforms, I was able to commission an extensive custom serif family, which includes text, allowing me to gather fresh information for my next chapter on newspaper fonts.

References

Ahrens, T., Questions Design, 27 January 2007

Anon (1995) Customized type makes new Sun easier to read. *The Baltimore Sun*, http://articles.baltimoresun.com/1995-09-18/news/1995261066_1_text-type-new-sun-ionic, accessed 21 May 2015

Andrlik, T. (2014) London Gazette: the Crown's official mouthpiece. http://allthingsliberty.com/2014/02/london-gazette/, accessed 21 May 2015

Lang, P. (1946). Times Roman: A Revaluation In Alphabet and Image 2. (Shenval Press, London).

Schwartz, C. (n.d.) Amplitude. http://www.christianschwartz.com/amplitude.shtml, accessed 21 May 2015.

ZeCraft (n.d.) Online at http://www.zecraft.com/fonts/Mencken, accessed 21 May 2015.

Chapter 13

Perception of fonts: perceived personality traits and appropriate uses

Dawn Shaikh and Barbara Chaparro

This chapter discusses the personality traits of onscreen typefaces and the perceived appropriateness of typefaces for a variety of onscreen document types including website ads, written assignments, email, résumés, spreadsheets, and web pages. Results from two studies will be discussed. In Study 1 participants rated the perception of 40 typefaces' personalities using 15 semantic differential scales. The results of a factor analysis revealed three correlated factors named Potency, Evaluative, and Activity based on Osgood, Suci and Tannenbaum [1957] that explain the perception of onscreen typeface personalities. Potency describes the ruggedness and masculinity of a typeface, Evaluative describes the perceived beauty and value of a typeface, and Activity describes the excitement, loudness, and speed of a typeface. Comparison of semantic differential charts for serif, san serif, display, and script typefaces revealed the serif and san serif typefaces to be neutral across factors; the bolder, blockier display typefaces were perceived as more Potent, more Evaluative; and the script typefaces were perceived as less Potent, more Evaluative, and less active. In Study 2, typeface appropriateness was evaluated for a variety of document types. General findings imply that for documents such as website ads, the most appropriate typefaces are those that have personalities congruent with the featured product's personality. For all other onscreen documents the most appropriate typefaces were those that were higher on Potency and Evaluative than Activity, and higher in perceived legibility.

1.1 Introduction

Standing at any bus stop or sitting in any airport terminal one quickly notices that reading from a screen is now the norm. According to a 2014 study by Mary Meeker of Kleiner Perkins, Americans spend approximately five hours a day in front of a computer, smartphone, or tablet; the Chinese average 6.5 hours a day in front of these devices [Epstein, 2014]. In Canada, folks who own a smartphone claim to spend 86% of their time consuming information on a screen [The Globe and Mail, 2014]. Newsfeeds warn of email apnea, distracted driving, and electronic screen syndrome. All signals point to the fact that consumers are spending more and more time staring at screens.

With screen-based information consumption on the rise, typeface design has shifted from print to screen focus. Services like Google Fonts and TypeKit popularized the concept of web fonts and quickly brought proprietary and open source typefaces to screens. Google's Open Sans (by Steve Matteson), Roboto (by Christian Robertson), and Droid Sans/Serif (by Steve Matteson) were specifically designed for use on screens. According to Google Fonts, these three typeface families receive approximately 90 trillion views monthly [Google.com, 2014]. Microsoft's Advanced Reading Technologies team has pioneered fonts for screens through their ClearType efforts and most recently the release of Sitka, by Matthew Carter, for the Internet Explorer 11 reading view featured in Windows 8.1 [Blogs.msdn. com, 2014]. Sitka is the first Microsoft-designed typeface 'with scientific legibility studies integrated directly into the design process' [Blogs.msdn. com, 2014].

Onscreen typeface research often focuses on legibility and layout issues. This chapter focuses on the perception of onscreen typefaces - in terms of personality and the perceived appropriateness of typefaces for various document types [Shaikh, 2007].

1.1.1 *Semantic differential scale*

The application of the semantic differential scale (SDS) to typeface connotation research has become a standard. Since the introduction of SDS in 1957, 15 of the 20 studies reviewed employed some variation of SDS. The number of semantic scales (adjective pairs such as good/bad, old-fashioned/modern, etc) used in these studies varied from 10 to 28. Osgood *et al.* [1957] defined semantic meaning as 'the relation of signs to their significance' (p. 3). The semantic differential 'relates to the functioning of representational processes in language behavior and hence may serve as an index of these processes' (p. 9). In his seminal text, Osgood justified the use of the semantic differential scale as follows – to allow us to use

> 'linguistic encoding as an index of meaning we need (a) a carefully devised sample of alternative verbal responses which can be standardized across subjects, (b) these alternatives to be elicited from subjects rather than emitted so that encoding fluency is eliminated as a variable, and (c) these alternatives to be representative of the major ways in which meanings vary' (p. 19).

Researchers use a 7-point scale to allow participants to judge both direction and intensity of their responses. The semantic differential provides participants with the concept (e.g., a sample of type) and a set of bipolar adjectives on a scale that has varying points of intensity.

In repeated tests of SDS, Osgood *et al.* [1957] consistently found three factors to explain the meaning of various stimuli: evaluative, potency, and activity. The names of the factors were based on the highest loading scale and have become the standard factors to explain semantic meaning. Osgood *et al.* reported that SDS will work with virtually any concept: personality traits, sonar signals, aesthetics, advertising, politics, mass communication, and art. Other researchers have applied SDS to typeface personality, writing sample evaluations, art, advertisements, and much more. The evaluative factor measures worth of items (good/bad, beautiful/ugly). The potency factor indicates the strength or power of items being judged (strong/weak). The activity factor implies the action level of the stimuli (active/passive, fast/slow).

1.1.2 *Semantic differentials scales and typeface connotation research*

The use of adjectives scales to rate typefaces was first done by Ovink [1938] who used adjectives such as force, strength, precision, fineness, warmth, and comfort. Participants rated the typefaces on a 5-point scale denoting how appropriately the typeface represented the idea. His analyses resulted in three categories of typeface connotation: (1) luxury/refinement, (2) economy/precision, and (3) strength.

The idea of using semantic differential scales (SDS) to determine typeface connotations is attributed to J. Brinton [1961]. SDS use a 7-point scale with bipolar adjective pairs as anchors. The methodology (or some variation of it) quickly became popular in this area of research and has been used by 15 of the 20 reported typeface personality studies since 1961.

A factor analysis of semantic scale data was first conducted by Tannenbaum, Jacobson, and Norris [1964]. Based on 25 scales (adjective pairs) Tannenbaum *et al.* found four factors describing typeface personality: Evaluation, Potency, Activity, and Complexity. Using a similar methodology, Wendt [1968] based his study on a German researcher's (Hofstätter) SDS. Wendt created a typeface-specific set of scales and subsequently found four factors: (1) weight, strength or firmness v. looseness or laxity, (2) tradition, despondency, paltriness v. progress and generosity, (3) order and reliability, and (4) extraordinary v. ordinary. Five factors were identified by Rowe [1982]. She labeled her factors as Potency, Elegance, Novelty, Antiquity, and Evaluation. Similarly, Bartram [1982] evaluated type with scales created specifically for type by designers and found four factors: Evaluation, Potency, Mood, and Activity. More recently, Henderson, Giese, and Cote [2004] used SDS and factor analysis to determine 'impressions' of type which generated four factors: pleasing/displeasing, engaging/boring, reassuring/unsettling, and prominent/subtle. Osgood's dimensions of Evaluative, Potency, and Activity formed the basis for a 2006 study by Doyle and Bottomley. Breaking away from the traditional SDS, this study used an 11-point scale and three single-item scales. The single-item scales used adjective clusters from Osgood's dimensions as anchors (for example on the positive side of Activity the researchers put the adjective cluster active, lively, young, fast and on the negative Activity side was a cluster containing passive, still, old, slow). The researchers claimed this allowed them to assess the same semantic dimensions without as much time investment. However, the use of three single-item scales eliminated the ability to differentiate one typeface's personality from another.

Brumberger's [2001] study used bipolar adjectives split on their own 7-point scale. She established 3 factors describing typeface personality which she labeled as elegance, directness, and friendliness. Mackiewicz and Moeller [2004] followed Brumberger's example of not using bipolar adjective pairs by correlating personality ratings with subjective comments from participants.

The use of SDS confirms that readers attribute personality traits to typefaces. With some level of consistency, Osgood's dimensions of Evaluative, Potency, and Activity show up as constructs to describe typeface personalities.

1.1.3 *Addressing methodological concerns with previous studies*

Two primary methodological concerns were identified with previous typeface personality studies: stimuli selection and semantic scales.

1.1.3.1   *Stimuli*

The most commonly used stimulus has been the alphabet in upper and lower case with a set of numbers and sometimes symbols [Tannenbaum *et al.,* 1964; Kastl and Child, 1968; Wendt, 1968; Benton, 1979; Bartram, 1982; Walker *et al.,* 1986; Brumberger, 2001; Mackiewicz and Moeller, 2004; Shaikh *et al.,* 2006]. The problem with using the alphabet is that it does not adequately represent the visual pattern of words and continuous text. The letter combination 'uvw' does not occur in text but only as a pattern in the English alphabet. The use of the alphabet removes any 'effect created by the visual pattern of the letters' [Morrison, 1986, p. 237]. The need for realistic strings of text is reinforced by Matthew Carter: 'A letter only has properties relative to the letters around it' [as cited by Boser, 2003, p. 46]. Other researchers have used text from the Declaration of Independence [Poffenberger and Franken, 1923], the quote 'Now is the time for all good men...' [Davis and Smith, 1933], the letters NRESTA [Tantillo *et al.,* 1995], and unspecified lines of text [Brinton, 1961]. Such famous text samples invoke connotations for many users and may vary depending on age and related demographics. Morrison [1986] and Ovink [1938] avoided the alphabet and meaningful text by using samples that were a third-degree approximation to English [Morrison] or nonsense text [Ovink].

The studies presented below rely on third-degree approximation to English. Such text appears to be English by mimicking the visual patterns of the language but has no meaningful content. Third-degree approximation to English ensures that each trigram within a 'word' is a combination that routinely appears in English (the word eating has the following trigrams: eat, ati, tin, and ing). Third-degree approximation also addresses the issues of content-based confounds since it has no inherent meaning.

1.1.3.2   *Semantic scales*

The selection of semantic scales has varied by study as well. In some cases, the scales are based on Osgood's [1957] initial research; but in other cases, the selection is left up to designers who may not use the same terminology as laypersons. Additionally, some of the studies did not ensure that the semantic scales used were connotative in nature. Using terms that are denotative for typefaces can create confounds and factors that are challenging to explain. Outside of Osgood's work, which has been applied to a variety of areas, no other standard approach exists for choosing the bipolar adjectives.

In order to choose semantic scales in our studies, a literature review was completed of 20 previous studies. Content analysis was conducted on all of the adjectives. The most commonly used adjectives were identified. Additionally, guidance was taken from Osgood's [1957] seminal research and recommendation for choosing bipolar adjective pairs:

1. Choose approximately three closely-related scales to represent each factor
2. Try to choose scales that load maximally on one factor and minimally on other factors
3. Choose scales that are relevant to the concept being tested
4. Choose scales that are connotative rather than denotative in nature
5. Ensure the anchors are considered polar opposites in terms of positive and negative

The final scales chosen included at least three scales from the main factors found in Osgood's work (evaluative, potency, and activity). The scales were used in several typeface studies which indicated they were relevant in the field of typeface research and had been established by previous work to be bipolar opposites in this context. All scales were connotative in nature rather than denotative.

1.2 Study 1: perceived personality of onscreen typefaces

Typographers routinely describe typefaces using personality descriptors. Secrest [1947] labeled Baskerville as 'a bit of a bore' and 'exact and mechanical' while calling Caslon full of 'quiet dignity'. Roboto, the font encountered by one billion Android smartphone users, is described as friendly, 'like a friend's handwriting' [Daily Intelligencer, 2014]. De Groot's Calibri, the default font in Microsoft Office applications, is 'warm' and 'soft' [Lucasfonts.com, 2014] (Figure 1). Since typefaces are often similar, Secrest speculated that designers must think of typefaces as they think of people - by minute distinguishing details and in terms of personalities. Do casual consumers of onscreen information consistently attribute such personality descriptors to typefaces?

Baskerville

Caslon

Roboto

Calibri

Figure 1: Baskerville, Caslon, Roboto, and Calibri fonts.

An online survey using semantic differentials was used to investigate this. Responses from 379 participants revealed a consistent approach to personifying 40 select onscreen typefaces (see Table 1).

Table 1: Typefaces evaluated using semantic differential scales.

Serif	Sans Serif	Display	Script/ Handwriting
Calisto	Arial	Agency	Bradley Hand
Cambria	Berlin Sans	Bauhaus 93	Brush Script
Centaur	Calibri	Chiller	French Script
Courier New	Century Gothic	Broadway	Gigi
Georgia	Consolas	Curlz	Informal Roman
High Tower Text	Corbel	Impact	Kristen
Lucida Bright	Lucida Console	Jutce	Lucida Handwriting
Perpetua	Incised 901 Lt BT	Papyrus	Viner Hand
Poor Richard	Trebuchet	Playbill	Monotype Corsiva
Times New Roman	Verdana	Tempus Sans	Vivaldi

Participants rated a 40-word nonsense text sample (third order approximation of English) on 15 semantic scales allowing respondents to judge both direction and intensity of their responses [Osgood *et al*, 1957]. Figure 2 shows the passage and semantic scales.

Humb exas frop moof? A seart shing 0183 dureck de poch. Fiss pla th marticather wishell owney lival.
Jo Lecry poss mar, adel wook daustion gre questraw deny. Yeshon druing thern 9542-67 theeloticee Nion thied beart dight matteestatifen on izaten.

Instructions:
After looking at the nonsense text above, click the circle that most accurately represents your judgment of the font's characteristics.

Passive	○ ○ ○ ○ ○ ○ ○	Active		Happy	○ ○ ○ ○ ○ ○ ○	Sad
Warm	○ ○ ○ ○ ○ ○ ○	Cool		Delicate	○ ○ ○ ○ ○ ○ ○	Rugged
Strong	○ ○ ○ ○ ○ ○ ○	Weak		Calm	○ ○ ○ ○ ○ ○ ○	Exciting
Bad	○ ○ ○ ○ ○ ○ ○	Good		Feminine	○ ○ ○ ○ ○ ○ ○	Masculine
Loud	○ ○ ○ ○ ○ ○ ○	Quiet		Hard	○ ○ ○ ○ ○ ○ ○	Soft
Old	○ ○ ○ ○ ○ ○ ○	Young		Fast	○ ○ ○ ○ ○ ○ ○	Slow
Cheap	○ ○ ○ ○ ○ ○ ○	Expensive		Relaxed	○ ○ ○ ○ ○ ○ ○	Stiff
Beautiful	○ ○ ○ ○ ○ ○ ○	Ugly				

This typeface is legible.
Agree ○ ○ ○ ○ ○ ○ ○ Disagree

3 of 20   Next Font--->

Figure 2: Examples of text sample, semantic scales, and legibility question.

Results from a factor analysis revealed three factors to describe the typefaces: Evaluative, Potency, and Activity. The three factors accounted for approximately 66% of the variance. Osgood *et al.,* [1957] described these factors as follows:

• Potency reflects typefaces judged as strong, powerful, or forceful

• Evaluative reflects typefaces viewed as valuable, worthy, or important.

• Activity reflects typefaces considered to be full of energy, movement, and action.

The factors were correlated; Potency and Activity were positively correlated, and Potency and Evaluative were negatively correlated. The typefaces viewed as high in Potency were likely to be higher in Activity. Conversely, the Potent typefaces were likely to be lower on the Evaluative factor. The typefaces seen as more Potent, less Evaluative, and more Active tended to be the bold, dark, block-like typefaces (Broadway, Agency, Playbill). Scripted typefaces (Vivaldi, French Script, Monotype Corsiva) tended to be less Potent, more Evaluative, and less Active. Serif and Sans Serif typefaces generally represented the middle of each factor.

Figure 3 shows the differences across typeface classes on the scale. Script/Handwriting typefaces were distinctly more feminine, beautiful, expensive, soft, delicate, relaxed, quiet, happy, weak, and warm. Display typefaces were characterized as ugly, cheap, and bad. While sans serif and serif typefaces had much in common, subtle differences were noticeable: serifs were more delicate, beautiful, expensive, warm, and old.

Within each class (Figures 4-7), typefaces varied across the scales to reveal typeface-specific perceptions of personality. Among the serif typefaces, Courier New stood out as the extreme on many scales - masculine, hard, stiff, ugly, cheap, bad, passive, weak, cool, and old. Poor Richard was characterized as the most feminine, active, and exciting of the serifs. The two monospaced sans serif typefaces, Lucida Console and Consolas were both outliers on the sans serif scale - more masculine, rugged, stiff, and cheap. Incised 901BLT was the most soft, delicate, relaxed, and passive of the sans serifs. The most feminine sans serif typeface was Century Gothic. Within the display typefaces, Curlz was the most feminine and Impact was the most masculine, hard, rugged, stiff, ugly, and sad. Vivaldi, from the script/handwriting group, was labeled as feminine, delicate, expensive, and old. The loudest, most exciting, and happiest of the script/handwriting typefaces was Gigi.

Typeface Classes

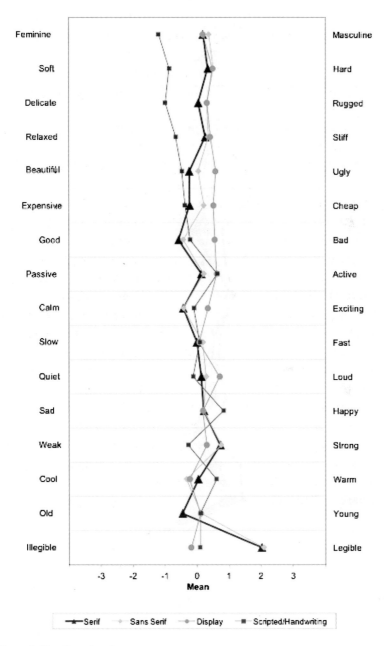

Figure 3: Typefaces by class.

Serif Type Class

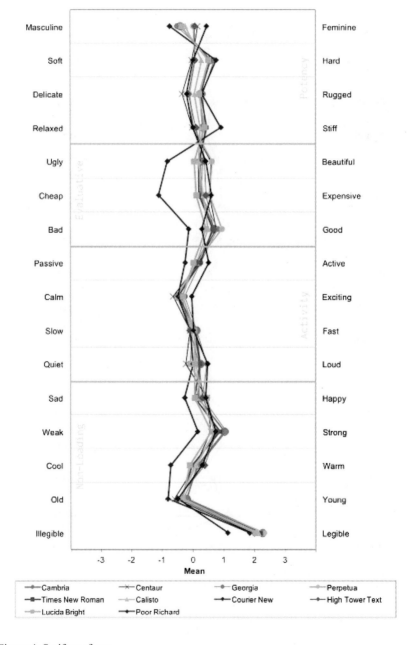

Figure 4: Serif typefaces.

Sans Serif Type Class

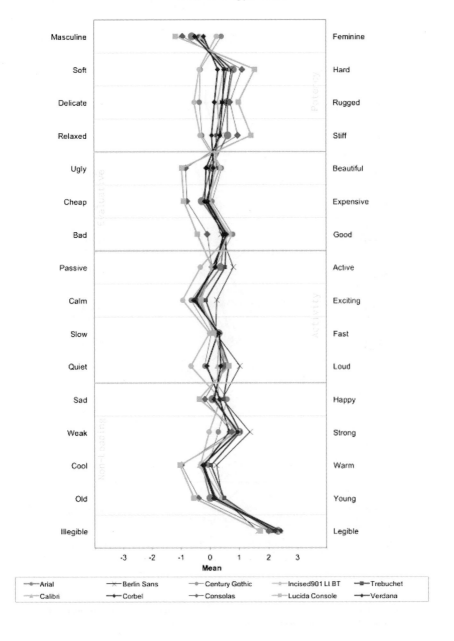

Figure 5: Sans Serif typefaces.

Digital fonts and reading

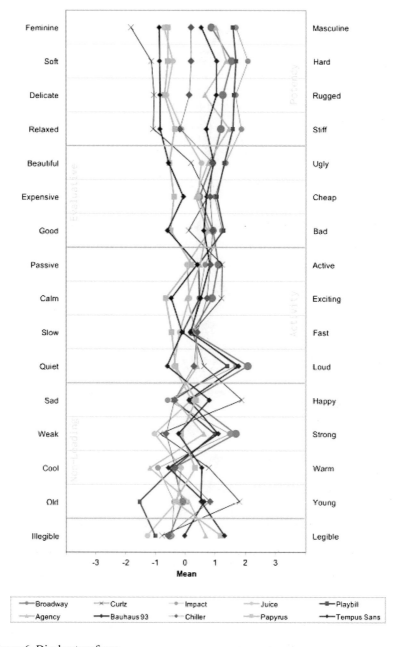

Figure 6: Display typefaces.

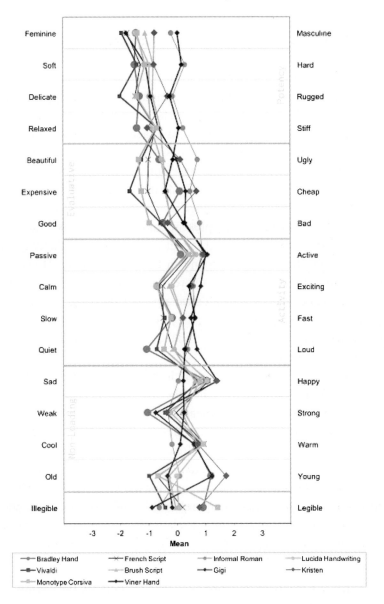

Figure 7: Script/Handwriting typefaces.

Previous research on typeface personality has utilized a variety of semantic scales which have resulted in variations of the factors proffered by Osgood *et al.* [1957]. For example, Tannenbaum *et al.* [1964] found an Evaluative, Potency, and Activity factor containing semantic scales very similar to those found in this study. However, they found two additional factors labeled as Complexity and Physical. Wendt [1968] found only two factors that did not have anything in common with the results of this study. His factors were described as a feminine factor and a poorly defined factor. The work of Rowe [1982] resulted in five factors with some similarity to the ones identified in the present study. Rowe established a Potency factor very similar to the one found. She also found an Elegance factor that was comparable to the factor labeled as Evaluation in the current study. However, she found a Novelty, Antiquity, and Evaluation factor that did not correspond to the factors in the present study. Similarly, Bartram [1982] also discussed factors labeled as Evaluation, Potency, and Activity which were equivalent to the factors found in the present study. However, he also had a Mood factor. All of these previous studies share some common methodological concerns: they all used alphabet samples; they all used at least one denotative semantic scale; they did not control for x-height of the typefaces when presenting stimuli; and they all used samples sizes that are too small for factor analysis.

Based on Osgood's [1957] research, the Evaluative factor typically accounts for more variance than the other two factors. This has also been found in typeface personality research by Tannenbaum and colleagues [1964] and Bartram [1982]. However, the results of our study indicate that the Potency factor (36.1%) accounts for a larger percentage of the variance than the Evaluative (17.9%) and Activity (11.8%) factors. Rowe [1982] also found the Potency factor to account for the most variance. The three factors found in our study were correlated. No previous typeface personality studies have reported factor correlations; in fact, most of them have reported using orthogonal/varimax rotations.

1.3 Study 2: perceived appropriateness of typefaces for various document types

Typefaces are often designed for a specific purpose - Inconsolata was 'designed for code listings' [Levien.com, 2014]; Vivaldi is 'ideal for invitations, announcements, and other work requiring a distinctive, formal appearance' [Myfonts.com, 2014] (Figure 8).

Inconsolata

Vivaldi

Figure 8: Inconsolata and Vivaldi.

Typographers, communications experts, and marketing professionals often attribute appropriateness to different typefaces – 'Fresh produce always seems to want an improvised, handwritten sort of message, while high-tech applications demand a cool, technocratic look' [Spiekerman and Ginger, 2003, p. 126]. Studies have confirmed that in paper-based studies, participants are able to identify typefaces that are more appropriate for specific purposes [Haskins, 1958; Walker, Smith, and Livingston, 1986; Brumberger, 2003a, 2003b; Doyle and Bottomley, 2006]. Additional research focused on print has shown that user success and happiness increased when uses and typefaces were congruent [Brumberger, 2001; Doyle and Bottomley, 2004]. Do casual consumers of onscreen text perceive typefaces to be more appropriate for certain types of documents?

Data was collected for 261 participants using an online paired comparison activity where stimuli were compared two at a time with a forced choice question - which is more appropriate? Participants evaluated website ads for seven products and résumés for seven careers. Using the data from Study 1 discussed above, typefaces were aligned with products and careers that were determined through additional research [Shaikh, 2007] to be similar on the three factors (Potency, Evaluative, Activity). Additionally participants evaluated a school assignment, email, spreadsheet, and sample of website text. For these text-heavy documents, typefaces were selected across the three factors with a consideration for legibility. Similar to Study 1, all text was third order approximation of English to avoid a content confound. Samples of stimuli are shown in Figures 9-11. The careers used in the résumés included a Florist, DJ, Paralegal, Butcher, Human Resources

Assistant, Statistician, and Webmaster. The products used in the ads included a hammer, perfume, luggage, cakes, burglar alarm, insulation, and cooking oil.

Figure 9: Website ad for cakes, perfume, and luggage.

Figure 10: Assignment sample.

Figure 11: Email sample.

Data revealed that participants consistently agreed on the typefaces that were most appropriate for each of the six document types. However, when choosing appropriate typefaces, legibility trumped congruency for all document types except website ads. When choosing type for website ads, appropriate typefaces were more likely to share similar perceived personality factors (Activity, Potency, and Evaluative) for the product advertised. For example, website ads for items strong on the Potency factor (hammer) were reported to be most appropriate when displayed in a typeface strong on the factor (Impact, Bauhaus93); ads for items weak on the Potency factor (cakes) similarly were reported to be most appropriate with typefaces weak on the factor (French Script, Vivaldi). The same was true for the Evaluative factor - items like perfume that were viewed as high on the Evaluative factor were best represented by a typeface that was high on the Evaluative scale, such as French Script or Vivaldi. The Activity factor showed similar, but less pronounced patterns.

The website ad stimuli findings were similar to those of Poffenberger and Franken [1923] where he found a similar typeface to be appropriate for perfume and building material advertisements. Data from Doyle and Bottomley [2006] support the idea that typeface personality should match the content in logos and advertisements. Doyle and Bottomley also theorized that the Evaluative factor was the most important factor in determining appropriate typefaces for products. Our findings do not support their theory. Our study results are based on fewer products than the studies conducted by Doyle and Bottomley and the typefaces that were high on the Evaluative factor differed considerably between the two studies. Our study suggests the impact of the Evaluative factor is much less that what Doyle and Bottomley found.

For all text-heavy documents (including résumés for specific careers), the most appropriate typeface was the most legible which corresponded to the typefaces reported to be neutral across all factors. The legible, neutral typefaces were typically serif and sans serif. These findings are similar to those of Brumberger [2003b] where participants perceived the typeface Arial as most appropriate for all text passages she evaluated. The scripted typeface in her studies was judged to be least appropriate regardless of content.

1.4 Summary

Results of this research indicate that there are three underlying factors which explain the perception of onscreen typeface personality - Potency, Evaluative, and Activity. In addition, the research suggests that online readers are able to identify appropriate typefaces for a variety of documents commonly encountered. Overall, typefaces that are viewed as neutral in terms of personality and high on perceived legibility are deemed as appropriate typefaces for most onscreen documents (assignments, email, résumés, spreadsheets, and website text). For website ads, the appropriate typeface is most often the one that is congruent with the product in terms of personality.

References

Bartram, D. (1982). The perception of semantic quality in type: Differences between designers and non-designers. *Information Design Journal*, 3, pp. 38-50.

Benton, C. L. (1979). The connotative dimensions of selected display typefaces. Paper presented at the Annual Meeting of the Association for Education in Journalism, Houston, TX.

Blogs.msdn.com, (2014). *MSDN Blogs*. [online] Available at: http://blogs.msdn.com/b/ie/archive/2014/03/04/introducing-reading-view-in-ie-11.aspx [Accessed 20 Sep. 2014].

Boser, U. (2003, September 1). A man of letters. *U.S. News & World Rep*ort, 135, pp. 44-46.

Brinton, J. E. (1961). The 'feeling' of type faces. *CA Magazine*, 3, pp. 43-45.

Brumberger, E. R. (2001). The rhetoric of typography: Five experimental studies of typeface personality and its effects on readers and reading. PhD. New Mexico State University, Las Cruces, NM.

Brumberger, E. R. (2003a). The rhetoric of typography: The awareness and impact of typeface appropriateness. *Technical Communication*, 50(2), pp. 224-231.

Brumberger, E. R. (2003b). The rhetoric of typography: The persona of typeface and text. *Technical Communication*, 50(2), pp. 206-223.

Daily Intelligencer, (2014). Google Is Designing the Font of the Future. [online] Available at: http://nymag.com/daily/intelligencer/2014/07/google-is-designing-the-font-of-the-future.html [Accessed 20 Sep. 2014].

Davis, R. C., & Smith, H. J. (1933). Determinants of feeling tone in type faces. *Journal of Applied Psychology*, 17, pp. 742-764.

Doyle, J. R., & Bottomley, P. A. (2004). Font appropriateness and brand choice. *Journal of Business Research*, 57, pp. 873-880.

Doyle, J. R., & Bottomley, P. A. (2006). Dressed for the occasion: Font-product congruity in the perception of logotype. *Journal of Consumer Psychology*, 16(2), pp. 112-123.

Epstein, Z. (2014). Horrifying chart reveals how much time we spend staring at screens each day. [online] BGR. Available at: http://bgr.com/2014/05/29/smartphone-computer-usage-study-chart/ [Accessed 20 Sep. 2014].

Google.com, (2014). Google Fonts. [online] Available at: https://www.google.com/fonts#Analytics:total [Accessed 20 Sep. 2014].

Haskins, J. B. (1958). Testing suitability of typefaces for editorial subject-matter. *Journalism Quarterly*, 35, pp. 186-194.

Henderson, P. W., Giese, J. L., & Cote, J. A. (2004). Impression management using typeface design. *Journal of Marketing*, 68, pp. 60-72. Retrieved online September 15, 2006, from http://www.new-edgeinc.com/pdf/Typeface.pdf.

Kastl, A. J., & Child, I. L. (1968). Emotional meaning of four typographical variables. *Journal of Applied Psychology*, 52, pp. 440-446.

Levien.com, (2014). Inconsolata. [online] Available at: http://levien.com/type/myfonts/inconsolata.html [Accessed 20 Sep. 2014].

Lucasfonts.com, (2014). LucasFonts | Case Studies > Calibri + Consolas. [online] Available at: http://www.lucasfonts.com/case-studies/calibri-consolas/ [Accessed 20 Sep. 2014].

Mackiewicz, J., & Moeller, R. (2004). Why people perceive typefaces to have different personalities. Paper presented at the International Professional Communication Conference, Minneapolis, MN.

Morrison, G. R. (1986). Communicability of the emotional connotation of type. *Educational Communications and Technology Journal*, 34, pp. 235-244.

Myfonts.com, (2014). Vivaldi™ - Webfont & Desktop font « MyFonts. [online] Available at: https://www.myfonts.com/fonts/linotype/vivaldi/ [Accessed 20 Sep. 2014].

Osgood, C. E., Suci, G. J., & Tannenbaum, P. H. (1957). The measurement of meaning. Urbana, IL: University of Illinois Press.

Ovink, G. W. (1938). *Legibility, atmosphere-value and forms of printing type*. Leiden, Holland: A.W. Sijthoff's Uitgeversmaatschappij N.V.

Poffenberger, A. T., & Franken, R. B. (1923). A study of the appropriateness of type faces. *Journal of Applied Psychology*, 7, pp. 312-329.

Rowe, C. L. B. (1982). The connotative dimensions of selected display typefaces. *Information Design Journal*, 3, pp. 30-37.

Secrest, J. M. (1947). Personalities in type designs. *Printer's Ink*, 218(7), pp. 52-53.

Shaikh, A. D., Chaparro, B. S., & Fox, D. (2006). Perception of fonts: Perceived personality traits and uses. Retrieved February 01, 2006, from http://psychology.wichita.edu/surl/usabilitynews/81/PersonalityofFonts.htm

Shaikh, A. (2007). Psychology of onscreen type: Investigations regarding typeface personality, appropriateness, and impact on document perception. PhD. Wichita State University.

Spiekermann, E. and Ginger, E. (2003). *Stop stealing sheep & find out how type works*. 1st ed. Berkeley, Calif.: Adobe Press.

Tannenbaum, P. H., Jacobson, H. K., & Norris, E. L. (1964). An experimental investigation of typeface connotations. *Journalism Quarterly*, 41, pp. 65-73.

Tantillo, J., Di Lorenzo-Aiss, J., & Mathisen, R. E. (1995). Quantifying perceived differences in type styles: An exploratory study. *Psychology & Marketing*, 12, pp. 447-457.

The Globe and Mail, (2014). Digital overload: How we are seduced by distraction. [online] Available at: http://www.theglobeandmail.com/life/relationships/digital-overload-how-we-are-seduced-by-distraction/article17725778/?page=all [Accessed 20 Sep. 2014].

Walker, P., Smith, S., & Livingston, A. (1986). Predicting the appropriateness of a typeface on the basis of multi-modal features. *Information Design Journal*, 5, pp. 29-42.

Wendt, D. (1968). Semantic differentials of typefaces as a method of congeniality research. *The Journal of Typographic Research*, 2, pp. 3-25.

Chapter 14

Legibility and readability of Arabic fonts on Personal Digital Assistants PDAs

Mrouj Almuhajri and Ching Y. Suen

Electronic reading opens new avenues especially with the advance of modern reading devices. The new generation of Personal Digital Assistants PDAs is more popular and more affordable. Therefore, it is necessary to re-evaluate typefaces used in these devices as they form a substantial component in reading. In this chapter, we present a survey which has been conducted to identify Arab community preferences among some selected fonts on PDAs, to infer the popularity of using these devices for reading. The results were taken as a basis to conduct experiments in order to investigate six Arabic fonts on PDAs from the perspective of legibility and readability to come up with the best fonts. Two experiments were conducted to evaluate the legibility of the selected fonts using a novel method named M-Short-Exposure method for isolated Arabic letters and connected letters. Then, another experiment for readability was also performed considering reading speed and comprehension of running texts. Thus, our findings identify the most legible and/or readable Arabic font(s) among the tested fonts. Moreover, some recommendations have been made on better use of legible and/or readable Arabic fonts for different purposes.

1.1 Introduction

The E-book market has blossomed because of the appearance of Personal Digital Assistants (PDAs) which have become more durable, more colorful, and more multifunctional. Hence, many improved features of these digital devices stimulate e-reading in a significant way leading to the need to test typefaces used on them.

Reading legibility and readability are two important concepts in this study. Tracy [1986] defined legibility as the ability to read and recognize letters in a clear and an easy way. In contrast, readability is described as how comfortable visual processing is while reading, and how comprehensible the long text is.

1.2 Related work

Legibility and readability are two concepts with a relationship which may cause confusion between them due to some overlap in their test methods. High legibility is very important for reading as it affects reading speed and the effort needed to identify letters in the right way. Based on history, we see many methods have been produced to determine the level of legibility of typefaces. Based on Beier [2012] the main test methods for legibility are: reader's preferences, visual accuracy threshold, search task, and continuous reading. Moreover, readability is related to reading performance as it tests the quality of text and the ability to recognize it in meaningful groupings. To test readability, several methods are used with running text including reading speed, word-search speed, eye-tracking, comprehension, and reader fatigue. Nevertheless, many aspects can influence readability, such as spacing, margins, use of words, and reader knowledge and skills.

1.2.1 *Methodology of testing legibility and readability*

1.2.1.1 *Reader's preferences*

People's opinion is a concern in this method where participants are asked to rank their preferences based on typefaces, sizes, styles, etc. Shaikh [2007] has evaluated 40 Latin typefaces through 15 semantic differential scales (SDS) as pairs of opposite adjectives including legibility. Her results reveal that serif and sans serif typefaces are more legible than display and script typefaces. Following the same procedure, Nikfal [2011] investigated 20 Arabic typefaces with four personalities. As a result, some fonts were defined with high legibility like Times New Roman and Simplified Arabic and they were recommended to be used in official documents, reports, and forms. Voorhees [2011] evaluated the congeniality of reading on digital platforms in comparison with paper of high resolution by reading five short text stories (one per device) in different orders. Feedback was collected from participants considering device type and features available for reading. The Kindle was recorded as the favorite, and the laptop and iPod touch were the least preferred. Also, the ability to change typeface and page layout were rated the most desirable feature.

1.2.1.2 *Visual accuracy threshold*

In this method, the focus is on identifying letters and words regardless of their comprehension. To measure visual accuracy, several approaches have been suggested such as the rapid exposure method. Participants are exposed to the stimulus for a very short time in which the eye is unable to move from one fixation to another. The tachistoscope was one of the earliest tools used, known as Flash Recognition Training (FRT), to measure recall of visual information. It has been used to rank the legibility of a set of characters and numerals [Suen, 1986]. Nowadays, these tools have been superseded by computers.

The short-exposure method of a single character was used in Beier and Larson [2010] based on Macromedia Flash MX. Each letter was exposed for 43 milliseconds, and then participants had to name it. Thus, accuracy of visual characters was measured, and hence type legibility. Moreover, the legibility of two Latin ClearType fonts compared to traditional serif fonts has been investigated using the short-exposure method [Chaparro, Shaikh and Chaparro, 2006]. A collection of letters, digits, and symbols were exposed for 34 milliseconds. Findings were positive for the new fonts of ClearType. However, the old style digits used in Constantia font like 0, 1, and 2 caused confusion with letters o, l, and z.

1.2.1.3 *Continuous reading*

This method is used to measure readability of typefaces by testing them in running texts. One technique used to evaluate the reading process is to measure the reading speed and comprehension or accuracy. However, many factors could be considered in these measurements like leading and spacing in text [Chaparro, Baker, Shaikh, Hull and Brady, 2004]. From the reading speed and comprehension level, it was revealed that margins gave better performance despite a lower speed. On the other hand, leading did not affect the performance of reading but influenced the participant's satisfaction. Another factor is font size and style which are considered in measuring legibility and readability. Ramadan [2011] conducted an experiment on university students who were asked to read 24 passages on a computer screen with four Arabic fonts in three font sizes. After recording reading speed and testing comprehension by answering given questions, the outcomes showed that both variables (font style and size) are significant.

Another technique to estimate reading performance and behavior in running text is eye tracking. It provides rich data from eye movements related to the process of reading. The effect of font size and font type on online reading has been examined through eye-tracking [Beymer, Russell and Orton, 2008]. Fixation durations were significantly longer with smaller size (10 pt) type leading to slower reading. Also, serif fonts gave slightly better reading performance than sans serif fonts. In addition, another study has been conducted on Arabic typefaces of different sizes using eye-tracking measurement [Al-Wabil and George, 2010]. Participants read aloud electronic passages on a computer screen and eye movements and oral reading were recorded. The finding suggests bigger sizes (16 or 14 pt) produce better reading performance.

1.3 The survey

In this survey, we aimed to collect data about the popularity of using Personal Digital Assistants PDAs, such as the iPad, for reading in Arab Communities; and Arab preferences regarding the fonts used on those electronic devices.

1.3.1 *Font selection*

Certain Arabic typefaces were selected for this survey. It was difficult to make a decision among a huge number of Arabic typefaces based on a short line of text. The Arabic Font Specimen Book [2009] was used as a reference.[a] Therefore, 13 typefaces, shown in Figure 1, were chosen considering six factors: type function, style classification, publisher, compatibility with platforms, format, multi-script support and, previous studies.

1.3.2 *Methodology*

Participants were recruited through the Arab association living in Montreal, Canada. The final analysis was based on 53 participants (36 male and 17 female) in which 39 of them reported that they do use PDAs for general reading and e-book reading.

---

[a] The quality of this publication has been strongly challenged by experts in the field [Nemeth, 2009].

The text used is shown in Figure 2, part of a poem written by one of the earliest Arab lexicographers and philologists, Al-Khalil Al-Farahidi, which has all Arabic alphabetical letters in the same text. Also, it is showing all alphabetical letters in isolated shape standing alone beside each other. Although the size was fixed for all 13 fonts in this survey, the height of each font was different. Therefore, we needed to normalize all fonts to the same height considering the ratio between height and width. Figure 2 shows examples of two fonts (Deco Type Naskh and Uthman Script Hafs) before and after normalization.

Apple iPad OS 6.1.3 devices with retina display were used to run the survey. Among several Apple survey applications, iSurvey v 2.10.7 was chosen to build and run the survey because it has the required features.

نص حكيم نص حكيمـ ﺽ ﺣﻜﻴﻢ نص حكيم نص حكيم نص حكيم نص حكيم

| Tanseek Modern Pro | Hemear LT | Hasan Enas | Geeza Pro | DecoType Naskh | Badiya Reg | Almohannad |

نص حكيم نص حكيم نص حكيم نص حكيم نص حكيم نص حكيم

| Yakout Reg | Uthman SH | Times New Roman | Tahoma | Myriad Arabic | Janna Reg |

Figure 1: Fonts used in the survey.

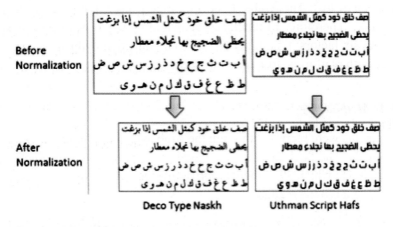

Figure 2: Normalization process for two different fonts.

1.3.2.1 *Design and procedure*

Each participant went through two different sections in the survey and completed them. The first section was about personal information and reading habits using Personal Digital Assistants PDAs. The second section introduced the 13 selected fonts to be rated. Each font image was shown one at a time in the middle of the screen and followed by three descriptions: Legible, Easy to read, and Comfortable for eyes. Participants were asked to rate each font image using five-point scales ranging from Strongly Agree to Strongly Disagree.

1.3.3 *Results and discussion*

General information showed that Apple devices, iPad and iPhone in particular, are the most commonly used devices in personal Arabic e-reading activities with a total of 73.02%. Kindle and similar devices which use e-ink gave low usability, and the reason behind this was suggested because of the lack of Arabic language support up to the time of the survey. Figure 3 illustrates the number of users for each specified gadget.

The second section gave us rich data about the selected fonts. The top six fonts preferred by participants were: Almohanad, Geeza Pro, Hasan Enas, Times New Roman, Uthman SH, and Yakout Reg. These fonts got the highest agreement and lowest disagreement scores for the average of all descriptive characteristics. In contrast, Tanseek Modern Pro has the lowest legibility rate, and Deco Type Naskh was considered as the hardest to read and the least comfortable for the eyes. Therefore, we avoided these two fonts in our final decision due to their poor performance. Finally, we minimized the number of fonts regarding our results, analyses, and comparisons among fonts. Thus, a group of six fonts only were selected for the next experiment: Almohanad, Badiya Reg, Geeza Pro, Hasan Enas, Uthman Script Hafs, and Yakout Reg.

1.4 Experiments and results: legibility experiments

Among the methods mentioned in the related work section to test font's legibility, the short-exposure method of a single character was chosen as the basis for our test. Although it has not been tested on Arabic yet, we

Digital fonts and reading

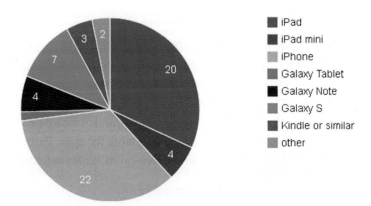

Figure 3: Number of users for each specific gadget in the survey.

thought that we cannot use it for many reasons. First of all, the Arabic language has different features and clear structure which influence the way of recognizing letters. Isolated letters could be simply identified if they are shown in a single presentation. For example, although the letters in Figure 4 have the same structure, the number and the position of diacritic dots would distinguish a letter and make it recognizable from others. In addition, unlike the Latin language, letters should be connected in order to create words, and each Arabic letter could have several forms depending on its position. It has been claimed that when an Arabic word contains two or more connected letters which have dots, it becomes difficult to differentiate among them especially in smaller sizes [Abubaker and Lu, 2012]. So, applying the same technique with Arabic typefaces to discover their legibility might give an inaccurate result.

Figure 4: Different letters of the same shape but different number and position of diacritic dots.

1.4.1 *Pilot Test*

To emphasize our thoughts, we ran a pilot study using the same method of short-exposure of a single character on a small number of participants (6 male and 6 female). Six fonts selected from the survey were prepared in which each letter in each font produced an image of 1.3 × 1.3 square inches in size 18 pt. All letters stood on a fixed virtual baseline in the middle. A small tool was developed in order to implement the test in Google Chrome browser.

Test material is located in the area of fixation point where participants were asked to focus on. The distance between the participants and screen was set to 50 cm approximately. Participants were asked to press the next button to trigger an exposure of a single character, and name it aloud. Exposure time was fixed for each letter at 50 milliseconds which is half of the time suggested for the human eye to not only receive a photon, but to pass a signal to the brain for conscious response [Gibbs, 1996]. Each participant got six exposures of different fonts with random chosen letters and in a random order. A mask of black dots was exposed after each letter in order to remove the afterimage appearance after the original image ceased to control the timeframe on the retina [Beier and Larson, 2010]. Figure 5 shows an example of a test character and the image which followed.

As expected, the accuracy of all 72 exposures gave 97.2% correct results with a total of two errors only. That supports the need for a modified method to suit Arabic font features.

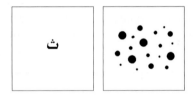

Figure 5: The test character (left) and after image (right) sample.

1.4.2 *Experiment 1: letter legibility*

Isolated letters are tested using the proposed method M-Short-Exposure, in which M refers to modified.

1.4.2.1 *Participants, material, and apparatus*

A total number of 138 participants (53 male and 85 female) engaged in the legibility and readability experiments. All were students who speak Arabic as their native language.

For each of the six fonts, a 3 × 3 matrix was prepared using Adobe Photoshop CS6 with nine Arabic isolated letters in which each letter takes a place in a single cell. The size of the matrix image was fixed at 4.5 × 4.5 square inches. Letters have been normalized in size to avoid the influence of font size. Six common Arabic nouns of three letters, which is the basic word structure, and with positive meanings have been assigned to each matrix. One and only one word can be generated from each matrix in some specific directions. The six remaining cells in each matrix were filled with random letters. Figure 6 shows an example of the matrix used in this experiment. Numbers and symbols are excluded in this study. Directions for words assigned in each matrix are limited to right-left, top-down, and diagonals from right to left only. All other directions are discarded from this study due the nature of Arabic language. Figure 7 illustrates the allowed and eliminated directions.

ح	س	ن
ف	ش	أ
ض	ج	ذ

Figure 6: Matrix sample for letter legibility experiment.

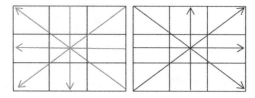

Figure 7: Allowed directions (left) and eliminated directions (right).

Two Apple iPads and one iPad mini OS 6.1.3 devices with retina display were used to conduct the experiment. Each device was set to full bright display, however, subjects were able to adjust the brightness setting as they prefer. Also, landscape mode and auto correction and completion were turned off. Furthermore, an Apple application named 'i3arabi' was designed and coded using Xcode and Objective-C programming language to implement the experiments.

1.4.2.2 *Design and procedure*

Three participants at a time took part using the three available PDAs. At the beginning, general instructions were given. Then, the six matrix samples were shown respectively. Each matrix image was located in the fixation point on which subjects had been asked to focus. The distance between participants and devices was flexible according to their personal preferences. Once the start button is pressed, a matrix is exposed for 1000 millisecond which is equal to the time we used in a pilot study to expose a single character multiplied by nine and added to 550 millisecond for direction complexity. Next, a mask of black dots is exposed too for the same period of time to remove the afterimage effect on the retina. After that, multiple choices were given including three different words of the same number of letters to choose from or choose 'I cannot recognize the word'. Each participant got six exposures in the same order in which each one represents a font involved in this study. There were six words assigned to six matrices, each one represented in a single font. Although the participants received matrix samples in order (font1, font2, font3,…, font6), they still got them in random order of words, i.e. word1 may be presented in font4 to one participant, but in font6 to another.

1.4.2.3 *Results and discussion*

In the M-Short-Exposure method of Arabic isolated letters, 80 results were recorded for iPad devices and 58 results for iPad mini for each font. So, we employed independent samples and got the Z -score-table, and it presented no differences between iPad and iPad mini at $p > 0.01$. Therefore, if the participant correctly identified the word from the presented letters on any device, the trial was counted as correct. The mean values for all fonts on the two devices are shown in Figure 8. It is obvious that Geeza Pro and Hasan Enas fonts were the most legible fonts in isolated letter presentation. Moreover, Almohanad and Badiya Reg fonts showed better performance on the smaller device (iPad mini) which may be due to their larger design on smaller preview.

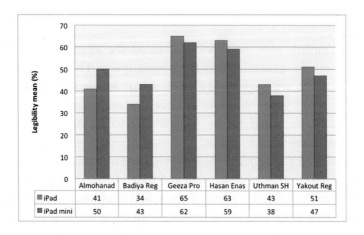

	Almohanad	Badiya Reg	Geeza Pro	Hasan Enas	Uthman SH	Yakout Reg
■ iPad	41	34	65	63	43	51
■ iPad mini	50	43	62	59	38	47

Figure 8: The mean values of letter legibility test on iPad and iPad mini.

1.4.3 *Experiment 2: word legibility*

This experiment is an extension to the previous experiment to promote M-Short Exposure method considering connected Arabic letters.

1.4.3.1 *Material*

Three text material groups were prepared for this experiment. A collection of 18 common Arabic nouns of different complexity were chosen. The complexity is measured by the number of letters in the word. Least complex: three letters; medium complex: four letters; and most complex: five or six letters. Words were scattered among the three groups with the same balance of complexity. Then, fonts were assigned to words in which each font appears once only within a group, but three times at three different complexity levels within all groups. Hence each font got the chance to appear three times in each level of complexity but with different words. For each group, words were scattered randomly in a bounded area of size 3 × 1.7 square inches. Figure 9 shows a sample of the text material for the first group.

Figure 9: A sample text material for word legibility experiment.

1.4.3.2 *Design and procedure*

General instructions were given at the beginning so that the participants had a trial sample to absorb the idea, then three samples were displayed sequentially in the fixation zone they were asked to focus on. Once the sample is triggered, it lasts for 1000 millisecond which is the same period used in the previous experiment. As done before, a mask of black dots is displayed after for the same duration to control the after-image impact. Next, participants were asked to fill six text boxes using a virtual touch keyboard with words they remember. Although abilities of short-term memory in participants may differ, it has been found that the average number of items people may remember after a short appearance is four [Machizawa, Goh and Driver, 2012]. By this way, we ensure that the most recognizable font among six words will catch the participant's attention first. So, there is no problem at all if participants could not remember all the words. Although spelling mistakes could lead to incorrect results, the selected words had been chosen to be easy to spell and commonly used. Therefore, the possibility of a typo was expected to be low.

1.4.3.3 *Results and discussion*

First of all, the results have been gathered for the six tested fonts based on participants' correct answers in each group over both PDAs. Then, the mean value of all groups for each font was calculated. When the results were analyzed using ANOVA among the three groups to see the impact of complexity levels on participants' answers, a significant difference within each font reached the F value critical at 99%. That means, words' complexity level had their impact on fonts legibility. Therefore, we took the mean of all three groups for both devices as shown in Figure 10 to deduce the most legible font in this study. Hence, Uthman SH was observed to be the most legible font regarding connected letters (words) while Yakout Reg font was the least.

1.4.3.4 *Final legibility results and discussion*

Integration between the two experimental results was needed to get legibility result as a single component. In particular, the average results coming from the three groups of words experiment have been calculated and then added to the letter legibility results. Figure 11 demonstrates the combined results for the examined fonts. Legibility of Geeza Pro, Uthman SH and Almohanad fonts in order was the highest while the remaining fonts showed lower legibility with large differences.

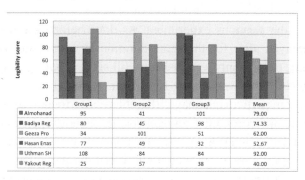

	Group1	Group2	Group3	Mean
■ Almohanad	95	41	101	79.00
■ Badiya Reg	80	45	98	74.33
■ Geeza Pro	34	101	51	62.00
■ Hasan Enas	77	49	32	52.67
■ Uthman SH	108	84	84	92.00
■ Yakout Reg	25	57	38	40.00

Figure 10: The results of word legibility experiment.

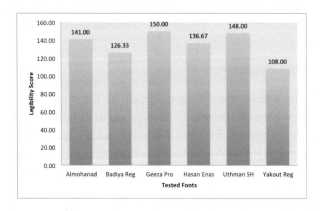

Figure 11: The combined results of legibility experiments.

1.5 Readability experiment

1.5.1 *Material*

Text passages for the readability experiment were taken from Qiyas test [National center for assessment in higher education, 2001]. However, we slightly modified them to bring them to the same level of difficulty with a mean number of 113 words. Six passages of different general topics were randomly assigned to each font we tested. The contents do not contain extremely rare words or technical terms. The size for all used texts was fixed at 18 pt. For each passage of each font, two multiple choice comprehension questions were picked.

1.5.2 *Design and procedure*

Participants were instructed to read at normal speed as they usually do, and informed in advance that reading speed will be automatically recorded. Furthermore, participants were told to read with concentration because if they passed the passage to the question page, they could not go back. Post-reading comprehension test may lead participants to scan text rather than reading it and looking for the answers [Darroch, Goodman, Brewster and Gray, 2005]. They began reading when the 'Start Reading' button was pressed to display a passage and trigger the timer. Upon completing the passage, a 'Done' button was pressed and reading speed was recorded. Figure 12 demonstrates the button strategy used in this application. Then, the comprehension questions page was displayed. Participants kept reading the passages displayed in order of the appearance of different fonts, and answered the related questions.

1.5.3 *Results and discussion*

For each font, the results of two comprehension questions were used to measure the comprehension level. Furthermore, reading speed (RS) was calculated by dividing the total number of words included in the passage by the total time elapsed to finish reading in seconds. To analyse these results, we tried to find the correlations between these two factors. The correlation coefficient value of all fonts showed negligible value between comprehension and reading speed.

Figure 12: Sample of readability experiment.

With respect to devices, the effect of device display size has been studied statistically. For both factors: reading comprehension and reading speed, we employed two independent samples regarding device type with a different number of observations to all the tested fonts. At p>0.01, there is no significant difference for comprehension factor of all fonts. However, some fonts showed significant differences in reading speed. In particular, Almohanad, Geeza Pro, and Yakout Reg fonts showed a positive impact when devices were varied. To be specific, the reading speed increased when the size of display becomes smaller. That could suggest awareness of font usage based on the targeted display type. This might have happened because these fonts have thicker strokes compared to the others. Thus, their similar design may feature them on iPad mini with a clearer view. Figure 13 and Figure 14 illustrate comprehension and reading speed means for all tested fonts. Almohanad and Yakout Reg fonts produced the highest levels of comprehension. In addition, the fonts which achieved the highest reading speed were Yakout Reg and Uthman SH.

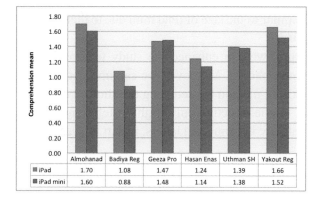

	Almohanad	Badiya Reg	Geeza Pro	Hasan Enas	Uthman SH	Yakout Reg
iPad	1.70	1.08	1.47	1.24	1.39	1.66
iPad mini	1.60	0.88	1.48	1.14	1.38	1.52

Figure 13: Mean values of reading comprehension for all tested fonts.

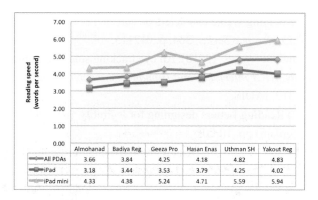

	Almohanad	Badiya Reg	Geeza Pro	Hasan Enas	Uthman SH	Yakout Reg
All PDAs	3.66	3.84	4.25	4.18	4.82	4.83
iPad	3.18	3.44	3.53	3.79	4.25	4.02
iPad mini	4.33	4.38	5.24	4.71	5.59	5.94

Figure 14: The mean values of reading speed for all tested fonts.

1.6 Conclusion

Several studies have been published regarding fonts' legibility and read-ability using different screen types. Yet, with the abrupt change in screen size and the advance of e-reading features, the demand of testing new devices has been raised. Arabic fonts were tested from the legibility and readability point of view on PDAs. From our results, some deductions, recommendations, and suggestions have been proposed: Arabic e-reading becomes more popular among Arab communities using Apple devices; recommendations could be provided for Uthman Script Hafs and Geeza Pro fonts to be used in e-books which require high legibility; it is recom-mended for Almohanad, Geeza Pro, and Yakout Reg fonts to be used when displays are similar to the size of iPad mini due to their better performance at a smaller size.

In the future, we can enhance the study to examine other types of tablets and smart phones. Moreover, we can improve the functionality of M-Short-Exposure method by: reducing the allowed directions in isolated letters matrix to one direction only (right-to-left), and by fixing the level of word complexity in connected letters, in part to keep the focus on fonts' performance.

References

Abubaker, A. and Lu, J. (2012), The optimum font size and type for students aged 9-12 reading arabic characters on screen: A case study," *Journal of Physics: Conference Series,* 364, p. 012115.

Al-Wabil, A. and George, R. (2010). An eye tracking study of arabic typography readability, *IHCI Interfaces and Human Computer Interaction,* pp. 309–312, IADIS.

Beier, S. (2012) Reading Letters designing for legibility. (BIS Publishers, 1057 DT Amsterdam) pp. 10-20.

Beier, S. and Larson, K. (2010). Design improvements for frequently misrecognized letters, *Information Design Journal,* 18, pp. 118-137.

Beymer, D., Russell, D. and Orton, P. (2008). An eye tracking study of how font size and type influence online reading, *Proc. 22nd British HCI Group Annual Conference on People and Computers,* 2, pp. 15-18.

Chaparro, B. et al. (2013). Reading online text: A comparison of four white space layouts, Usability News, Available: http://psychology.wichita.edu/surl/usabilitynews/62/whitespace.htm. [Accessed 22 Oct. 2013].

Chaparro, B., Shaikh, A. D. and Chaparro, A. (2006). Examining the legibility of two new ClearType fonts, *Usability News,* 8.

Darroch, I. et al. (2005). The effect of age and font size on reading text on handheld computers, *Lecture Notes in Computer Science,* 3585, pp. 253–266.

Gibbs, P. (2013), Can a human see a single photon? Available: http://math.ucr.edu/home/baez/physics/Quantum/see_a_photon.html. [Accessed 17 Jun 2013].

Machizawa, M., Goh, C. and Driver, J. (2012). Human visual short-term memory precision can be varied at will when the number of retained items is low, *Psychological Science,* 23, pp. 554–559.

National center for assessment in higher education (2001). Available: http://www.qiyas.sa/Sites/English/Pages/default.aspx. [Accessed 6 Jun 2013].

Nemeth, T. (2009). Complex Dutch Arab Complex. *TYPO,* 36.

Nikfal, S. (2011) English and Arabic typeface personas and arabic typefaces design charactersitics. Master's thesis, Department of Computer Science and Software Engineering, Concordia University, Montreal, Canada.

Ramadan, M. Z. (2011). Evaluating college students' performance of Arabic typeface style, font size, page layout and foreground/backgroujnd color combinations of e-book materials, *Journal of King Saud University - Engineering Sciences,* 23, pp. 89-100.

Shaikh, A. D. (2007) Psychology of onscreen type: investigations regarding typeface personality, appropriateness, and impact on document perception. PhD thesis, Department of Psycology, Wichita State University, U.S.A.

Smitshuijzen, E. (2009) Arabic Font Specimen Book, (Uitgeverij de Buitenkant, Amsterdam).

Suen, C. Y. (1986). Human recognition of handprinted characters and distance measurements, *Graphonomics: Contemporary Research in Handwriting,* Elsevier Science Publishers B. V., pp. 213-223.

Tracy, W. (1986) Letters of Credit: A View of Type Design. (David Godine, London) pp. 30-32.

Voorhees, G. (2011) Congeniality of reading on digital devices. School of Print Media, Rochester Institute of Technology, Rochester, U.S.A.

Index

Typefaces are indicated in italic